THOMAS STOTHARD

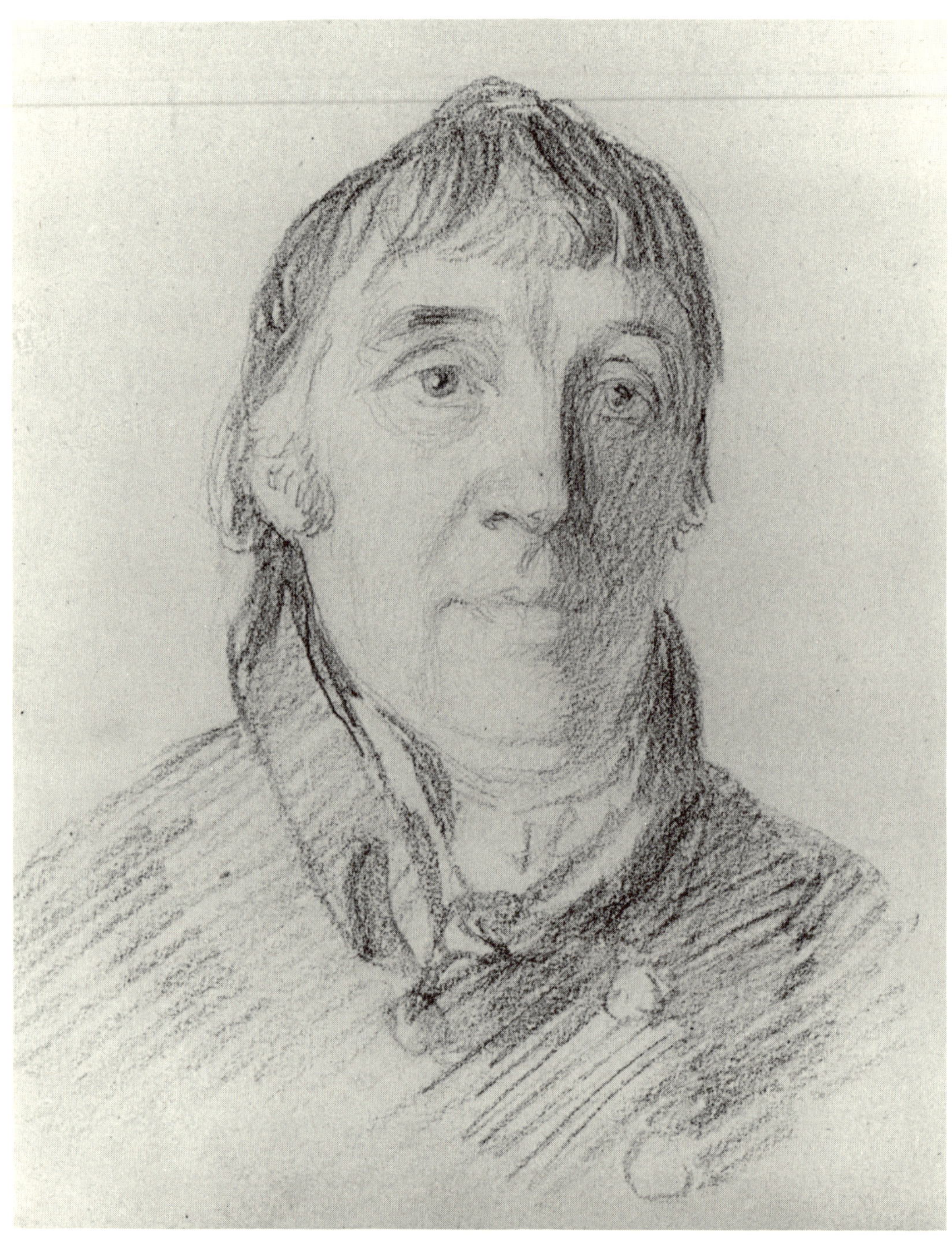

John Flaxman, "Portrait of Thomas Stothard," pencil, 7 x 5¼".

Shelley M. Bennett

THOMAS STOTHARD

The Mechanisms of Art Patronage in England circa 1800

University of Missouri Press
Columbia, 1988

∞™ This paper meets the minimum requirements of the
American National Standard for Permanence of Paper for
Printed Library Materials, Z39.48, 1984.

For photo acknowledgments, see p. 112.

Library of Congress Cataloging-in-Publication Data

Bennett, Shelley M., 1947–
    Thomas Stothard : the mechanisms of art patronage in
England circa 1800.

    Bibliography: p.
    Includes index.
    1. Stothard, Thomas, 1755–1834—Criticism and inter-
pretation. 2. Art, English. 3. Art, Modern—17th–18th
centuries—England. 4. Art, Modern—19th century—
England. 5. Art patronage—England. 6. Artists and
patrons—England. I. Title.
N6797.S76B46   1988   709'.2'4   87–19235
ISBN 0-8262-0644-6 (alk. paper)

PREFACE

Mr. Stothard is perhaps the first genius, after Mr. Fuseli and Mr. Flaxman, that the English school or modern Europe has known. —Sir Thomas Lawrence[1]

Mr. Stothard had the soul in him of a genuine and entire painter. He was a designer, a colourist, a grouper; and, above all, he had expression. . . . Since the days of the greatest Italian painters, no man felt or expressed the graces of innocence and womanhood as he did. . . . The VARIETY as well as grace of his productions soon put him at the head of designers for books, and there he has since remained. . . . He is one of the few English artists esteemed on the continent, where his productions are bought up like those of his friend Flaxman, who, we believe, may be reckoned among his imitators; for Stothard's genius was richer than his, and included it. —Leigh Hunt[2]

In the works of Stothard female beauty and elegance strongly prevail, and that in a degree infinitely beyond his contemporaries. . . . So versatile is the genius of this extraordinary man, that it embraces every subject, and it is really astonishing with what facility he has depicted the pastoral, the historic, the humourous, the pathetic, and the sublime. —Edward Dayes[3]

How is it possible that an artist of such renown in the late eighteenth and early nineteenth centuries has been relegated to a minor place in the history of English art? How did Stothard gain the high esteem of his contemporaries? Why was he such a popular artist?

Thomas Stothard (1755–1834) was probably the most prolific illustrator of his times, executing designs for everything from landscape, sculpture, and history painting to ceramics, silverwork, and book illustration. The resounding popularity of his art attests to the extent to which his decorative style and sentimental subject matter appealed to a wide range of his contemporaries. Nowadays, he is perhaps best known for his long and intimate association with John Flaxman and William Blake. Together these three close friends developed a reduced linear style to amplify the emotional resonance of their art. Stothard, Flaxman, and Blake also were among the first artists of note to become involved in the newly developing manufacture of mass-produced art commodities.

During the eighteenth century, several entrepreneurs began to exploit new techniques, such as the division of labor and specialization, in the production of quality craft items such as illustrated books, ceramics, and silverwork. In each of these fields, manufacturers turned out mass-produced luxury objects at relatively low prices in order to reach a new and lucrative market. Various commercial incentives encouraged late-eighteenth-century British artists such as Stothard to extend their activities into this booming area of art production. Stothard's career provides numerous insights into the effect these new market conditions had on the mechanisms of art patronage. His early and formative experience working for these new art markets determined the nature of his subsequent role as an artist. Conditioned by his early training in the Spitalfields silk industry and by his continual reliance for employment on book illustration, Stothard accommodated the tastes of both manufacturers of art commodities and individual, private patrons. His success lay in his ability to adjust to diverse commercial demands.

Stothard's consciousness of the marketplace formed the basis of his prolific employment, financial success, and popularity. It was not, however, incompatible with his identity as a venerated professional artist and Royal Academician. Nor did it hinder his attainment of success in more traditional areas, such as history painting. His employment in the production of art commodities did not cause his social status and reputation to suffer.

A reevaluation of Stothard's life also discloses the link between his artistic endeavors and broader social commitments. As he wrote of Dürer, "His genius was so universal that he followed the business of his profession and at the same time attended the affairs of the public."[4] To pursue these public affairs, Stothard was affiliated with several radical political organizations, particularly in his youth. The general spread of his fame and the rise of his prices must be measured against this background. His sentimental art is a challenge to the accepted notion that political artists produce only "tough" art. An account of Stothard's life, in particular of the special nature of his relation to his employers, reveals the increasingly complex role of the artist in an industrial society.

ACKNOWLEDGMENTS

For their advice and encouragement I would like to give special thanks to Ann Bermingham, Patricia Crown, and Robert Essick. I also am indebted to several other scholars for their generous help, in particular G. E. Bentley, Jr., Timothy Clifford, Susan Downey, Julius Kaplan, and Giles Mitchell. Alex Potts's perceptive reading of the manuscript was of invaluable assistance; while Robert Wark's impeccable scholarship served as an ideal model in the preparation of this book.

The liberal aid of the staff of numerous institutions made this project possible. I am especially grateful for the help I received in the Prints and Drawings Departments of the British Museum, the Boston Public Library, the Henry E. Huntington Library and Art Gallery, the Nottingham Castle Museum, the Victoria and Albert Museum, and the Yale Center for British Art. My work has been facilitated by a Dickson fellowship from the University of California, Los Angeles, a grant from the Paul Mellon Centre for British Studies, two research grants from the Huntington Library, and a fellowship from the British Academy.

S.M.B.
1 October 1987

CONTENTS

1 FORMATIVE YEARS

THOMAS Stothard was born on 17 August 1755, at the Black Horse Inn in Long Acre, London. Stothard's father, a native of Stutton near Tadcaster, and his mother, from Shrewsbury, had moved from Stutton to London in 1750. Once settled in Long Acre, Stothard's father began business as a publican of the Black Horse Inn.[1]

In eighteenth-century London, taverns ranged from common beer-houses to more dignified middle-class affairs like the Turk's Head. The larger taverns also functioned as social centers for concerts, dinners, and club meetings. A contemporary source indicates that the Black Horse Inn was frequented by coach-makers,[2] a class of skilled artisans, well into the nineteenth century. As late as 1837, it is noted that "the body makers are the wealthiest of all and compose among themselves a species of aristocracy to which the other workmen look up with feelings half of respect, half of jealousy."[3] The coach-makers considered themselves the social equals of masters, shopkeepers, or professional men. Thus, the Black Horse Inn was probably a tavern of a more middle-class nature. As a member of this prosperous new class, Stothard's father was able to send his delicate only child, Thomas, to day and boarding schools in the country and to leave his widow and son £1,200 at his death in 1770.[4]

Born into a bourgeois family, Stothard reaped the benefits of an early schooling. He was sent to day school at Acomb in Yorkshire when he was from five to eight years old and to day school at Stutton when he was from eight to thirteen or fourteen years old. In 1769, at age fourteen, he attended a boarding school for not more than one year at Ilford, Essex.

As a consequence of his schooling, Stothard was always a great reader. Although there is no indication that he ever mastered the use of another language, he relished the many romantic novels of his time written or translated into English. His interest in art also was encouraged from an early age by the teacher in whose care he was placed in Acomb, Yorkshire, when five years old. Late in life, Stothard recounted to Allan Cunningham:

She had two sons in the Temple, London, who sent her a present of some of the heads of Houbraken, framed and glazed; likewise an engraving of the blind Belisarius, by Strange; and some religious pictures from the unrivalled graver of the same artist. I looked often and earnestly at those productions. . . . I gazed till a love of art grew within me, and a desire to imitate what was on her walls. I could see that my hand was improving, and I had sketched some things not amiss, when, at eight years old, I was removed to Stutton, the birth place of my father. Before this, I should have mentioned that my father, pleased with my attempts, had sent me boxes of colours, which I knew so little how to use, that I applied to a house painter for some mixed paint, which he gave me in an oyster shell, and the first man I painted was in black. I had no examples; you know how necessary they are; Literature may be taught by words, Art must come through signs.[5]

Following the death of his father in 1770, Stothard went to live with his mother in Stepney Green, London. To allow him to pursue his interest in drawing, Stothard's mother apprenticed her son to John Vansommer, a Huguenot silk weaver and designer living in Spital Square. At the age of fifteen, Stothard was exposed to Spitalfields, a strongly radical district in eighteenth-century London.

Spitalfields was one of the older working-class communities and was noted for its anti-authoritarian disturbances throughout the century. Violently affected by all trade fluctuations, the weavers had a long record of militancy. The prosperity in the silk industry during the Seven Years War, when the French trade was temporarily taken over, was followed by a period of depression and unemployment in the 1760s and 1770s. The result was widespread rioting, loom-cutting, and bitter disputes over wages in Spitalfields. In 1773, this turbulence culminated in a joint approach to Parliament by masters and journeymen. In the resulting Spitalfields Act, combinations were outlawed and prices for weaving were fixed. Although the Act brought peace to Spitalfields, there are numerous accounts of misery and starvation among the weavers until the end of the century.

As an apprentice to a Spitalfields silk weaver, Stothard was at the heart of radical politics developing in England during these decades. He also was exposed to the strong intellectual tradition of the Spitalfields weavers. As a type, the Spitalfields weaver is often taken as an example of an intelligent and skilled craftsman. There are even contemporary claims that weavers customarily read a book on some philosophical subject while working at their looms.[6] Although such accounts are subject to doubt when extended to the majority of silk weavers, there is reason to believe that these intellectual proclivities were characteristic of the Huguenot colony of silk weavers. In the early part of the eighteenth century the Huguenot colony in Spitalfields was enriched by societies for Mathematics, History, Horticulture, Entomology,

Music, a Recitation Society for the reading of Shakespeare and other authors, and so forth. Stothard was undoubtedly familiarized with this side of Spitalfields by his Huguenot master, John Vansommer, to whom he was apprenticed from 1770 to 1777.[7]

Vansommer had received his training from the Huguenot silk-weaver Joseph Dandridge, an entomologist, botanist, and ornithologist who knew several artists and engravers and also was acquainted with Voltaire. In 1727, Vansommer came out of apprenticeship and set up business as both a silk weaver and a designer, an unusual combination in England. Since there were few silk designers at that time in England, he quickly made a reputation for himself, gaining both prestige and financial success. By 1750, Vansommer was a wealthy man, residing in Spital Square, the most exclusive area of Spitalfields.

Vansommer was probably in continual contact with French culture through correspondence with French designers and possibly visits for his firm to France. He is most likely the man to whom Voltaire addressed a letter on the topic of man's natural inclination to war, dated June 1768. Through Joseph Dandridge, Vansommer may have met Voltaire in 1726–1727 when Voltaire was in exile in England. Although it is unlikely that their correspondence extended over the years, the Frenchman's published writings undoubtedly remained a constant source of interest for Vansommer. At the early age of fifteen, Stothard was probably exposed to the social and political philosophy of this influential French writer-philosopher.

During his apprenticeship, Stothard also began friendships of importance to the future development of his art. He met George Cumberland, a young man who shared and encouraged the progressive sympathies nurtured by Vansommer. Upon Stothard's death on 27 April 1834, Cumberland noted in his pocket annual, "Tho. Stothard died at 1 o'clock in the day. He was my old & revered friend from 17 years of age."[8] Since Cumberland was born in 1754, this would date the beginning of their friendship to 1771 or 1772, depending on whether the "17 years of age" refers to Cumberland or Stothard.

In 1771, George Cumberland's father died, leaving his family in reduced circumstances. George was forced to seek employment as a clerk in the Royal Exchange Assurance Company. He remained there until his resignation upon receipt of a small inheritance in 1785. Even when fettered by the restrictions of the life of a clerk, Cumberland's restless temperament drove him in pursuit of diverse intellectual and artistic interests. Some of these energies found expression in his fourteen publications, in his compilation of a large collection of prints centering around Marc Antonio Raimondi and Guilio Bonasone, in his activity as an amateur artist, in his friendships and correspondence with several of the influential patrons and artists of his day, and in his voluminous correspondence with his brother Richard Denison Cumberland. The best known of George's publications, *Thoughts on Outline,* which appeared in 1796, discussed the merits of outline in antique, Renaissance, and contemporary art.[9] The views expounded in this short treatise reflect several of the artistic values shared by Stothard.

In addition to his progressive activities in the arts, Cumberland held strong antiministerial political views that he voiced in the London evening paper *The General.* George admitted to his brother on 17 September 1779, "[I] compose 20 paragraphs every week for the General Evening Postscript and have for some time, but they are seldom news—little essays on the times, conjectures, encouragement, &c. In short, I try to lead the public sentiment right."[10] One of his most admired friends was the radical politician and scholar Horne Tooke.[11]

Although there is only one letter from Stothard to Cumberland among the vast collection of Cumberland manuscripts in the British Library, frequent references are made to him throughout the papers. The earliest mention of Stothard's name appears in 1778 in conjunction with two fellow artists, the miniaturists Samuel Shelley and Richard Collins.[12] These young men seem to have formed such a tight-knit association that Cumberland refers to them in 1780 in his correspondence with his brother as "the Club."[13]

In May 1774, John Vansommer died. Stothard finished his seven-year apprenticeship under Vansommer's wife, Ann, who carried on the business. By 1775, there was such a decline in the silk industry that Stothard had more leisure time. It was probably during this period that Stothard formed his first close ties with the group of aspiring young artists that included Cumberland, Shelley, Collins, [James or Samuel] Scarlett, William Darcey, and others. These associations during the final years of his apprenticeship helped sway the balance in Stothard's decision to pursue a career as an artist. In 1777, upon completion of his indentures, Stothard went on a ten-day trip to Shrewsbury, his mother's birthplace, and to North Wales; then in September he went to Portsmouth to visit his friend Darcey. On 30 December, Stothard entered the Royal Academy schools in Maiden Lane.

The earliest surviving example of Stothard's art is found on a draft of a letter dated "Portsmouth Sp. 1, 1777"[14] and probably written by Stothard shortly before entering the Royal Academy schools, while visiting his friend Darcey in Portsmouth. This rough sketch of stick-like figures in contemporary dress illustrates that Stothard's training in the Spitalfields silk industry had not led him to any advancement in the art of figure drawing. A slightly later sketch by Stothard of "July 23, 1778" is still crude in its overall treatment, but now there is greater flow and continuity to the lines.[15] Before the end of 1779, Stothard's abilities had shown such a marked improvement that he was able to gain steady employment as a draftsman.

While pursuing his artistic development, Stothard was affiliated with several progressive political organizations instrumental in the propagation of revolutionary principles and popular agitation in Britain. The Gordon Riots in June 1780 were one of the first outbursts of the emerging radical consciousness in late-eighteenth-century England. The Protestant Association and, in particular, its president, Lord George Gordon, were the major instigators of this violent uprising.

The Protestant Association was formed in 1779 to obtain a repeal of the Catholic Relief Act of 1778. The keynote of this organization was its religious fanaticism and cry of "No Popery." Lord George Gordon, a member of the House of Commons, was elected president of the association in November 1779, and he proceeded to call several public meetings to harangue against popery. In May 1780, Stothard exhibited at the Royal Academy a painting entitled *Protestant Association*.[16] On 2 June 1780, the Protestant Association summoned a gathering of about sixty thousand supporters to present a petition to Parliament against Catholic toleration. The House of Commons refused to debate the petition. Inflamed by the speeches of Lord George, the crowds turned into violent mobs. A pandemonium of rioting, burning, and pillaging broke loose until order was restored on 8 June.

Although the Gordon riots were deliberately fostered by the Protestant Association, the precise nature of the connection between the association and the populace who constituted the majority of the rioters remains unclear. There was certainly a strong antiministerial element to the Protestant Association's desire to repeal the Catholic Relief Act. The Spitalfields weavers sympathized with this aspect of the riots and mustered to take part in the protest.

There is no record of Stothard's connection with this pressure group beyond the exhibition of his painting of the association; yet Stothard's continued appearance on the fringe of several other radical groups over the next thirty years suggests that he sympathized with the antiministerial goals of the Protestant Association. From what is known of Stothard's mild temperament, it is hard to imagine him participating in the actual riots. As others, he was probably concordant, however, with the new political tactics of this well-organized group. The Protestant Association was one of the first organizations to make use of the Platform, that is, to use petitions, meetings, speeches, and political association to push "extra-parliamentary" measures.

It is also likely that Stothard sympathized with the goals of the Society for Constitutional Information. He designed for them a print, *The Declaration of Rights,* engraved in 1782 by the political reformer William Sharp. Founded in 1780, this popular group promoted advanced theories of reform based on purifying the constitution. The most active period of the society was during the early 1790s under the guidance of Horne Tooke and the adherents of Thomas Paine's *Rights of Man.*

The political agitation in Britain reached an intense peak in the early 1790s, culminating in government action against the reform groups in 1795. This brought about the end of the Society for Constitutional Information and the demise of the equally influential London Corresponding Society. This active organization was composed mostly of artisans, with a strong contingent from among the Spitalfields weavers. In December 1795, Stothard attended the last great demonstration of the LCS, which was held in Marylebone Fields.[17] There he heard the speeches of John Thelwell and others against the politically repressive measures of William Pitt and King George III.

In addition to his radical political sympathies, the writings of Voltaire probably encouraged Stothard to take up Deism. Although he never went to church, Stothard was noted for being a very pious man. The religious views of the Huguenot Protestants also may have swayed Stothard in his youth, as his affiliation with the antipopery cause of the Protestant Association indicates. Yet none of his letters or other writings hints of any particular religious inclination. He was evidently an advocate of toleration, for he married a woman who was an Anabaptist, part of the old Dissenting tradition.

Stothard is described in the *Morning Chronicle* a few days after his death: he was of "about the middle size, of a compact make and exceedingly active and enjoyed almost uninterrupted Health. When about 60 years of age he walked almost 20 miles a day . . . . For many years of his life he was exceedingly deaf [probably beginning about 1800]." The anonymous writer continues, "as a man Stothard could have no enemy. His character was simplicity itself."[18] One gathers from contemporary accounts that Stothard was well-liked by his fellow artists and was esteemed throughout his life as a warmhearted man. His art reveals his sentimental disposition, his absorption in romance novels, and his gentle sense of humor. Although he is reported in old age to have "hated all collusion with bustling, arrogant men,"[19] several of his friendships in his younger days indicate a more tolerant and open attitude.

As a contemporary biographer remarked, Stothard

stood forth at once an example of genius without eccentricity, of industry without parallel, and of devotedness to his profession which appeared to absorb every consideration, whether it regarded the

health of his body or the tone of his mind. Such recreations as he allowed himself to take were always with reference to his studies and his art; his walks became a source of inventive results, and every object which attracted his regard, whether the design on the top of a ballad, or examples of animated nature, was to him a model that would live in his remembrance till the occasion occurred when it would be required.[20]

Stothard was mild, sweet tempered, and tremendously responsive to his surroundings. This aspect of his personality undoubtedly contributed to his success with a wide variety of patrons.

During the final years of his apprenticeship or during his years as a student at the Royal Academy schools, Stothard began his lifelong employment in the production of mass-produced art items. Among Stothard's first employers was Josiah Wedgwood. By concentrating on improvements in materials and in the processes of production, Wedgwood was able to manufacture high-quality, reasonably priced ceramic ware in his factory at Etruria. His greatest success came with his development of jasperware, an imitation of Roman cameo glass. To attain a lower price range and thus reach a broader market, Wedgwood was quick to apply new techniques, such as specialization and the division of labor, to the production of this popular art commodity.

With the increased use of these industrial techniques, the role of the designer became more and more autonomous, separate and distinct from the technical skills associated with the different crafts. Once a division had been made between the labors of designing and of making, the design became the self-conscious, specialized task of the "artist" rather than the spontaneous product of the craftsman. Similarly, the control of the designer over the final art product was now considerably reduced.

Wedgwood was forever aware, however, of the designer's importance to the success of ceramic ware; thus he was generous in his remunerations.

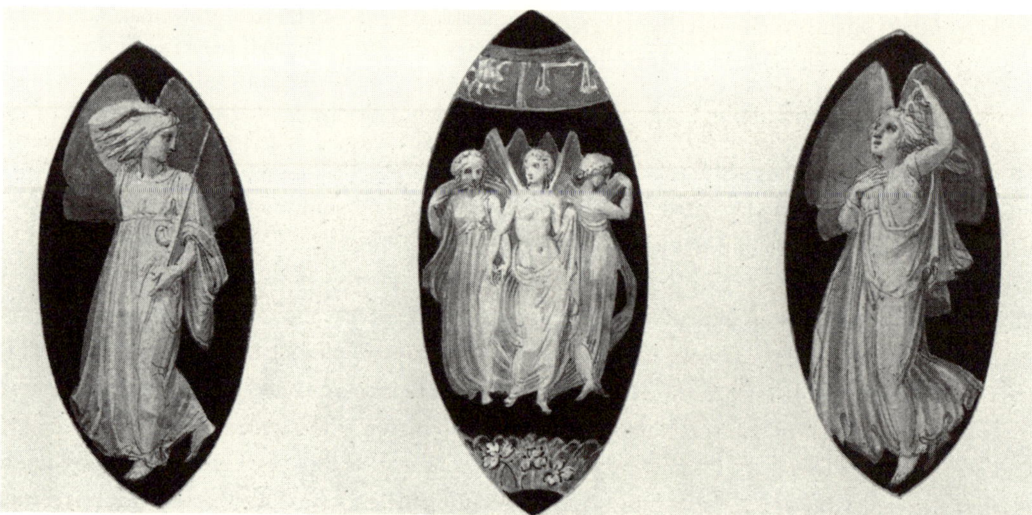

Fig. 1. Thomas Stothard, three untitled designs for Wedgwood, pen and wash, 3¹/₄ x 1¹/₂″ each.

Furthermore, Wedgwood employed several artists of note, such as George Stubbs and John Bacon at Etruria, and was always in search of new talent to create original designs for his booming international business in jasperware.

As opposed to later manufacturers, Wedgwood was deeply involved in every stage of the production of his high-quality, moderate-cost commodities. This policy extended to his personal commitment to the artists he employed. For example, he assisted Stothard's close friend John Flaxman in his artistic development with both a monetary advance and recommendations that enabled Flaxman to travel to Rome in 1787. Wedgwood was Flaxman's first and one of his most constant patrons.

Beginning in 1775, Flaxman created several of his most renowned designs, such as his famous relief of the *Dancing Hours* (1778), for Wedgwood's jasperware. This design and many other of his commissions for Wedgwood were based on classical prototypes gleaned from the prints published in 1766–1767 after Sir William Hamilton's collection of vases or from publications such as the *Catalogo Degli Antichi Monumenti . . . Di Ercolano,*

complied by O. A. Baiardi, which began appearing in 1755.[21] In addition to exploiting the contemporary taste for antiquity, Wedgwood was ever conscious of the possibilities of a new market; thus, he commissioned Flaxman to design a Gothic chess set in 1785 to appeal to the concurrent taste for medieval themes. Flaxman continued his employment on these various designs for Wedgwood throughout his life. Stothard's other close friend from his youth, William Blake, did not begin his connections with the Wedgwood firm until late in his career, probably from 1815 to 1816. During this time he engraved about 185 of Wedgwood's pottery models.

Stothard was probably employed by this industrial pioneer in the early 1780s. He executed drawings that served as the models for a pattern utilized by Wedgwood on a variety of pale and dark blue jasper perfume bottles (Figs. 1 and 2). Stothard's drawings of these classical zephyrs are executed in his more amateurish style of the early 1780s, while the jasper perfume bottles date to about 1785.[22]

Stothard probably based his designs on similar examples in the *Catalogo Degli Antichi Monumenti . . . Di Ercolano* (Fig. 3). His personal touch can be

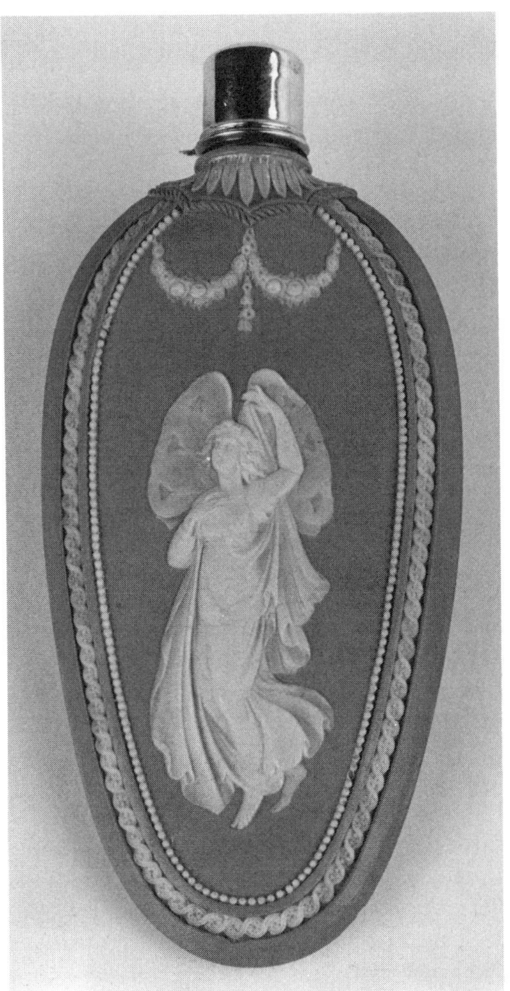

Fig. 2. Wedgwood jasperware perfume bottle, circa 1785.

subsequent development of his style and the nature of his relations to his patrons.

As a result of his early training in the Spitalfields silk industry, Stothard easily adapted to the role of a specialist, contributing to the production of an art commodity over which he had no direct control. This role necessitated a collaborative and rather subordinate attitude, ever responsive to the diverse needs of his employers. This conception of his function as an artist became standard for Stothard throughout his career.

At this early stage in his artistic career, Stothard also began his lifelong employment in another expanding area of skilled craft production, book illustration.[23] In the late eighteenth century, printsellers-booksellers began to cater to the increasing demand for books, especially with

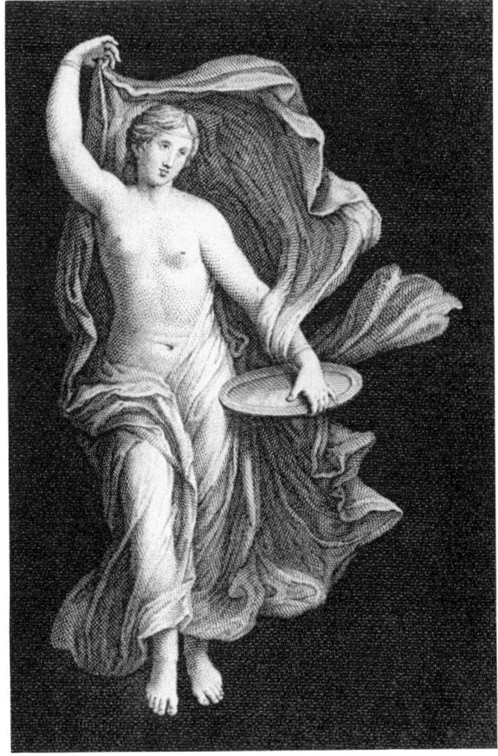

Fig. 3. O. A. Baiardi, illustration to *Catalogo Degli Antichi Monumenti . . . Ercolano* (Naples, 1754/5), engraving, image 11³⁄₈ x 8³⁄₄".

seen in the addition of his beloved butterfly wings to these personifications of the gentle breezes. Stothard utilized a silhouette technique of placing light-colored figures against a dark background emulating vases and gems. Stothard's and Flaxman's employment in producing silhouette designs for Wedgwood's jasperware was undoubtedly a strong stimulus to their concurrent interest in the development of a reduced linear style. Stothard's early experience in designing for this new, expanded market for mass-produced craft items was an important influence on both the

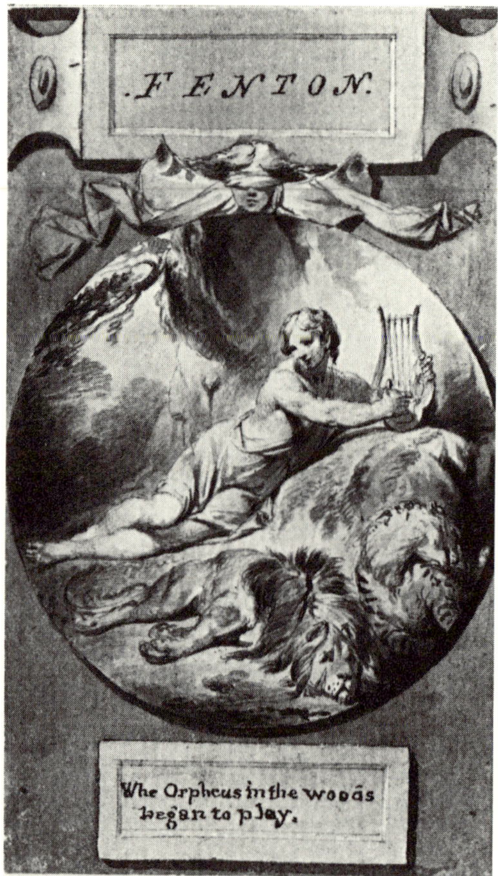

Fig. 4. Thomas Stothard, illustration to Fenton, published in Bell's *Poets of Great Britain* (1779), pen and wash, 4¼ x 2½", bound into an extra-illustrated Bray's *Life of Stothard.*

illustrations. The proliferation of book illustration at the end of the eighteenth century is closely tied to the rise of a reading public. This new market was to provide Stothard with a consistent source of patronage throughout his life.

Due to the high cost of new publications, the market for many books was limited, however, to the upper and upper-middle classes. Although the number of new novels published each year began to multiply at the end of the eighteenth century, the selling prices also continued to climb to considerable heights. The book-buying public was a relatively exclusive market.[24]

A notable exception to this luxury market for books were the "numbers" or "series" publications. After the revocation of the perpetual copyright law in 1777, booksellers such as John Bell, John Harrison, and John Cooke began to issue collections of reprints. To maintain a low price, they adopted an older practice of issuing publications in parts. These weekly numbers sold at about sixpence each, a rate not beyond an apprentice's buying power. Although there is no evidence concerning the size of these editions, their consistently low cost indicates that their publishers were attempting to reach a wider market than the limited one for new publications.[25]

It was Stothard's work for numbers publications that established his reputation and popularity. One of the earliest indications of Stothard's ability to satisfy a popular taste comes from the cover of the separate numbers of Harrison's *Novelist's Magazine:*

It is foreign to our Plan to take any sort of notice of letters received by the Publishers, and we do not mean to repeat it; but in justice to that most astonishing artist, the truly ingenius Mr. Stothard we cannot suppress the Happiness we feel, from the numerous encomiums in his favor, which have been transmitted to us by several of the greatest Connoisseurs in these kingdoms; all uniformly declaring him the first Genius of the ages in this department, and earnestly recommending us to procure as many drawings as possible from the animating pencil of so distinguished and aspiring an Artist.

The appeal of these cheap reprint series, such as Bell's *British Theatre* and *British Poets* and Harrison's *Novelist's Magazine,* lay in their illustrations as much as in their literary content. Bell, like other early pioneers of mass-produced art commodities, realized that high-quality illustrations would assure the financial success of his publications; thus, he was known to have selected his designers

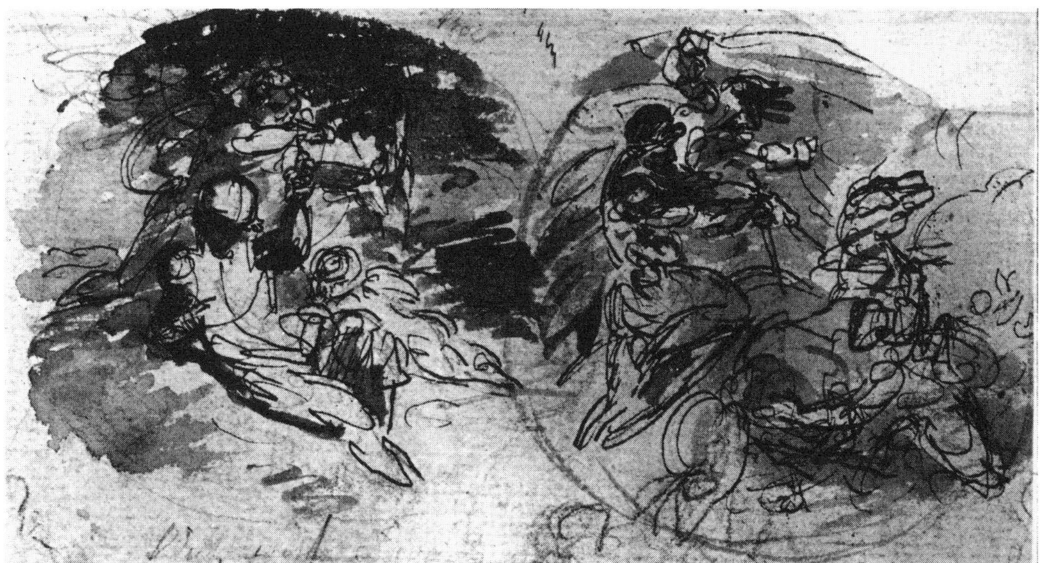

Fig. 5. Thomas Stothard, untitled, pen and wash, 5 x 2⅞", bound into an extra-illustrated edition of Bray's *Life of Stothard.*

and engravers for their excellence rather than their cheapness.[26] Contemporary commentators praised Bell and his fellow publishers for the positive effects these commercial policies had on the arts. As one newspaper critic noted in 1790:

The pretensions to public patronage which Mr. Bell holds out in his new publications of the British Theatre, are reputable to the fine arts and the Belles Lettres. . . . To enterprises like the above is Britain indebted for the extension of her literary fame: no small portion of which has been derived from the wide circulation of the British classics, promoted by the elegant & accurate manner in which they have been produced: - indeed we may date the revival of, if not the original taste for, fine painting & elegant book embellishments in England, to the enthusiasm & perseverance of Mr. Bell in that line of business—for the productions of the press may be said to have been in a barbarous state in this country, until he awakened public curiosity, & incited emulation by his beautiful editions of the Poets of Great Britain, & our immortal dramatic Bard. From the avidity with which those elegant publications were received, may be attributed the present spirited plans of Boydell & Macklin.[27]

Clearly, Stothard's early book illustrations, such as his design for a passage from Richard Fenton (Fig. 4) for Bell's *Poets of Great Britain* (print published 29 December 1779), contributed to the success of these publications. Although this drawing displays a notable lack of accuracy in the proportions of both the figure and the animals, Stothard has successfully developed the rhythmic relationships in the contours of the figures. Another early pen-and-wash sketch (Fig. 5), which in style and format is similar to the illustrations for Bell's *Poets of Great Britain,* reveals the rococo style that underlies the finished drawing for Fenton. In both, all spatial play is repressed by the strong two-dimensional organization of the composition even to the exclusion or distortion of the proper foreshortening of the limbs. The wash is arbitrarily dashed across the drawing with little or no attention to three-dimensional modeling. Stothard's concern is with surface pattern and animation. The wash adds to the sense of excited movement on the surface of the design created by the elaborately curving pen lines. The rhythmic,

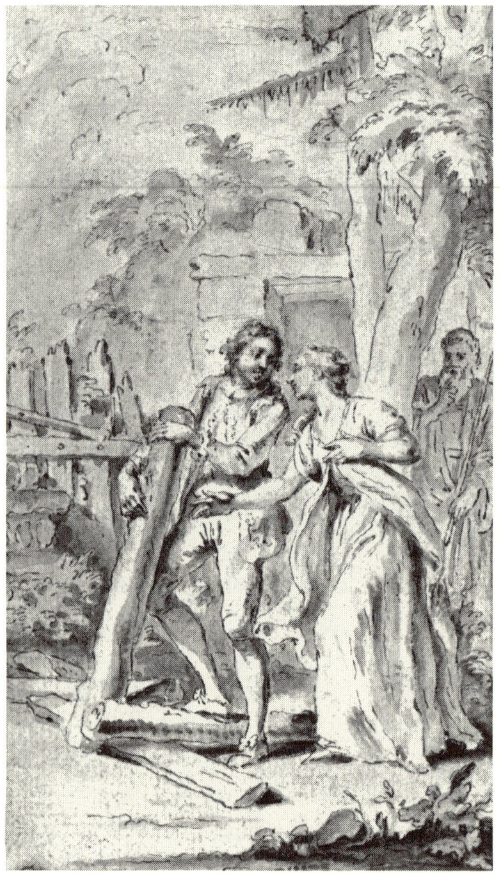

Fig. 6. Hubert Gravelot, illustration to Shakespeare's *Tempest* (act 3, scene 1), published by Lewis Theobald (1740), pen and wash, 3 x 5″, bound into an extra-illustrated edition of Boydell's *Shakespeare.*

continuous lines are the foundation of the design and the prime elements in the overall elegant and decorative effect.

The heads of Houbraken that hung on the walls of his schoolmistress's home in Acomb, Yorkshire, no doubt introduced Stothard to this rococo style at an early age, in particular to the style of Hubert Gravelot (Fig. 6), who designed the elaborate rococo frames in the Houbraken prints. Gravelot was one of the key figure in the development of the rococo style in England in the 1730s and 1740s. Stothard also was influenced in his choice of a rococo style by his apprenticeship to the silk weaver John Vansommer. In the eighteenth century, Spitalfields silks closely followed the latest French patterns. As in their French prototypes, the elegant, playful, and decorative rococo style predominated throughout the century in the floral designs of the Spitalfields silks and brocades.[28]

Stothard never lost his early predisposition for this elegant style of decoration. He modified, however, the type of rococo art practiced by Gravelot and his immediate followers in England. He reversed Gravelot's procedure, using line rather than wash as his basic means for creating decorative effects. In contrast to Gravelot's technique, Stothard employed wash merely to supplement his continuous, cursive lines. As Stothard began to investigate the new avenues of artistic expression that opened up to him during his years at the Royal Academy schools, he simplified and modified even further this rococo manner of surface animation, but he never broke completely from this decorative mode.

During the last years of the eighteenth century and the beginning of the nineteenth century, Stothard designed illustrations for Thomas Cadell's many recent fiction reprints, for Thomas Tegg's remainders and reprints, for John Sharpe's reprint series of Bell's *British Poets* and *Classics,* for F. J. Du Roveray's and Thomas Pickering's reprints of the classics, for John Suttaby's *Miniature Library* reprints, and others (see Appendix 2). His early experience in the specialized role of the designer in ceramic ware and book illustration prepared Stothard for the demands of diverse media such as silverwork, separate prints, sculpture, and oil painting.

2 ENTRY INTO THE ART WORLD

IN ADDITION to his work in the production of mass-produced art commodities, Stothard also utilized the standard artistic outlet, the annual art exhibition, to place his work before the public. In 1777 he contributed three pictures to the Society of Artists exhibition: two landscapes from his trip to North Wales and a battle scene from the fourth book of the *Iliad*. Throughout his life, Stothard continued to exploit artistic organizations, especially the Royal Academy, to further his career. He pursued his commitment to the profession of artist by enrolling in the Royal Academy schools where he spent the usual seven years, from 1777 until about 1783.[1] Stothard did not marry until 1783, when the imminent completion of his term as a student would have allowed him to make a more permanent arrangement.

Although the Academy schools did not require fees, a student had to provide his own materials. Stothard supplemented his meager income from the interest on his father's bequest by working for the booksellers and by painting portraits of intimate acquaintances.[2] Stothard seems to have acquired enough monetary self-sufficiency to be able to move from his mother's residence at Mr. Summer's near the Blind Beggar in Bethal Green. Probably on his return from a second visit to his friend Darcey in Portsmouth, Stothard took up lodgings in 1778 with Samuel Shelley in the Strand. A letter of 19 May 1780 from George Cumberland to his brother passes on the latest "news of the Club": Shelley had married and moved to Covent Gardens (where he resided from 1780 to 1794), and Stothard had moved to New-

port Street.[3] Stothard, Cumberland, and their friends also shared several nonartistic interests, often going on sailing trips during the late 1770s and early 1780s before marriage and growing responsibilities called a halt to their more carefree outings. There are records of their sailing excursions in 1779 up the Medway River[4] and in 1781 to an unknown destination.[5]

The memorable events surrounding one of these sailing trips up the Medway, perhaps that of 1779,[6] were described most fully by Stothard's daughter-in-law, Anna E. Bray, in later years.[7] On this sailing expedition Stothard, William Blake, and their friend Ogleby were arrested on suspicion of being French spies. They were held until word was received from members of the Royal Academy verifying that they were British citizens. Such a humiliating experience at the hands of the representatives of the crown was sure to reinforce whatever republican sympathies Stothard and Blake already shared.

Blake had been introduced to Stothard in 1779 by the engraver Thomas Trotter, who was lodging with Shelley at the time. A close friendship quickly sprang up between these two young artists. They continued on intimate terms until the shady dealings by the engraver Cromek in the 1806 *Canterbury Pilgrims* commission irreparably destroyed their fruitful relationship. Between 1780 and 1786, a particularly close artistic association existed between Blake and Stothard, with Blake engraving many of Stothard's designs for the booksellers.

Although Stothard's temperament was quite

different from Blake's eccentric, visionary, defiant character, the two men shared many radical political and artistic beliefs. Like Stothard and Cumberland (whom Blake probably met at this time through Stothard), Blake held strongly anti-ministerial views. Like Stothard, Blake also appears on the fringe of several radical political groups during the 1780s and 1790s.

John Flaxman was the third member of this fertile artistic trio. After admiring Stothard's designs for the *Novelist's Magazine* in a shop window, Flaxman introduced himself to their designer in 1779 or 1780,[8] and Stothard, in turn, presented Flaxman to Blake. Flaxman and Stothard remained lifelong devoted friends; Flaxman's close relations with Blake began to falter after 1806, when he appears to have sided with Stothard in the bitter *Canterbury Pilgrims* controversy.

In contrast to Stothard, both Blake and Flaxman had strong artistic training in their youths. Born of a relatively prosperous middle-class hosier, Blake began studying art at the age of ten at Shipley's School under William Pars. Four years later, in 1771, he was apprenticed to the fashionable engraver James Basire. Upon completion of his apprenticeship, Blake enrolled in the Royal Academy schools in 1779. After a short and tempestuous period as a student, he broke all further ties with the Academy. During his lifetime, Blake never attained wide recognition as an artist and often had to fall back on his training as an engraver to maintain his meager existence.

Flaxman, on the other hand, had a more traditional and more successful career as a professional artist. Trained as a sculptor in the workshop of his father, a plaster caster and modeler who worked for Louis François Roubiliac and Peter Scheemakers, Flaxman exhibited works at the Free Society of Artists when he was twelve years old, and in 1770 he entered the Royal Academy schools at the age of fifteen. In 1775, Flaxman began designing and making wax models for the popular jasperwares of Josiah Wedgwood. Flaxman continued in this regular employment until his departure for Italy in 1787. Following the popular success of his outline designs for the works of Homer in 1793, Flaxman returned to England and a highly successful career as a sculptor of funerary monuments. Contrary to Blake's example, Flaxman operated through the standard artistic channels and became an Associate Royal Academician in 1797, full Academician in 1800, and Professor of Sculpture in 1810.

This trio of young artists shared an admiration for the works of their older contemporaries, James Barry and John Hamilton Mortimer. These two powerful artistic personalities had a direct impact on several artists in the late 1770s and early 1780s. Blake often mentioned Barry in his writings as the preeminent example of genius thwarted and neglected by an ignorant public and patrons. Blake saw himself as continuing the historical and moralistic painting tradition of Barry and Mortimer. The eccentric, rebellious, and highly romantic natures of both of these older artists struck a responsive cord in Blake. Although mild-mannered Stothard was repulsed in his later years by the often insolent and abusive nature of Barry's attacks on his fellow Academicians,[9] he was probably more sympathetic to the views of this outspoken man in his youth. Stothard's political affiliations often overlapped with Barry's. As early as 1783, Barry was an intimate friend of the arch-radical William Godwin. Among those with whom Godwin and Barry met over the years were several close associates of Stothard's, such as Henry James Richter, a student of Stothard's, and William Sharp, the engraver of many of Stothard's early designs.[10] The republican aspect of Barry's beliefs as well as the direct example of his art undoubtedly attracted and influenced the young Stothard as well as his friends Blake and Flaxman.[11]

Very little documentation remains concerning this seminal period in the relationships among Stothard, Blake, and Flaxman. Blake's friendship with Flaxman remained of special importance to him throughout most of his life, with Flaxman soliciting work for Blake as an engraver and explaining his eccentricities to his patrons.[12] Stothard's friendship also was valuable to Blake for many years. Blake's own artistic sentiments were so closely in tune with Stothard's that when he opened his own print shop in partnership with James Parker in 1784, the only prints to be issued were after Stothard's designs of *Zephyrus & Flora* and *Callisto*.[13]

Of very similar dispositions, Flaxman and Stothard were always the closest of friends. Although prudish at times, Flaxman was a man "of even temperament and of great purity and simplicity of character."[14] In addition to his generous aid to Blake, Flaxman also assisted Stothard in obtaining employment. As Stothard related to Allan Cunningham late in life, "I knew Flaxman well; he was very kind to me, for he introduced me to some valuable friends who patronized my earliest works."[15]

These early patrons of Stothard's were probably the Rev. Anthony Stephen Mathew and his wife Harriet. In the early 1780s, all three young men were frequenting the salon of Harriet Mathew, a minor bluestocking. Flaxman became acquainted with the Mathews in 1769 during his boyhood days in his father's plaster-cast shop. Flaxman introduced both Blake and Stothard into the Mathews' circle shortly after their acquaintance in about 1779.[16] This gathering of intellectuals shared a taste for Gothic and Italianate literature, music, and art. A literate woman, Mrs. Mathew read the works of Homer to Flaxman in Greek and encouraged an interest in Shakespeare and the pre-Romantic poets.

The Mathews gave Flaxman one of his first commissions, the decoration of their back parlor in the Gothic style. He remained on intimate terms with them for most of his life. Although Blake broke with the Mathew circle in about 1784 and bitterly satirized them in *An Island in the Moon*, it was through the Mathews that Blake published his first volume of verse, *Poetical Sketches*, in 1783.[17]

Although no record exists of the Mathews commissioning a work from Stothard, a tentative link exists between Stothard and one famous member of the Mathew circle, the chemist-philosopher-reformer Joseph Priestley. It was probably through the Mathews that Stothard acquired the commission to design for Priestley the illustration of *Experimental Philosophy Pushing Aside the Clouds of Darkness from the Garden of Science* in about 1782.[18]

In his mention to Allan Cunningham of "valuable friends," Stothard may equally well have been referring to another influential promoter and patron of the arts, William Hayley. Stothard was probably introduced to this eminent poet of the sensibility cult by Flaxman, who mentions Stothard in his letters to Hayley as early as 18 October 1784.[19] Flaxman was introduced to Hayley by George Romney in 1783 and became an intimate acquaintance, spending many summers at Hayley's country house at Felpham. Hayley's acquaintance with Blake began long before the date in 1800 when his acts of patronage set Blake up in residence at Felpham. Hayley was an indefatigable patron of the arts, supporting and encouraging such artists and poets as George Romney, Joseph Wright of Derby, and William Cowper. One of Hayley's favorite words was *benevolence*.[20]

Although no documents exist that would establish a direct link between Stothard and Hayley or Stothard and Romney during the 1780s, Stothard was probably an early friend of Romney's and like Flaxman and Blake was probably introduced to Hayley at an early date. Flaxman had known Romney since a year or two after Romney's return from Italy in 1775. Another of Stothard's close friends, Cumberland, was an avid admirer of Romney, composing two odes to him upon his return from Italy.[21]

Another influential artist with whom Stothard came into contact in his youth was Henry Fuseli. Stothard probably became acquainted with Fuseli at the Royal Academy after Fuseli's return to England from Italy in 1779. Outside of their association in routine Royal Academy business, there is no record of a close relationship between Stothard and Fuseli until the year 1812, when they often dined together with their fellow Royal Academicians Joseph Farington, Nathaniel Marchant, James Northcote, and Robert Smirke.[22] Their political affiliations may have brought Stothard and Fuseli together at an earlier date. Fuseli was a member of the circle of radicals that clustered around the publisher Joseph Johnson and included Godwin, Thomas Paine, Thomas Holcroft, Mary Wollstonecraft, and Priestly.

Johnson began commissioning designs from Stothard in 1780 and employed him on several publications in the 1780s and subsequent years. Stothard was involved in several causes that were supported by this circle of intellectuals, in particular the political goals of reform promoted by the Society for Constitutional Information, which was supported by Paine, Holcroft, and several others of this circle.

Stothard was acquainted with Holcroft by 1784 when he designed an illustration for *Witt's Magazine,* which Holcroft edited. The print, entitled *The Temple of Mirth,* was engraved by Blake. Stothard may have met Holcroft's friend, the prominent reformer Godwin, at this time or later through Henry James Richter, whom Stothard instructed in art in 1787 or 1788. Stothard and Ritcher remained close friends over the years,

with Stothard referring to the frequent visits of "our friend Richter" in a 1799 letter to his wife.[23] Stothard was probably the intermediary who introduced Richter to Blake, with whom Richter also became an intimate. Henry and his brother John, who was one of the leaders of the Society for Constitutional Information indicted in the 1790s, were often associated with Godwin.

Another connection between Stothard and this circle of radicals existed through the engraver William Sharp, who was a friend of Horne Tooke, Holcroft, and Godwin and a leading member of the SCI in the 1790s. Sharp was associated with Stothard via the many engravings he made after Stothard's designs between 1780 and 1786, including his engraving of the print Stothard designed for the SCI in 1782. Sharp was admired by Blake and was a friend of Flaxman.[24] Cumberland also knew Sharp, for he noted in his pocket annual in 1786 that he dined with Stothard and Sharp.[25] Whether Sharp or another friend was the intermediary, Stothard was probably introduced into the circle of Holcroft and his fellow reformers during the 1780s. As late as 1809, Henry Crabb Robinson noted a meeting of Holcroft's friends that included Stothard, Godwin, and John Thelwell.[26]

These were the artists, writers, philosophers, and radical politicians Stothard associated with during his maturity. The general spread of Stothard's fame, reputation, and success and the rise of his prices must be measured against this background.

After his marriage in 1783 to Rebecca Watkins, a twenty-three-year-old Anabaptist, and their move to Henrietta Street in Covent Gardens, Stothard's reputation as a successful artist gradually began to increase as his work for the booksellers found a receptive audience. Stothard's rise in reputation can be measured by the increasing demand from publishers for his illustrations for both reprints and new publications.

By the late 1780s, Stothard's talent for capturing a popular sentiment was recognized by one of the most distinguished of the booksellers, the alderman Thomas Cadell. Cadell became one of the chief employers of Stothard for the next twenty-five years. In addition to issuing cheap reprint series of the classics in numbers or parts, Cadell and his partner after 1793, William Davies, specialized in publishing relatively expensive editions of recent fiction that were directed to an upper- and upper-middle-class market.

Another sure indicator of Stothard's ascending stature as an artist is the rise in his prices. When Stothard first began illustrating in 1779, he received a half-guinea per design from Bell and Harrison. The popularity of publications with his illustrations allowed Stothard to quickly raise his charge in 1780 to £1.1 for each of his designs for Harrison's *Novelist's Magazine*.[27] By 1793, Stothard was charging £1 for a slight drawing for a pocketbook for Robinson. By 1797 he was receiving two and a half guineas per drawing from Cadell and Davies for illustrations to William Shenstone's *Poems*,[28] and he received the same from Miller for *Don Quixote* illustrations in 1799–1800.[29]

Stothard's prices continued to climb over the following decades with Cadell and Davies paying him £5.1 for each of his designs on woodblocks for Robert Burns's *Poems* in 1809. When figuring the charge for his absence from home while carrying out a commission in 1809, Stothard estimated in his bill that he made £10 per week at his trade.[30] During the next five years, Stothard's prices jumped phenomenally in part due to the wartime inflation. In 1813 he charged Ballantyne 20 guineas per illustration for Walter Scott's *Rokeby*.[31] In 1822 Stothard disclosed to a patron that his usual price for even a vignette was £5.[32] By 1824, his earning potential had jumped to £20 per week.[33] As the price for Stothard's designs for book illustrations increased, so too did his average price for easel paintings, rising from approximately 30 guineas in the 1790s to 50 guineas in the 1810s. A successful and industrious artist, Stothard died in prosperous circumstances, leaving £5,000.[34]

Although his chief financial support came from his employment by the booksellers, Stothard did not see this as inconsistent with his aspirations to become a respected member of the Royal Academy. In the late eighteenth and early nineteenth centuries, because of the lack of opportunity for exhibition outside the Royal Academy, artists were unlikely to obtain public recognition or private patronage except through the official channels of the Academy. Throughout his long career, Stothard held the distinction of Royal Academician in high esteem. As noted in an obituary, "Mr. Stothard considered the profession of an artist, and most especially the distinction of R.A. (as it ought to be), the passport to gentility,"[35] and by analogy to prosperity.

Stothard's training in the Royal Academy schools also influenced many of his subsequent artistic interests. Stothard, Blake, and Flaxman were encouraged to pursue their study of the art of antiquity, the middle ages, and the trecento by the teachings at the Royal Academy schools and the Royal Academy exhibitions.[36] What they saw exhibited at the annual shows also fostered their interest in a linear style and their search into ever widening areas for new sources of subject matter.

For example, the 1779 Royal Academy retrospective of the works of John Hamilton Mortimer probably inspired Blake to follow the precedent set by Mortimer in turning to British history in his series of drawings executed in 1779–1780, including *Boadicea Inspiring the Britons against the Romans*. Stothard also illustrated this rare subject from British history (Fig. 7) during the early 1780s.[37] During the late 1770s and early 1780s,

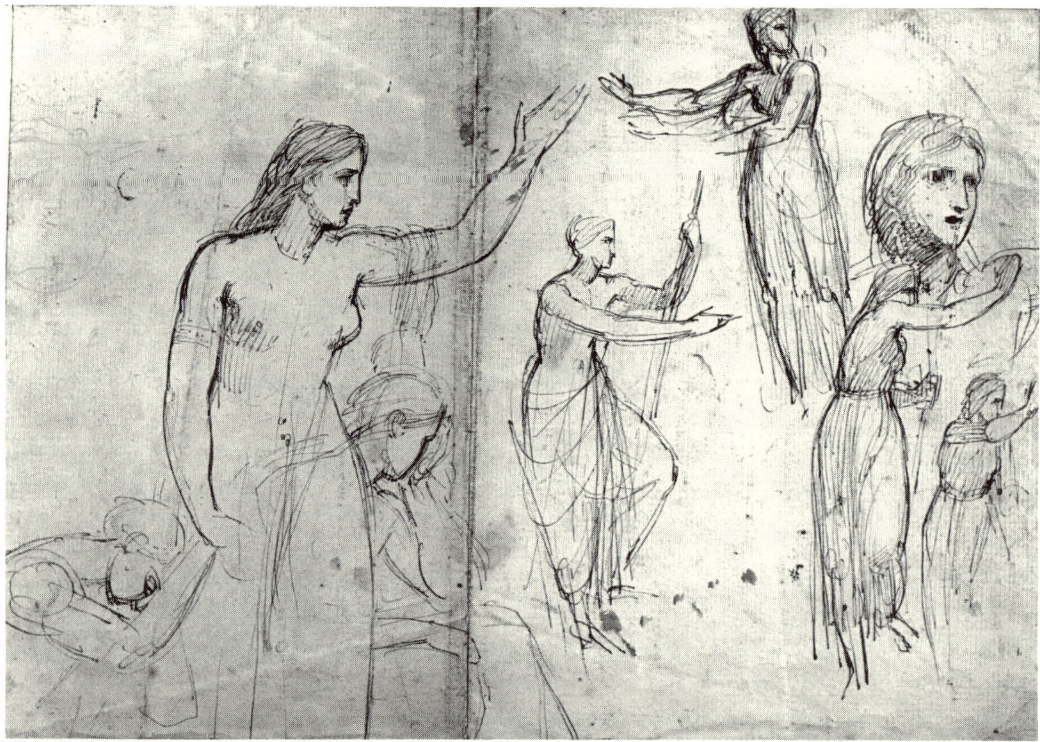

Fig. 7. Thomas Stothard, *Boadicea Inspiring the Britons against the Romans,* pencil & pen, 9¹/₂ x 13¹/₄″, bound into an extra-illustrated edition of Bray's *Life of Stothard.*

Mortimer's pen technique as well as his subject matter were imitated by several young artists, including Thomas Rowlandson, in addition to Stothard and Flaxman. Stothard's first contribution to the Royal Academy exhibitions was a banditti subject in 1779 similar to those of Mortimer. In fact, a few of Stothard's early drawings are in direct imitation of Mortimer in both style and subject matter. For example, his pen and ink drawing (Fig. 8) in the Boston Public Library illustrates a banditti subject of the type so closely associated with Mortimer and using his pen technique. Stothard's rhythmic, parallel lines echo the pattern of tight diagonal zigzags used by Mortimer to serve as a convention for modeling. Drawings by Stothard in this Mortimeresque style can be dated to this early period in his career through their relation to published prints.

A new direction in Stothard's style also appears in a series of early sketches associated with British history (Fig. 9). These drawings can be dated close to 1783 due to their similarity in both subject and style to a drawing by Flaxman of *The Massacre of the Britons at Stonehenge,* which is signed and dated 1783 (Fig. 10). In both Flaxman's and Stothard's drawings, there is a dramatic simplification of pictorial means. Interior detail is reduced almost to the point of elimination. The shallow, frieze-like space is never violated by the movement of the figures. This two-dimensional organization is emphasized by the elimination of modeling or any other plastic effects. Little or no foreshortening is used that might destroy the controlling flat surface design. Above all, line is the crucial means by which the composition is developed—a long, continuous line devoted to contours. Every pictorial

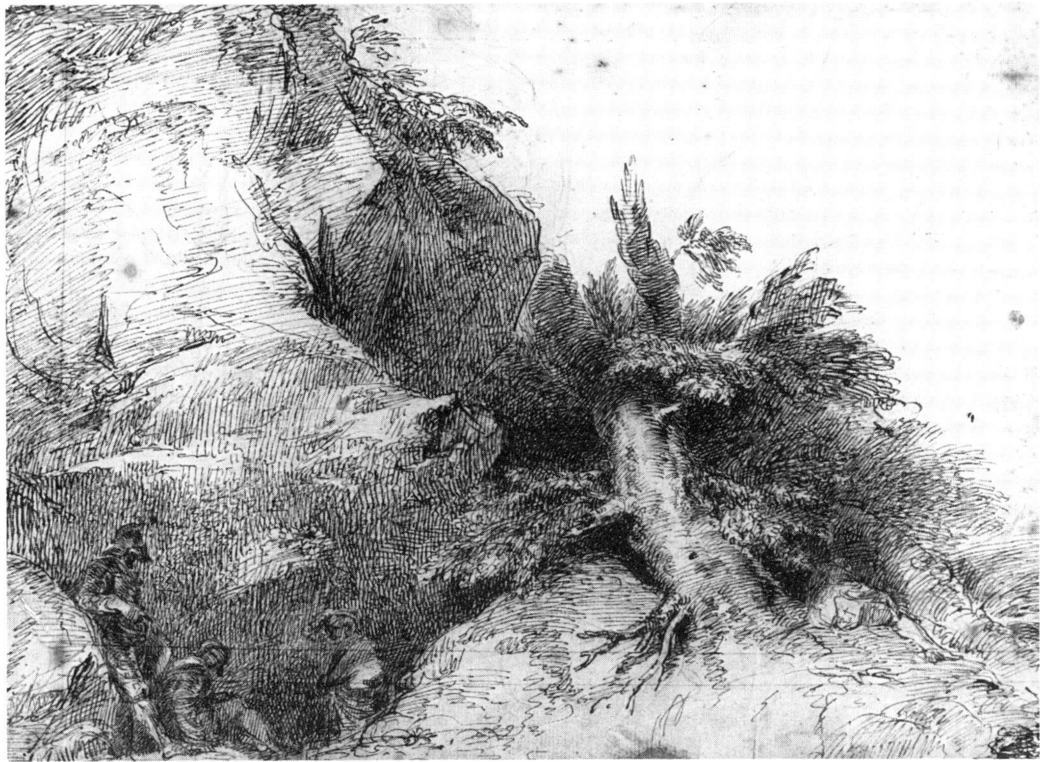

Fig. 8. Thomas Stothard, landscape drawing, pen and traces of pencil, 10 x 14″, bound into an extra-illustrated edition of Bray's *Life of Stothard.*

element of design that would distract attention from the outlines is suppressed or eradicated.

Other characteristics of this new linear style are displayed in one of a series of related drawings by Stothard of classical subjects for an unidentified project (Fig. 11). Forms are defined by their contours. Long, continuous lines describe the edges of the highly simplified figures. Shadows remain transparent and are subordinated to the linear articulation of the forms. The arbitrary light washes do not create a sense of three-dimensional solidity; instead, they contribute to the sense of abstract, flat pattern. In order to create a rhythmic pattern of lines, anatomical demands have been relegated to a minor status, if not ignored. To enhance the linear pattern, the figures have been elongated and radically simplified with little refer-

ence to their three-dimensional structure. Overlapping figures create a sense of depth, but only a shallow depth that is confined by the lateral orientation to a narrow frontal plane. By placing the light figures on a dark background, Stothard made the individual elements even more distinct, emphasizing their edges. Forms are reduced to their most characteristic and expressive silhouette. By means of this abbreviated linear vocabulary, meaning is quickly conveyed.

Blake developed a similar linear style at this time; in fact, all three young friends evolved this style simultaneously, during the early period of their association. It is important to remember that both Stothard and Flaxman were employed by Wedgwood at this time, mimicking classical designs for mass-produced ceramic ware. The

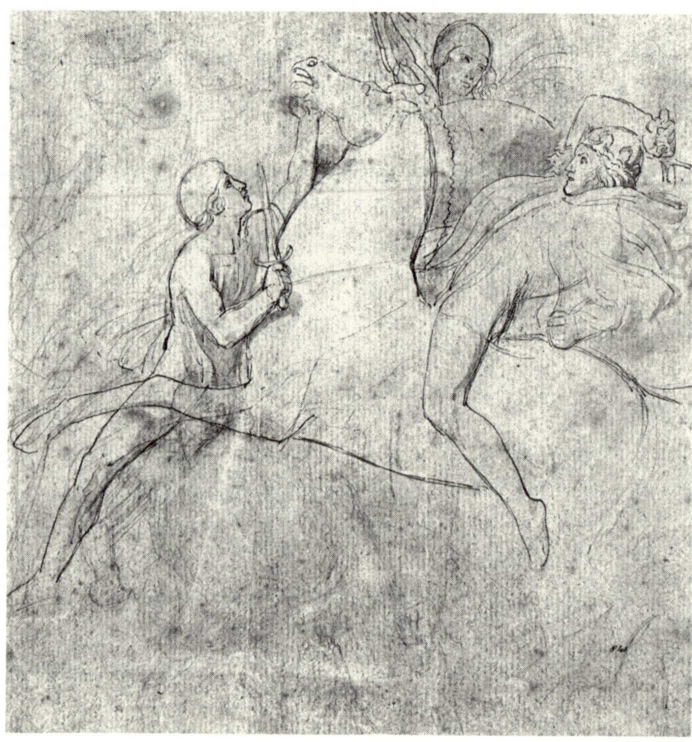

Fig. 9. Thomas Stothard,
untitled, circa 1783, pencil, pen,
and wash, 9 x 8²/₃″.

design requirements for this art commodity probably encouraged them to experiment with this more reduced linear vocabulary.

In addition, various economic considerations may have induced Stothard and his friends to develop this particular style. Outline engravings, such as the sets of engravings after classical excavations, preceded the development and popularization of outline drawing. These engravings (see Fig. 3) rely on a technique of placing a white silhouette on a dark foil. This juxtaposition gives a slight plastic sense to the group of light forms as if they were relieved from their background in emulation of classical sculpture. These engravings probably suggested to Stothard, Flaxman, and Blake the use of a silhouette technique. The success of outline engravings would have encouraged them to experiment with a similar linear style in hopes of reaching the same market.

Another economic factor also influenced their use of a reduced, outline style. In a letter that probably dates from the summer of 1822, Stothard wrote to his patron George Thomson of Edinburgh,

As to your request of the different charge for outline and coloured drawings, the outline I cannot ask less than 2 guineas and the coloured drawings shall be as heretofore 3 or 4 according to the number of figures—betwixt ourselves this is a secret I rely on your honour will go no further—for believe me, my good Sir, the price of my lowest charge here is 5 guineas even for a vignet.[38]

Although Stothard always quoted lower prices to this parsimonious patron, the figures reveal a significant difference in cost between outline and watercolor designs. The fact that outline drawings were less expensive undoubtedly contributed to their success.

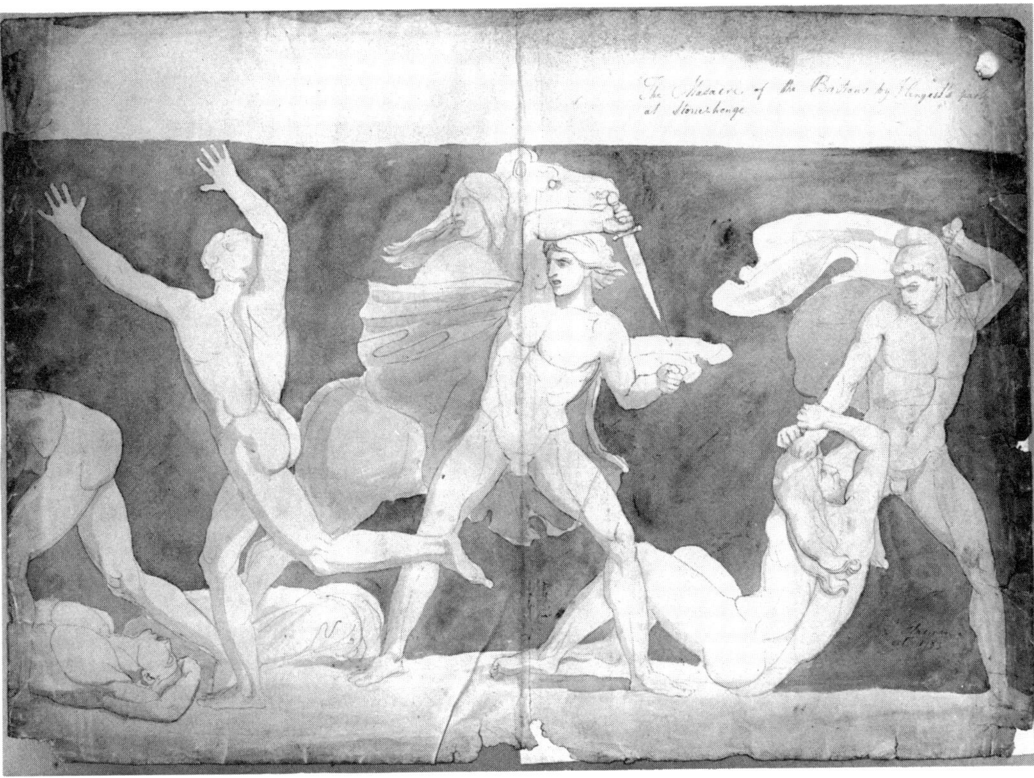

Fig. 10. John Flaxman, *The Massacre of the Britons at Stonehenge,* signed & dated 1783, pen and wash, 18¹/₃ x 25³/₄.

In 1805 Flaxman was charging £3.3 apiece for new outline designs for his editions of the *Iliad* and of the *Odyssey,*[39] while a scant four years later Stothard was receiving as much as £5.1 apiece for designs on woodblocks. This suggests that Flaxman also charged less for his outline drawings than the going rate for other designs. Although Stothard defended the merits of outline drawing to Thomson in another letter,[40] outline drawings probably required less time to execute than drawings by other processes, thus accounting for their lower price. This economic consideration helps explain why book illustrators continued to commission drawings in a linear idiom despite the increase in tonal methods of reproduction at this time.

Stothard's market-conscious attitude to his work led him, however, to use a variety of techniques when developing his designs, depending on the subsequent use of the design. For example, in many of his finished designs, such as his water-color illustration of Charlotte Smith's *Elegiac Sonnets,* published by Cadell in 1789, he reintroduced conventional modeling and illusionistic techniques (compare the study in Fig. 12 with the finished design in Fig. 13). The specific requirements of the engravers probably necessitated Stothard's reversion to tonal effects in his final designs for book illustration.[41]

Both economic and popular factors were considered in choosing the process and technique used in engravings for book illustration. The contemporary preference for tonal engraving effects in book illustrations is stressed in several letters from Flaxman to William Hayley. Flaxman wrote to Hayley on 12 August 1805:

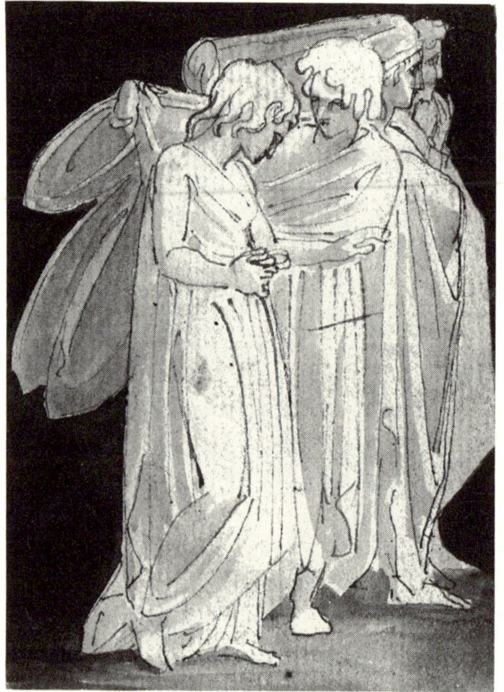

Fig. 11. Thomas Stothard, untitled, pen and wash, 3½ x 2⅝", bound into an extra-illustrated edition of Bray's *Life of Stothard.*

The Frontispiece of Cowper & Milton united as the Patrons of an Orphan, I cannot undertake; I have frequently mentioned that I am not in the habit of doing designs for books on a variety of accounts & you may assure yourself, that I have not sufficient practice in chiaroscuro requisite for that species of art to produce a happy effect when engraved, but Stothard would draw or paint this subject with peculiar beauty.[42]

On 17 September 1806 Flaxman wrote Hayley:

Indeed, indeed, My good Friend the drawing you desire of Milton & Cowper uniting to protect the orphan, is entirely out of my way for I am unused to shadow small drawings for engravers to copy, besides, from my constant practice in large I cannot touch small shadowed heads with the precision and spirit that Stothard does.[43]

After finally consenting to make this sketch for

Hayley, Flaxman wrote him on 10 December 1806: "It will be necessary for M. Stothard to reduce it to proper scale for your volume as well as to give the proper effect for the Engraver."[44]

Stothard was quick to respond to the special commercial requirements of book illustration and readily added chiaroscuro effects in his final drawings. The ease and facility with which he could adapt to the changing demands of the engravers contributed to his popularity among booksellers.

On the whole, the few other developments within book illustration, such as the popularization of wood engravings after 1800, can be traced to determining economic factors. Wood engraving was less costly and easier to work with than copper-plate engraving. For several decades the two processes existed as equal rivals; but by 1845 wood engraving had become the dominant process used in book illustration. As always, Stothard

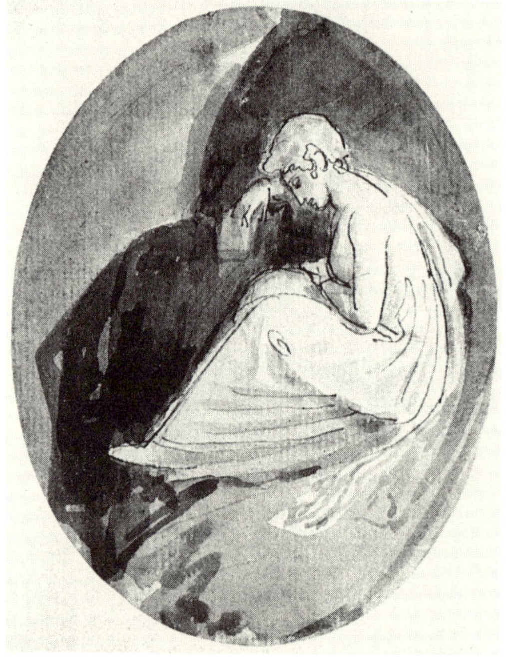

Fig. 12. Thomas Stothard, study for an illustration to Charlotte Smith's *Elegiac Sonnets,* published by Cadell (1789), pen and wash, 4½ x 3⅝.

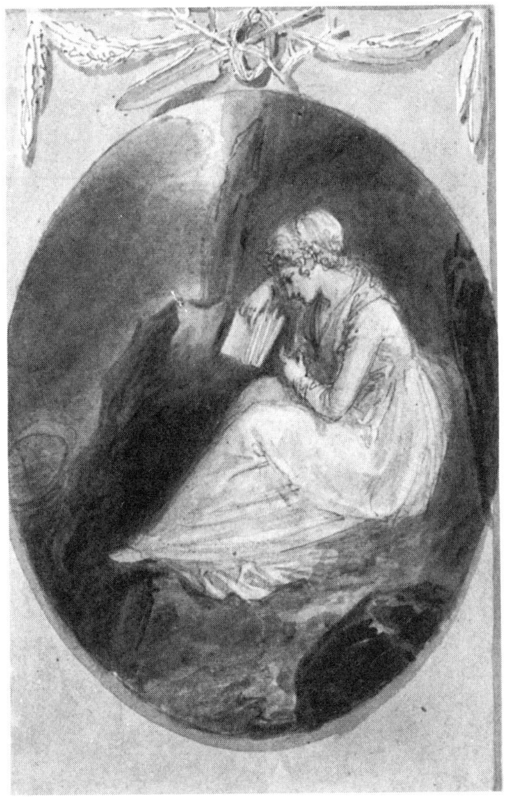

Fig. 13. Thomas Stothard, illustration to Charlotte Smith's *Elegiac Sonnets,* published by Cadell (1789), watercolor, 4 x 2¹/₂".

was one of the first illustrators to experiment with the latest technical developments.

As early as 1808, George Cumberland twice jotted down in his notebook that "Stothard draws his designs on Blocks with Pencil for the engravers."[45] And in Stothard's bill of 1809 for business completed for Cadell and Davies, he charged £25.6.0 for "five designes on Woodblocks" and £84.4.0 for four pictures from Chaucer.[46] Stothard's woodblock and vignette designs were considerably less expensive than his full-scale illustrations, for which he charged about £20 each during this same period.[47] Throughout his career, Stothard exploited a variety of different techniques to increase his market range.

3 ELEVATION IN STATUS AS AN ARTIST

THE RISE of Stothard's prices and the increase in his prestige in the art world were based on his ability to gain recognition through traditional artistic channels, such the Royal Academy, on his continued employment in the production of mass-produced art commodities, and on his work for influential private patrons, such as Samuel Rogers. The diversity of his artistic ventures demonstrates the complex mechanisms of patronage he developed at this stage in his career.

Since the inroad to artistic respectability was acceptance into the Royal Academy, Stothard also turned to that most exalted genre of art, history painting, to further his career. In 1780, soon after his entry into the Royal Academy schools, Stothard sent *The Retreat of the Greeks with the Body of Patroclus* to the annual exhibition. He exhibited three more history paintings in 1791, the year of his election as an Associate Royal Academician, and three in 1794, the year of his election to full Royal Academician.

The decades of the 1780s and 1790s were the heyday of history painting, culminating in several large-scale schemes of patronage: John Boydell's Shakespeare Gallery in Pall Mall, 1789–1805; Thomas Macklin's Poets Gallery in Pall Mall, 1788–1805, and his illustrated *Bible,* 1790–1800; and Robert Bowyer's Historic Gallery, 1790–1806, and illustrated edition of David Hume's *History of England,* 1806. Stothard's involvement in all of these ambitious projects did much to advance his artistic standing. Although Stothard did not send paintings to the Royal Academy exhibitions from 1786 to 1791, his con-

tributions to the schemes of Boydell, Macklin, and Bowyer placed his art before the public and his fellow artists in an equally exalted surrounding. His paintings for these projects were generally well received. As one newspaper reviewer said in 1788 of his *Amyntor and Theodora* from David Mallet's poem for Macklin's Poets Gallery:

This representation is at the point of time when Amyntor first views his beloved Theodora, after she is landed from the skiff. It is painted by Mr. Stothard, who by the performance, has shown himself an artist of great merit. The languid state of Theodora, Amyntor's surprise, and the characteristic manner of the group of islanders, are all beautifully expressed. In the composition of the piece, there is considerable skill and genius.[1]

Stothard's contribution to Boydell's Shakespeare Gallery in 1790, a painting depicting the meeting of King Henry VIII, Cardinal Wolsey, and Anne Boleyn (act 1, scene 4, *Henry VIII*), elicited even more effusive comments from another reviewer:

"Each heavenly piece enraptur'd we compare, / Match Raphael's Grace with thy lov'd Guido's air." In this very masterly and learned composition, which beams with taste and elegance, Mr. Stothard's apparent aim has been Grace, and grace is the presiding feature of this picture. In drawing and disposition of the figures, delicacy of marking, and nice discrimination of character, it has that simple and pure air which distinguishes the works of Correggio and Parmegiano. . . . Mr. Stothard's classical and correct taste, his perfect conception of character, and intimate acquaintance with the work of the best painters of antiquity, promise to place him very high among the very first of the profession.[2]

In November 1791, Stothard was elected an Associate Royal Academician and by January 1792 Townley could report to his friend Cumberland, "I hope poor Charles is getting into Employ— Stothard is finally."[3] So closely did Stothard equate the profession of artist with the Royal Academy, that even after he attained the highest honor of full Royal Academician in 1794, he remained closely associated with Royal Academy business for the rest of his life. Throughout his career, Stothard played an active role in the Academy as a Visitor to the Life Drawing Class or a member of the Council and later as the Royal Academy Librarian.

With recognition by the Royal Academy came an augmentation in authority on all matters of art. For example, in 1797 Stothard's opinion as an expert was solicited in the Jewdwine/Slade case questioning the authenticity of paintings by Claude, Cuyp, and Ruysdael.[4]

In the year of his election to full Royal Academician, Stothard was assured enough of his financial future to use the remainder of the capital left him by his father to buy a comfortably furnished house at No. 28 Newman Street for his rapidly growing family.[5] Newman Street was the "Artists Street," inhabited by Benjamin West, John Bacon, John Russell, James Ward, Henry Howard, and many others, amounting to almost forty artists. Stothard's geographic move represented a material sign of his success as a professional artist.

The culmination of Stothard's growing prestige in the art world came in 1799 when he received from Lord Exeter the important commission to execute three wall paintings at Burleigh (also spelled Burghley) House in Stamford,

Northamptonshire. Stothard received the considerable sum of about £1,300 for these large wall decorations, which occupied him for five summers, from 1799 to 1803. Stothard painted three historical compositions, *Intemperance,* also known as *The Banquet of Cleopatra* (Fig. 14), *The Horrors of War,* and *Orpheus and Eurydice.* Clearly, Stothard was esteemed by his contemporaries as a history painter in the grand manner, as well as a designer for mass-produced art commodities. As John Williams noted in 1796 about the Royal Academy Exhibition of 1794:

I congratulate the Royal Academy on the acquisition of such a member as Mr. Stothard, whose education and understanding enables him to rescue the general character of a Royal Academician from the imputation of ignorance, and whose urbane manners render his preeminence tolerable to all. I do not hesitate to assert, that this gentleman is the ONLY Artist in this country who can comprehend, with keen precision, a subject dependent upon historical fact.[6]

Although actively pursuing academic recognition through the traditional means of history painting, Stothard did not relinquish his radical political affiliations or his employment in mass-produced craft production. In his association with the banker-poet Samuel Rogers from 1792 onward, these two commitments coincided and contributed to his artistic eminence. Rogers inherited his father's liberal, nonconformist beliefs and embraced the political principles of close friends from the Whig opposition such as Charles James Fox, Richard Sheridan, George Cumberland, Horne Tooke, and Sydney Smith, and fellow enthusiasts of the French Revolution such as Paine and Priestley. Following the success in the fashionable world of his poem *The Pleasures of Memory* in 1792, Rogers became an arbiter of taste in all matters pertaining to literature. Among his literary friends, Rogers could name Byron, Cole-

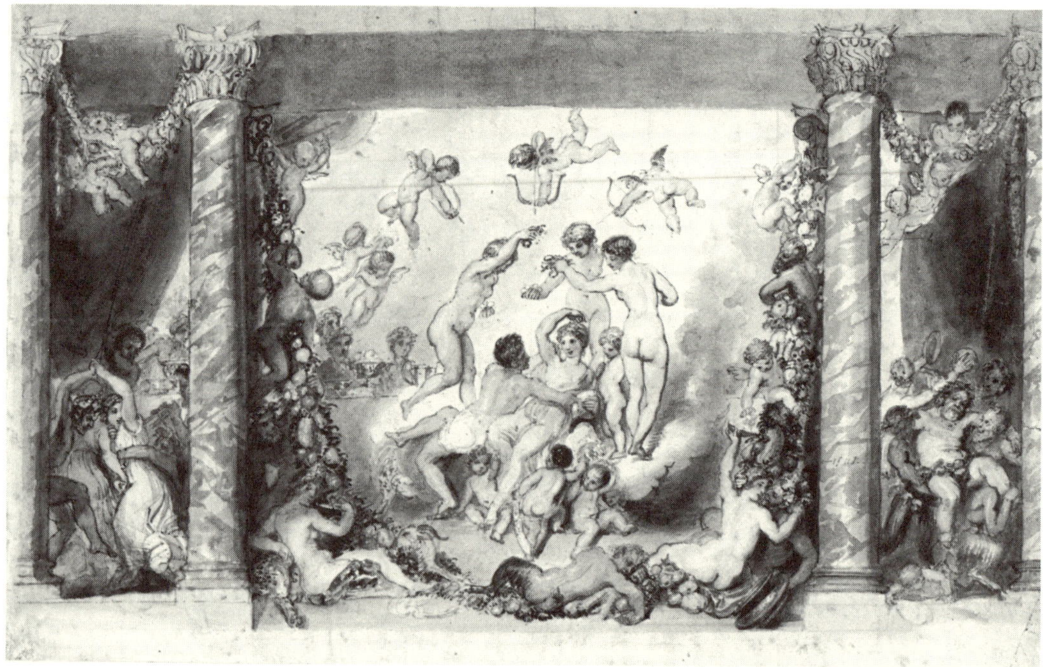

Fig. 14. Thomas Stothard, study for *Intemperance* in Burleigh House, 1799–1803, watercolor, 17 x 10¹/₂".

ridge, Wordsworth, Thomas Moore, Thomas Campbell, and later Dickens.

Rogers extended his reputation as a discriminating patron to the art world through his brother-in-law Sutton Sharpe, a wealthy brewer who studied drawing at the Royal Academy. At his house, Rogers met several artists including Stothard, John Opie, John Flaxman, and Thomas Bewick. Stothard is present at one of Rogers's celebrated breakfasts recorded in a large print (Fig. 15).

The first entry of Stothard's name in Rogers's diary appears on 13 November 1792 and suggests the common interests shared by the two men:

Dined at Sharpe's and met Boddington and Stothard. Stothard said: "If the Pantheon were in London I think I should be a happier man. I often take an evening walk in the park in summer to observe the figures, and at a distance they position themselves into those bold simple forms that were the delight of the Grecian artists."[7]

Rogers also attempted to capture the imagination of London society through the avant-garde decoration of his London house and turned to Stothard for contributions to his lavish artistic scheme. Rogers's treasures at 22 St. James's Place included one of the choicest collections of Greek and Roman vases in England. Rogers also collected paintings and drawings that would attest to his progressive artistic tastes. Of the old masters, he owned paintings both by the major Baroque masters, which he purchased from the Orleans Gallery sale, and by the Italian Primitives. Rogers also patronized contemporary artists. He owned all of Flaxman's drawings for Aeschylus and one of the largest contemporary collections of Stothard's drawings.[8] In addition, he commissioned Stothard to paint versions of his well-known paintings on a cabinet for his house. A contemporary article in *The Athenaeum* of 29 December 1855 describes this piece: "Opposite the chimney-piece a cabinet of lightwood is panelled with pictures by Stoth-

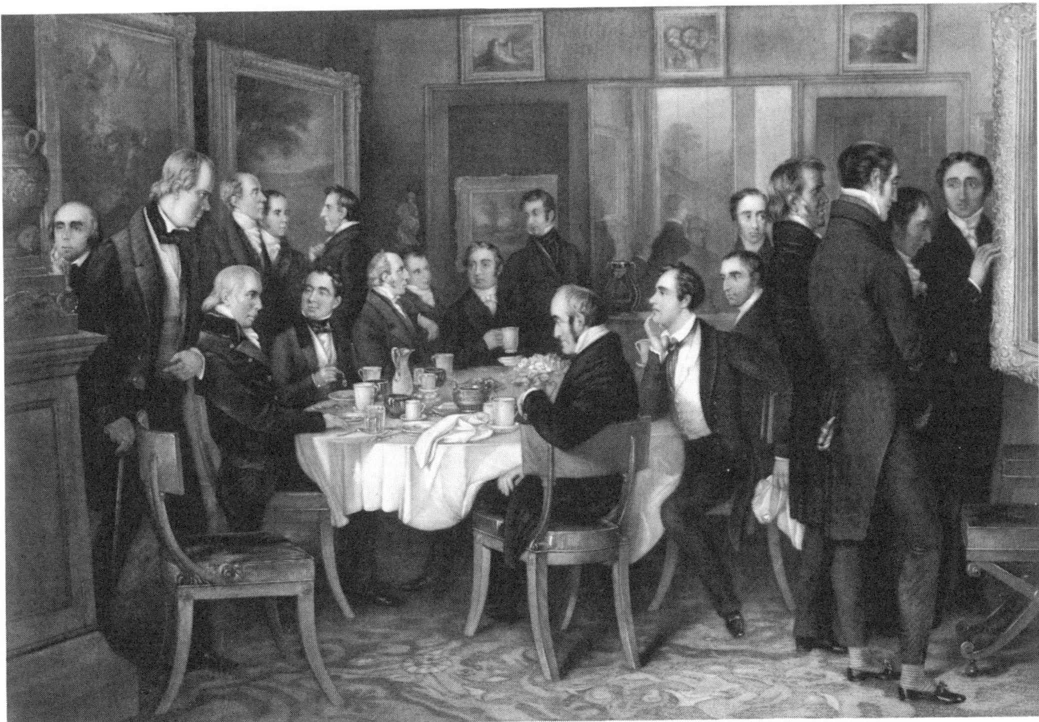

Fig. 15. Samuel Rogers's celebrated breakfast, engraved by C. Mottram (published 1815), 26½ x 35¾". From left to right, the figures are identified in the print as: John Flaxman, Walter Scott, James MacKintosh, Lansdowne/Sheridan, Thomas Moore, Sydney Smith/Wm. Wordsworth, Robert Southey, S. T. Coleridge, Washington Irving, Samuel Rogers, Byron, J. K. Kemel [?], T. Jeffrey, Thomas Stothard, Thomas Lawrence, J. M. W. Turner, and T. Campbell.

ard. The subjects are the characters of Shakespeare, the Canterbury Pilgrims, the characters of the Decameron, and the Sans Souci."[9]

When *The Pleasures of Memory* reached its sixth edition in 1794, Rogers decided to embellish the publication with two illustrations by Richard Westall and two by Stothard of *Hunt the Slipper* (Fig. 16) and *Her Senses Had Fled!* (Fig. 17). Stothard's illustrations were continued in many subsequent editions and contributed to the success of this popular work. By 1806, it had reached its fifteenth edition with most editions ranging from one thousand to two thousand copies.[10] As late as 18 March 1812, Farington noted:

Fuseli spoke of Rogers as a Poet & Said "He never wrote a line of Poetry in His life, all His good lines are *copies* from Poets, and in His 'Pleasures of Memory' He begins with Gray! For this work so popular does it continue to be, Rogers receives £100 a year from Booksellers for the privilege of publishing it."

Rogers was ever aware of the value of Stothard's illustrations to a book, for when a new edition of *The Pleasures of Memory* was published by Cadell in 1810, Stothard was chosen to design a set of thirty-four vignettes to be engraved on wood by Luke Clennell, a follower of Bewick. Likewise, Stothard was chosen to illustrate vignettes for Rogers's *Human Life* (1820) and for *The Pleasures of Memory* and *Italy, Part I,* which appeared in the *Royal Engagement Pocket Atlas* in 1808 and 1825.

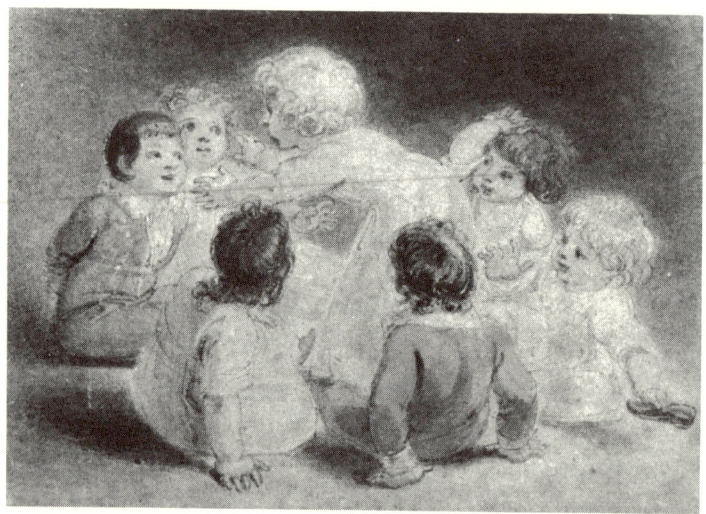

Fig. 16. Thomas Stothard, *Hunt the Slipper*, published in Rogers's *The Pleasures of Memory* (1794), watercolor, 1¼ x 3⅛".

To ensure the popular success of his publications of *Italy* in 1830 and of *Poems* in 1834 and to bolster his waning literary reputation, Rogers again turned to Stothard for illustrations. When *Italy* first appeared (anonymously) in 1822, it had received no critical attention; so Rogers decided to revise and reissue it in a sumptuous edition with illustrations by Stothard and J. M. W. Turner. The ten thousand printed copies of *Italy* cost Rogers the exorbitant sum of £2,016 for embellishments and a total of £7,335; but by May 1832, sixty-eight hundred copies had been sold, and the sales soon covered Rogers's initial financial output.[11] Rev. John Mitford noted in his "Recollections" (1847–1856), "Wordsworth to Dyce speakes of Rogers' Poems (Italy), 'The Plates mad[e] it sell, for in the Poetry there's nothing—absolutely nothing.'"[12]

Rogers asserted his control over all matters, choosing not only the illustrators but also the subject and the manner of illustration.[13] As Mitford noted in his "Recollections": "Rogers said Turner and Stothard entered into his views without difficulty in the illustrations of his Italy & Poems—assisted each other—did whatever he wished."[14]

Rogers told Rev. Alexander Dyce,

This vignette by Stothard was done from my description of what I actually saw—an Italian girl giving her little brother water to drink in the palms of her joined hands. I never had any difficulty with Stothard and Turner about the drawings for my works. They always readily assented to whatever alterations I proposed; and sometimes I even put a figure by Stothard into one of Turner's landscapes. The two figures in the foreground of vignette p. 151 are Stothard's; the standing figure in vignette p. 248 is also Stothard's.[15] [See Figs. 18–20]

Rogers decided to assign the figural subjects to Stothard. Turner, who was considered weak in his treatment of figures, was given all the landscapes and architectural vignettes.

The decisive proof of Rogers's determining control over most of the artistic decisions appears in the relationship between different versions of several of Stothard's designs. In his development of an illustration titled *The Gondola* (Figs. 21–23) for *Italy,* Stothard was evidently persuaded to alter his original placement of the male figure in his finished design. Rather than creating an entirely new drawing, Stothard used a device that deviated from his usual practice. He placed the altered version of the male figure on top of his original design

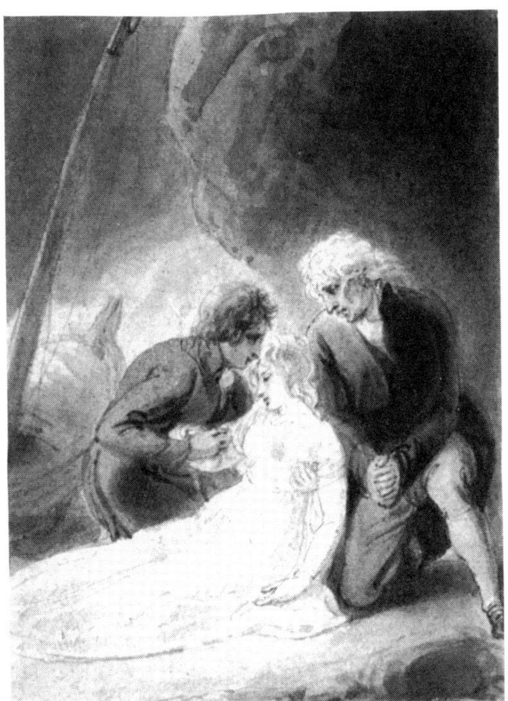

Fig. 17. Thomas Stothard, *Her Senses Had Fled,* published in Rogers's *The Pleasures of Memory* (1794), watercolor, 3¹/₂ x 2⁵/₈″.

(Fig. 22) so that it could be flipped up, allowing the two versions to be compared, evidently leaving the final choice up to Rogers. Rogers's control over the total production of these illustrations also is clearly demonstrated by the fate of *The Gondola.* Rogers was not satisfied with Stothard's adjustments to the composition; thus, he did not have this illustration engraved for the publication.

Rogers was able to exert his authority during any stage of this collaborative artistic venture. For example, Stothard was apparently required to alter his composition of *The Swing* (Fig. 24) for Rogers's *Poems* (1834) after it had already reached the engravers. Stothard pasted another version, this time altered in subject matter rather than style, over the proof state (Fig. 25). The steel-plate engravings Rogers decided to utilize for these editions required much time and labor. In fact, the

proofs for *Italy* were under way in 1827, yet not completed until 1829.[16] Thus this revision after the plate had been partially prepared would have called for lengthy and costly alterations. In this instance, Rogers chose to remain with Stothard's original version of *The Swing,* for that is the illustration that appears in the publication.

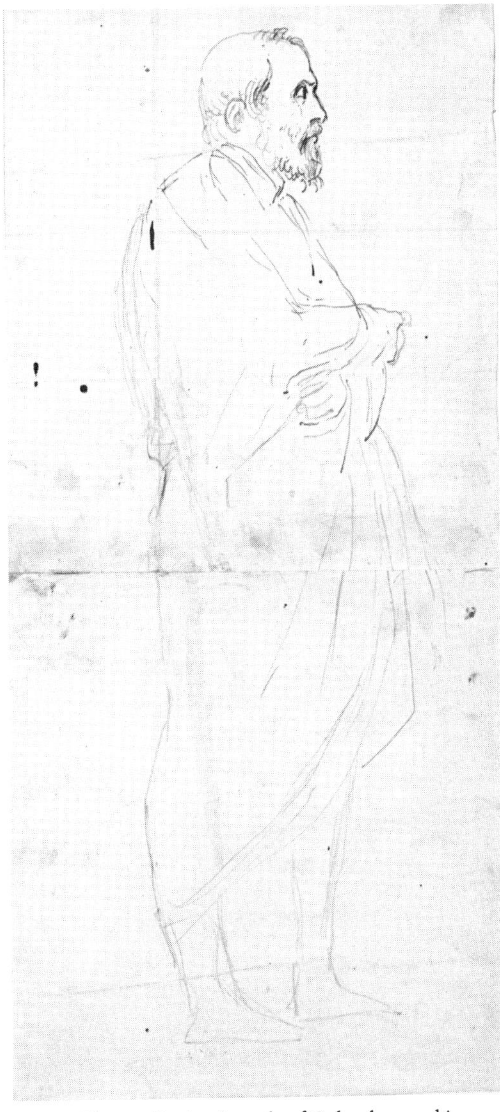

Fig. 18. Thomas Stothard, study of Columbus used in Turner's illustration of *Land Discovered by Columbus,* published in Rogers's *Poems* (1834), pencil and pen, 13¹/₂ x 6¹/₄″.

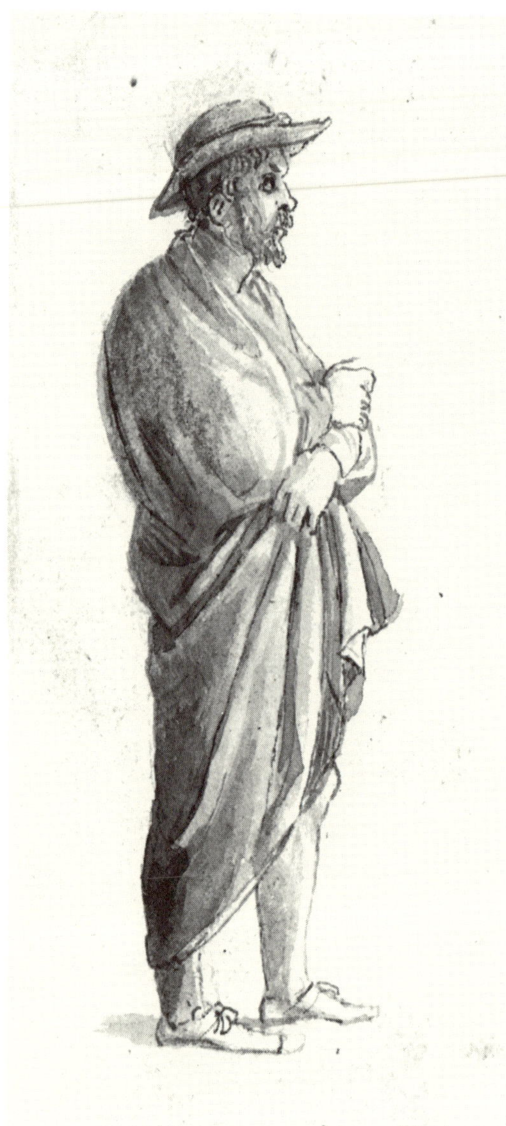

Fig. 19. Thomas Stothard, study of Columbus used in Turner's illustration of *Land Discovered by Columbus,* published in Rogers's *Poems* (1834), pen and wash, 6 x 4¼".

Rogers was the intermediary and guiding force in this commercial venture. His efforts were so successful that his publication of *Italy* remained popular for the next one hundred years.

The readiness with which Stothard complied with Rogers's requests indicates that his relations with this poet-publisher were similar to those he had already established with his professional publishers in London. In each case, his role in the creation of the final art product was that of a specialist, collaborating in the production of an art commodity. Stothard's pliable and submissive attitude to the demands of his publishers and patrons was probably an important factor influencing the booksellers in their frequent employment of his talents.

This may explain why publishers consistently chose Stothard to illustrate their publications, even though a more vitalized style of book illustration was available in the works of contemporary artists such as Henry Fuseli, Philip de Loutherbourg, Robert Smirke, or Edward Francis Burney. Burney, for example, created an energetic interpretation of the shipwreck scene (Fig. 26) for George Kearsley's edition of Fénelon's *The Adventures of Telemachus, The Son of Ulysses,* which was published in 1795. Burney's robust and vigorous design is a more sympathetic interpretation of Fénelon's narrative than Stothard's illustration

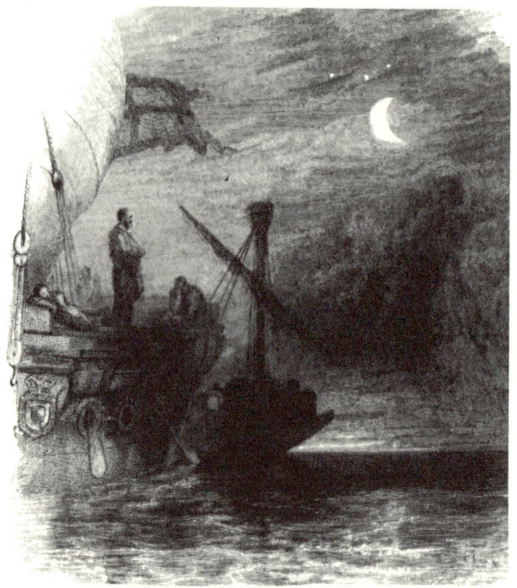

Fig. 20. J. M. W. Turner, *Land Discovered by Columbus,* published in Rogers's *Poems* (1834), engraving, image 3½ x 3".

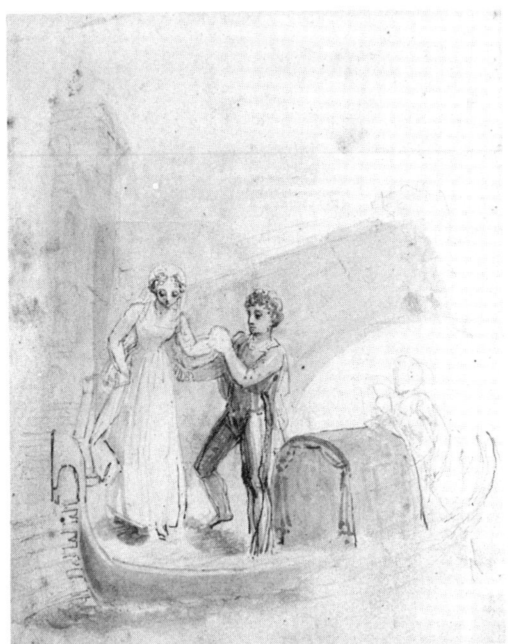

Fig. 21. Thomas Stothard, study for *The Gondola,* pen and wash, 5½ x 4½".

of the identical scene (Fig. 27) for this same edition. Line is the principal means of creating expression in both of these illustrations, but distinctly different types of expression. In this shipwreck episode, Venus is attempting to entice Telemachus, the son of Ulysses, away from his companion Mentor, who is Minerva in disguise. In the Stothard design, an innocent, adolescent, discreetly modest Venus arranges herself in a decorative arabesque pose that has no direct relationship to the action around her. Stothard's several studies of Venus's twisting pose reveal that he carefully considered her action in and of itself, but with little regard for its relation to the meaning of the whole composition. In contrast to Burney's reclining, mature Venus figure and his vigorously active male characters, Stothard has reversed the emphasis, throwing the expressive weight onto the female figure. Stothard often relied on the female figure as his chief expressive device to convey both grace and sentiment. But,

in this case, the qualities of grace and sentiment were not in keeping with the spirit of the text. The meaning of the passage is completely obscured in Stothard's illustration. While Burney's illustration represents an aggressive, vital Minerva (Virtue) who mirrors the moral overtones of the narrative, Stothard's sentimental interpretation of Venus (Vice) has subverted the didactic message of this scene. Burney's tight, hard, springing lines add to the overall sense of dramatic tension. In contrast, Stothard's swelling, gracefully curving outlines heighten the lyrical, decorative quality. Stothard's design rather than Burney's more appropriate interpretation was chosen, however, for publication in the 1795 edition of Fénelon's *Telemachus.*

Stothard's style and interpretation in this drawing of the shipwreck scene from *Telemachus* are typical of his narrative approach. No matter what the emotional tenor of the text, his illustrations are always attractive, decorative designs with little or no dramatic impact. His inability to render the full range of emotions reveals the expressive limitations of his style. Yet the majority of Stothard's

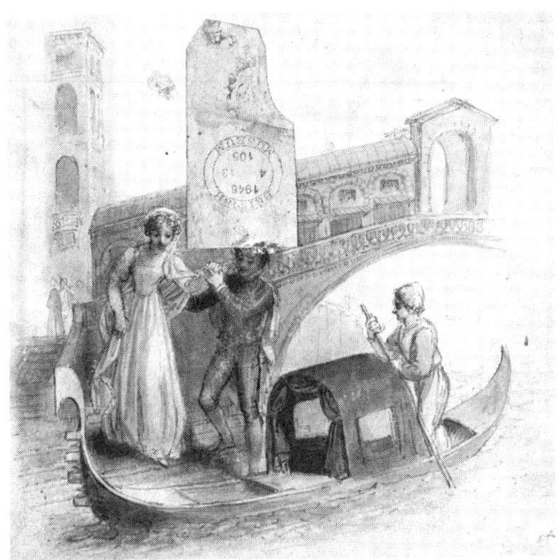

Fig. 22. Thomas Stothard, *The Gondola,* pen and wash, 5 x 5".

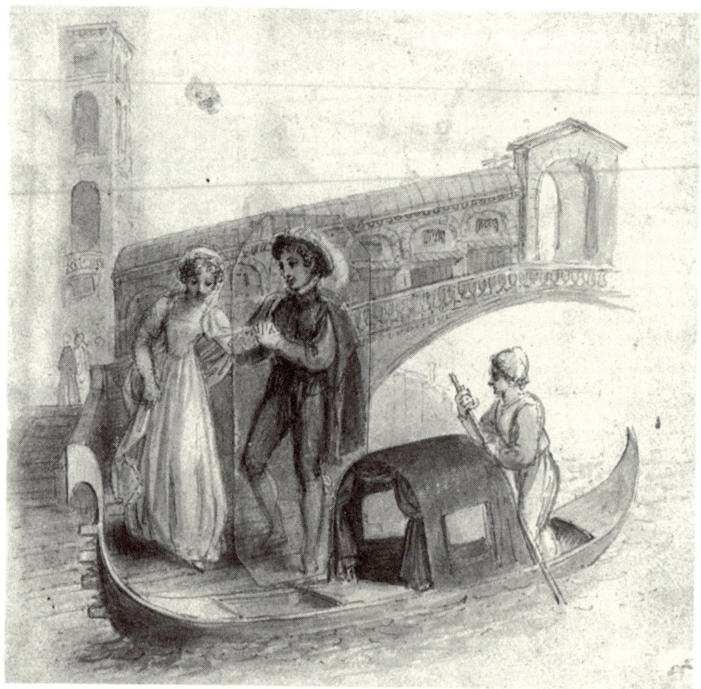

Fig. 23. Thomas Stothard, *The Gondola* with altered drawing pasted over Fig. 22,, pen and wash, 5 x 5".

contemporaries seldom, if ever, perceived these limitations. Quite to the contrary, Stothard was often lauded for his ability to capture a wide range of emotions. The words of a contemporary provide useful clues to this eighteenth-century point of view:

Of all our artists who have applied their talents to the illustration of books, he is unquestionably the most original in composition, the most varied, refined and characteristic. In this latter quality he is especially distinguished; it being wonderful to see with what spirit he identifies himself with his subject, and makes his compositions appear, as well in the character of their figures, as in their inferior adjuncts of scenery, buildings, costume, &c. to belong inseparably to the time and story which he treats. The great fertility of his pencil has not weakened this merit: nearly the whole of his productions having their "proper mark and likelihood" from delineating, with surprising verisimilitude, the *quaint, time-hallowed* humour and nature of old Chaucer, he will pass to the *artificial* manners of the reign of Queen Anne, which, in his

drawings for the Spectator "live and move, and have their being" once more. With Milton his is *primeval and angelical;* with Bunyan *dreamy* and Calvinistic: he represents the solitary moods of the mariner Robinson Crusoe on the uninhabited island, as if he had been cast away with him, and then he flutters with *infinite grace* in the courtly and sparkling scenes of Pope's "Rape of the Lock." With Spencer he is able to *escape from the world of realities,* and lose himself in the *shadowy domains* of Faery; and while nothing can be more *abstracted and ideal* than his designs for this poet, it would seem, on the other hand, in looking at his scenes from the modern novelists, that towns and drawing-rooms, boarding-school heroines, and ordinary society, were his proper and only sphere. The work before us [Stothard's illustrations to Boccacio's *Decameron*] is eminent indeed in this quality of adaptation to the subject matter.[17]

These themes are constantly reiterated in contemporary diaries, letters, and periodicals that stress the abstract, ideal, primitive, timeless quality of Stothard's art. It would seem that his art

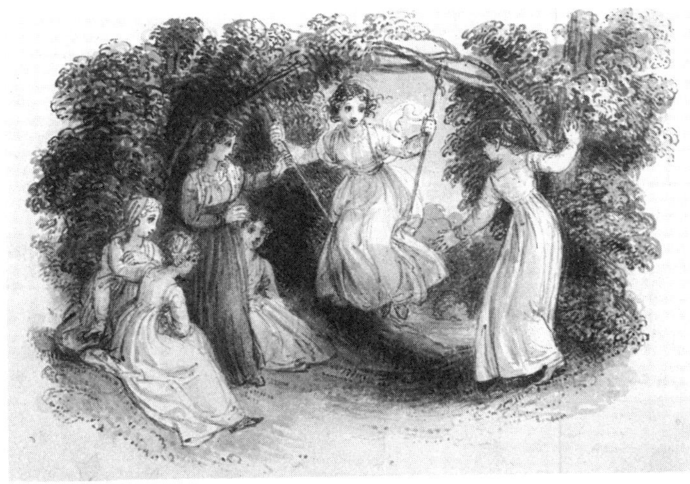

Fig. 24. Thomas Stothard, *The Swing,* published in Rogers's *Poems* (1834), pen and watercolor, 5⁷/₈ x 7¹/₈".

embodied those universal qualities that his contemporaries associated with "the classics" (that is, good literature). His visual interpretations effectively engaged the sympathies and emotions of this literary audience.[18]

Although Stothard's art covered a wide range of experience, most of his designs were directed to the widespread interest in sentimental subject matter. His illustrations are oriented to the new concern with tender sentiments in the late eighteenth century. More than any of his fellow artists, he satisfied the commercial demand for visual images that catered to this taste. To do so, Stoth-ard utilized various standard devices. In particular, the female figure became his primary vehicle for arousing the compassion of his audience.[19] Like numerous writers and artists during the eighteenth century, he exploited stock formulas, such as female virtue in distress, to stir up the benevolent emotions of his audience.

The popular conception of this ideal woman is captured in Stothard's rendition of Samuel Richardson's heroine, Clarissa (Fig. 28). In this scene, *Lovelace's Dream,* one of a large series of illustrations he designed for Richardson's *Clarissa,* published in 1784 in Harrison's *Novelist's Magazine,*

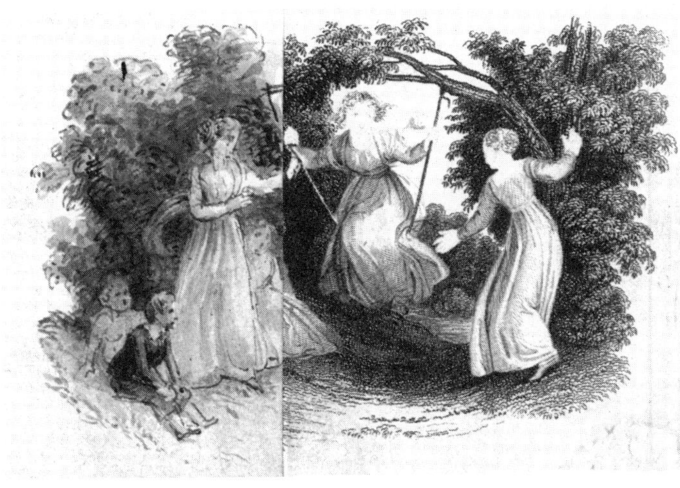

Fig. 25. Thomas Stothard, *The Swing* with altered drawing pasted over the engraved proof, image 2¹/₂ x 3³/₈".

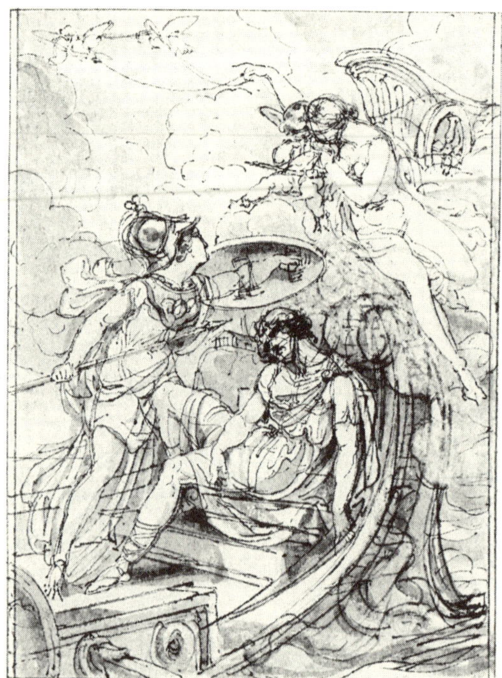

Fig. 26. Edward Francis Burney, illustration of the shipwreck scene for Kearsley's edition of Fénelon's *The Adventures of Telemachus* (1795), pen and wash, 7¼ x 7¼".

Stothard relied on the female form to embody the eighteenth-century concept of grace. The long, continuous contour lines of Clarissa's figure and dress are constantly varied by her animated poses. Stothard emphasized to the point of distortion the gliding, curving lines that describe the figure. Clarissa's proportions have been elongated in order to facilitate a maximum sense of fluid motion. Disregard for anatomy has been carried to such an extreme that Clarissa's figure is awkwardly short between her foot and knee in contrast to the exaggerated elongation of her figure in the area from her knees to her high waistline. Her body has been arbitrarily altered to enhance the flowing lines of her dress, which create a sense of liquid, graceful action.

Stothard quickly became renowned for his ability to capture in his art the eighteenth-century ideas of feminine grace and beauty. As a contem-

porary artist noted, "In the works of Stothard female beauty and elegance strongly prevail, and that in a degree infinitely beyond his contemporaries."[20] Or as noted by a newspaper reviewer of the 1790 Royal Academy Exhibition,

Stothard preserves this year the rank which was allotted to him in the last Exhibition by the general voice. The elegance and beauty of his female figures—the aerial softness and taste with which his subjects are endowed, give him title to our warmest praise and which justly increased by the diffidence with which he withholds his claims.[21]

Or as charmingly phrased by Leigh Hunt in a poem dedicated to Stothard,

Thy fancy lives in a delightful sphere,
Stothard, -fit haunt for spirit so beneign;
For never since those southern masters fine,
In whose blest shapes, unforced, unflattering, clear,
Manifest truth and sweet-eyed soul appear,
Has true woman's gentle mien divine
Looked so, as in those breathing heads of thine,
With parted locks, and simple cheek sincere.

Therefore, against our climate's chilly hold,
Thou hast a nest in sunny glades and bowers;
And there, about thee, never growing old,
Are these fair things, clear as the lily flowers,
Such as great Petrarch loved, —only less cold,
More truly virtuous, and of gladdening powers.[22]

Stothard evidently was conscious that this was his most effective expressive means; for he asked Flaxman to apply to Hayley for a suggested subject in which women were the vehicle of expression. As Flaxman wrote in about 1795,

I have a request to make of you in that gentleman's [Stothard's] behalf that at your leisure you will look over the old English writers, scriptures post Bedam, Matt. Weston Matt: Brisiesis & Guile Malmburiensis for 2 or 3 beautiful subjects in which women are intro-

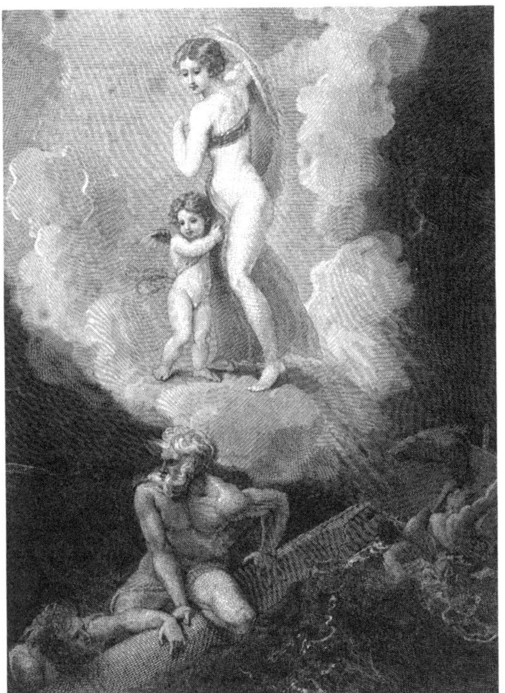

Fig. 27. Thomas Stothard, illustration of the shipwreck scene for Kearsley's edition of Fénelon's *The Adventures of Telemachus* (1795), engraving, 7½ x 5½".

duced for a Picture he is employed to paint for Boydel.²³

The extent of Stothard's influence in popularizing this visual mode of interpretation can be quickly demonstrated by examining the impact of one of his numerous illustrations to Oliver Goldsmith's *The Vicar of Wakefield.* This novel, more than any other literary work, marks the shift in taste to the sentimental.

The Vicar of Wakefield (1766) did not appear with illustrations until 1780 when Harrison published the novel with two prints by Daniel Dodd and William Walker in the *Novelist's Magazine.* These two illustrators depicted respectively the scenes of *The Vicar Confronting Burchell with the Letter* and *Burchell's Rescue of Sophia from the Coach.* The former scene is completely devoid of dramatic action. The figures are frozen in stiff, formal, rhetorical poses that convey little or no meaning. The latter illustration depicts one of the few physically violent moments in the narrative and is atypical of the novel's overall emotional tone. Neither exploits incidents in tune with the contemporary audience's tender sentiments.

In 1792 Harding published a new edition of the ever-popular *The Vicar of Wakefield* with six illustrations by Stothard. Stothard's interpretations were so entirely in sympathy with contemporary tastes that his illustrations set the standard for the many following illustrations of this novel. He chose to depict the scenes that would play strongly on the feelings of his audience; most characteristic is *Sophia Being Rescued from the Stream by*

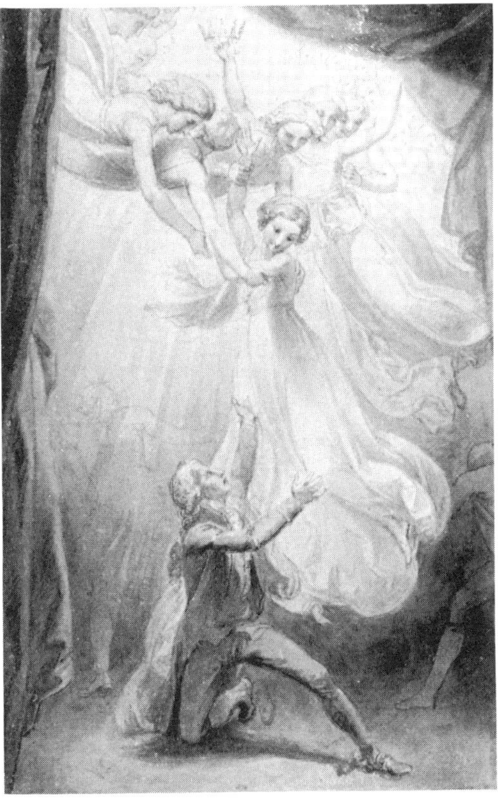

Fig. 28. Thomas Stothard, *Lovelace's Dream* for Richardson's *Clarissa,* published in Harrison's *Novelist's Magazine* (1784), pen and wash, 4½ x 3".

Burchell (Fig. 29). The delicate sensibility of the reader would be deeply moved by such a scene of beauty in distress and deeply thrilled by the sentimental rescue, which provided an incentive for Sophia and Burchell to fall in love. This scene is a hallmark of the cult of sensibility, and its repeated depiction by following illustrators attests to its ability to reach a wide audience.[24] Stothard's illustration of *Sophia's Rescue* set the precedent that was followed by Thomas Rowlandson in Rudolph Ackermann's 1817 edition, by William Mulready in an 1834 edition, and by John Masey Wright (1777–1866) in an illustration that was issued in the much later 1903 publication by Adam and Charles Black.

The few deviations in Stothard's art from this sentimental manner of interpretation were due to the special demands of his employers, as can be seen in his work for Thomas Hope. Hope was among the new arbiters of refinement in London society in the early nineteenth century. Through the lavish decorations and furnishings in his celebrated house in Duchess Street and through his highly acclaimed publications, such as *Household Furniture and Interior Decoration* (1807), Hope proselytized his eclectic notions on art, combining a taste for classical, gothic, oriental and various exotic cultures. From a wealthy family of Amsterdam bankers, Hope was able to finance his extravagant schemes. He patronized several of the greatest painters and sculptors of his day, collected antique art, acquiring part of Hamilton's second collection of Greek vases, and even tried his hand at creative writing. His most famous novel, *Anastasius, or Memoirs of a Greek written at the close of the Eighteenth Century* (1819), was based on his extensive travels.

In March 1805, Hope commissioned from Stothard a painting from Greek History of *Hector Bidding Farewell to Andromache* to add to his celebrated Picture Gallery.[25] This unique room was

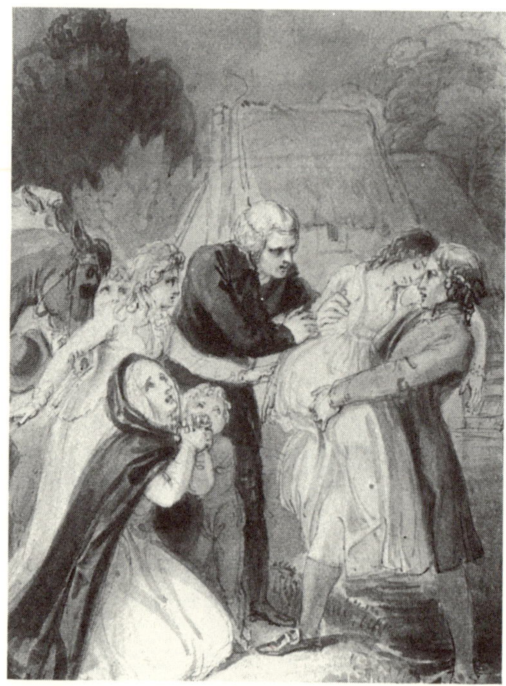

Fig. 29. Thomas Stothard, *Sophia Being Rescued from the Stream by Burchell,* published in Goldsmith's *The Vicar of Wakefield* (1792), pen and wash, 4³/₄ x 3¹/₄".

modeled on a combination of classical Ionic temples and was adorned with canvases of Greek mythology painted by Benjamin West, George Dawe, and Richard Westall.

The fame of Hope's house had spread far and wide after he opened it to public exhibition in 1804. This public exposure provided Stothard with another opportunity to advance his artistic status and reputation; thus, he made numerous studies for this commission. A series of related sketches (see Fig. 30), one of which is on the verso of a dated summons to a Royal Academy meeting on "12th December 1804," reflects the composition of the finished painting.[26] Stothard was preceded by Gavin Hamilton, David Allan, and Angelica Kauffman in his depiction of this subject from Homer's *Iliad*.[27] For his painting for Hope, Stothard followed Hamilton, basing his composition on the famous model in Nero's Golden House

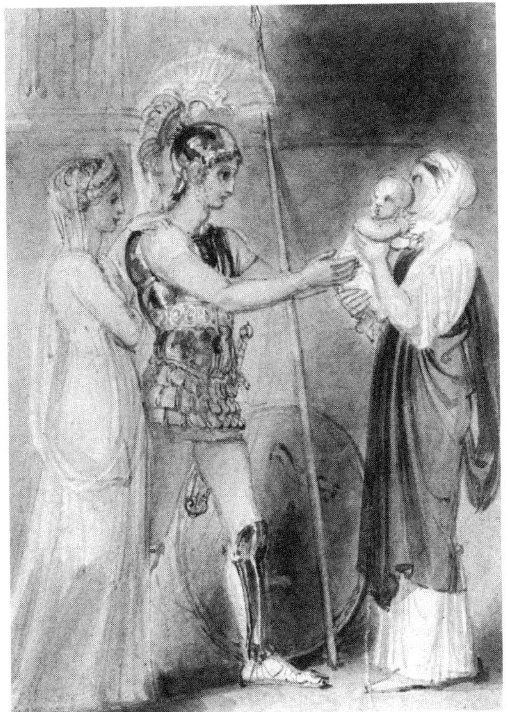

Fig. 30. Thomas Stothard, study for *Hector Bidding Farewell to Andromache*, commissioned by Thomas Hope in 1805, watercolor, 4 x 2⁷/₈".

in Rome that represents the moment in Hector's farewell to Andromache when his child recoils in fright from his helmet:

So speaking glorious Hektor held out his arms to his baby who shrank back to his fair-girdled nurse's bosom screaming, and frightened at the aspect of his own father, terrified as he saw the bronze and the crest with its horse-hair, nodding dreadfully, as he thought, from the peak of the helmet.[28]

When Stothard illustrated this same subject for Du Roveray's *Classics* in 1805, he completely altered the interpretation (Fig. 31). For the book illustration, Stothard depicted the next moment in Homer's narrative:

Then his beloved father laughed out, and his honoured mother, and at once glorious Hektor lifted from his head the helmet and laid it in all its shining upon the ground. Then taking up his dear son tossed him about in his arms, and kissed him.[29]

The differing demands of Stothard's employers account for these variations in choice of moment and interpretation. The emotional tenor of his design for Hope is in keeping with the solemn, almost religious significance of Hope's iconographic program for his temple of art. The interpretation he created for Du Roveray, with its exploitation of the sentimental overtones of this atypical passage from Homer, is characteristic of book illustration in general during this period. As always, Stothard was quick to respond to the diverse tastes and requirements of his various employers.

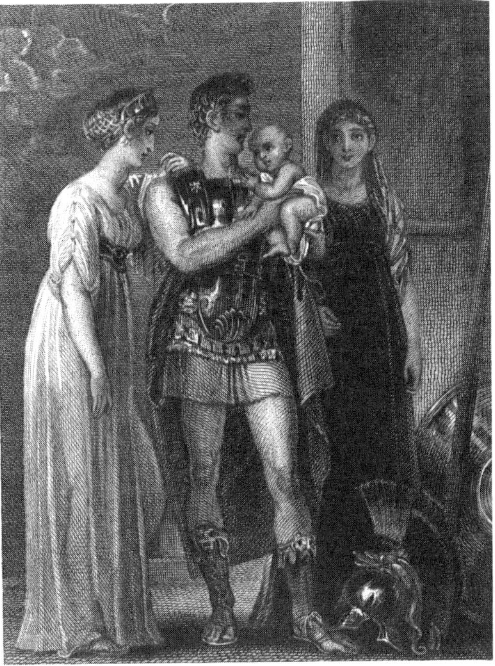

Fig. 31. Thomas Stothard, *Hector Bidding Farewell to Andromache*, published in Du Roveray's *Iliad* (1805), engraving, 4³/₄ x 3³/₄".

4 ADDITIONAL SOURCES OF INCOME

By the close of the century, Stothard had illustrated a wide range of literature, past and present. He would continue his work for book publishers at a prolific rate for many years to come, but at the beginning of the nineteenth century Stothard also began to design for a wide variety of new types of art, ranging from banknotes and theater tickets to silverwork and funerary monuments. Although he maintained his connections with radical reformers, Stothard increasingly channeled his energies into diverse artistic activities. Not only did he extend his employment for private patrons and his Royal Academy commitments, he also expanded into new areas, such as landscape drawing.

Before entering the Royal Academy schools, Stothard had displayed a strong interest in landscape. Two of his first three exhibited works at the Society of Artists in 1777 were scenes from his journey of that year to North Wales. One or two sketches survive from Stothard's various sailing trips up the Medway during his term as a student. Various contemporary sources attest to his lifelong interest in nature, in particular his enthusiasm for butterflies. While on a trip to the Lakes District in 1809, he discovered a species of butterfly, the Mountain Ringlet, then unknown in England.[1] George Phillips noted, "I have it from unquestionable authority that the late Mr. Stothard, R.A. possessed a large collection of mothes and flies, for the avowed purpose of reference to them as examples both of colouring and the disposition of ornament."[2]

On his frequent walks into the countryside surrounding London, Stothard also made numerous sketches of flowers, animals, and other aspects of nature. Yet there are no landscape drawings by him that can be dated between 1779 and 1805. His renewed interest in landscape drawing in the early nineteenth century is related both to the quickening of interest in landscape in general during this period[3] and to the influence of a new patron, Col. Thomas Johnes of Hafod.

In his work for Johnes, Stothard was probably closely directed by the personal tastes of his patron, as he was in his work for Rogers and Hope. In 1805 and maybe as early as 1803, Stothard began his summer employment for Johnes at his Hafod estate in North Wales as drawing master to his precocious, invalid daughter Mariamne.[4] As a wealthy landowner, Johnes was able to devote his time to literary pursuits. The spectacular, wild countryside surrounding Hafod and Johnes's frequent acts of patronage attracted many artists to this rather isolated spot in North Wales. Johnes gathered around himself a circle of artists that included at different times the sculptor Thomas Banks, the landscapists J. C. Ibbetson, John "Warwick" Smith, and Turner, the architect John Nash, Stothard's friend George Cumberland, and Johnes's cousin Richard Payne Knight and friend Uvedale Price. These men encouraged Johnes to develop the wilder character of his Cardinganshire estate. Well aware of the latest fashions, Johnes employed Thomas Baldwin of Bath to build him a Gothic house. His grounds also included a Garden of Eden, Alpine Bridge, and Druid Temple. When a fire burned down his house on 13 March 1807, Johnes had it rebuilt by Nash in an Indian

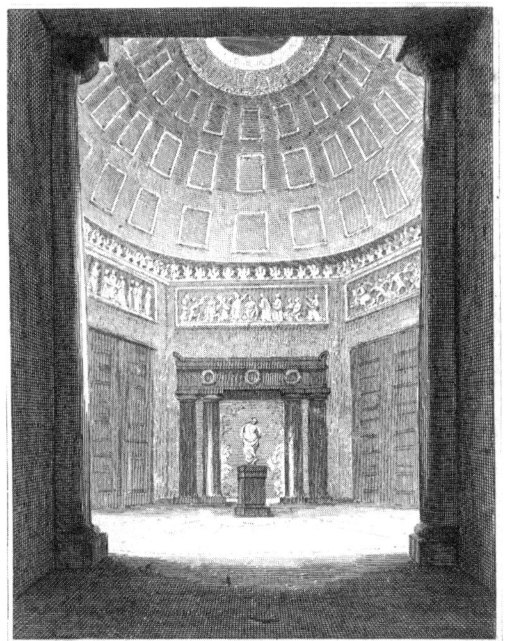

Fig. 32. Col. Thomas Johnes's Octagon Library at Hafod, illustrated in Thomas Dibdin's *The Bibliomania* (1842), engraving, image 4³/₄ x 3⁵/₈".

style with an octagon library to hold what remained of his valuable library.

When the house was completed in the summer of 1810, Johnes commissioned Stothard to decorate the upper part of this octagon library with eight panels *en grisaille* of chivalrous scenes from Monstrelet.⁵ Fuseli was commissioned to decorate the entrance hall with similar scenes from Froissart's medieval chronicles of the Hundred Years War. Based on the manuscripts in his library, Johnes had translated Monstrelet and Froissart and had published them at his private press at Hafod. Stothard realized the importance of this commission for his future employment. When he wrote to his wife to account for his lengthy stay of three months at Hafod, he proclaimed, "If I wish to succeed well with the subjects I am painting, to gain credit and future engagements, it is for your sake."⁶

By 1810, Johnes had issued the final volume of

his translation of Monstrelet. This was to be one of the last of his literary efforts; thus, Stothard's paintings were to mark the apogee of Johnes's literary career. Stothard was undoubtedly closely supervised in his selection of the subject matter for his eight panels.

A print from an 1842 edition of Thomas Dibdin's description of Johnes's octagon library in *The Bibliomania; or Book-madness* (Fig. 32) records what he saw on his visit in July 1814 and gives a vague indication of the subject matter of Stothard's scenes and of their placement. Of greater assistance in reconstructing this commission are sketches on the recto and verso of a sheet (Figs. 33–34) in an album of drawings, now in the Fitzwilliam Museum, that belonged to Stothard's close friend George Cumberland. Cumberland was also a friend of Johnes and a visitor at Hafod who composed *An Attempt to Describe Hafod* in 1796. These sketches are probably copies by Cumberland of Stothard's eight panels. In the sketch on the recto (Fig. 33), from the top frieze down, the scenes are identified by Cumberland as: "Murder of the Duke of Orleans by the Order Duke of Burgundy"; "The hasty council—the Duke refused admission"; "The Supplication of the Duchess of Orleans for Justice to Charles 6, He beloved his children also"; "Ni[?] compulsatory reconciliation of the family of Orleans with the Duke of Burgundy"; those in the sketch on the verso (Fig. 34) are identified as: "The Duke Murdered on the Bridge between Barniers—End of the Wars"; "Battle of Agincourt"; "Marriage of Hen. V with Catherine . . ."; "Coronation."

Stothard's precocious interest in medieval art prepared him for this commission. After his 1814 visit to Hafod, Dibdin declared that Stothard's scenes from Monstrelet were in his opinion far finer than the colored compositions he had done at Burleigh and "unquestionably were very much beyond what a foreign artist [Fuseli] has pre-

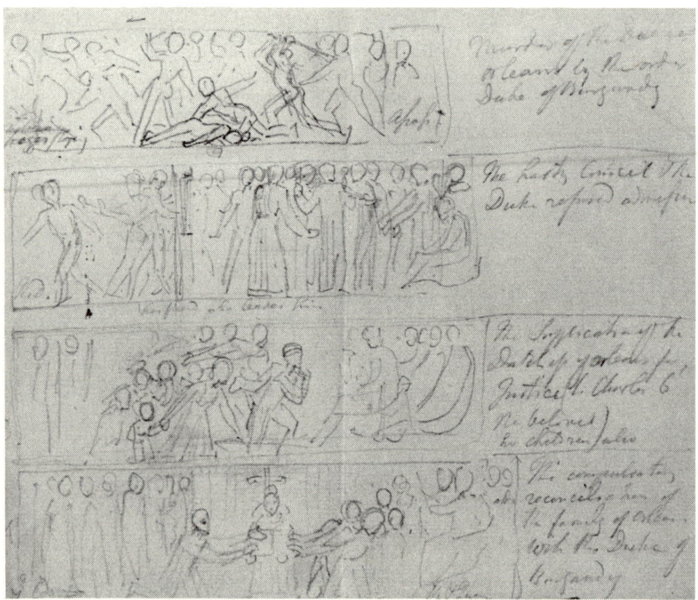

Fig. 33. George Cumberland, copy of Stothard's representations of scenes from Monstrelet for Johnes's Octagon Library, Hafod, pencil, 7¹/₂ x 8³/₄″.

viously effected in the same chiaroscuro style, on the sides of the entrance hall at Hafod, from Froissart's Chronicles."[7]

In addition to his work for Johnes as a mural painter and a drawing master, Stothard also provided him with designs for sculpture. He designed a Gothic fire screen[8] and a memorial to commemorate Johnes's beloved daughter Mariamne when she died at the age of twenty-seven. Johnes consulted Stothard about a design for this memorial soon after her death on 4 July 1811.[9] Stothard probably returned to Hafod in 1811 with his young friend Francis Chantrey to advise Johnes on this funerary monument. Typical of his collaborative artistic practices, Stothard supplied the design for the monument, which was then executed by Chantrey.[10] Stothard's son Robert also claimed that Stothard provided the designs for Chantrey's *Sleeping Children* in Lichfield Cathedral (1817).[11] Drawings by Stothard (Fig. 35) for this funerary monument (Fig. 36) substantiate Robert's statement and suggest that Stothard provided designs for Chantrey on other occasions as well. As in several of his diverse art activities, Stothard assumed a collaborative role, functioning as but one component in a complex art enterprise.

Ever responsive to his physical and intellectual surroundings, Stothard also was stimulated both by the Welsh scenery and by the theories of landscape he would have heard discussed at Hafod by Knight and Price, two prophets of the Picturesque school. Stothard never relinquished his interest in landscape. In subsequent years, with increasing frequency, he embarked on excursions into the English, Welsh, and Scottish countryside to pursue his landscape drawing (see Appendix 1). The numerous landscapes that Stothard executed throughout these years were rarely connected with a specific commission but rather reflected a more personal side of his art. Stothard's landscape drawings demonstrate, however, the same diversity and stylistic experimentation that can be found in the various other media he worked in throughout his career.

The nature of Stothard's response to his surroundings at Johnes's estate is typified by one example from among the many drawings he executed at Hafod. In a pencil drawing identified in an unknown hand as of "The Devil's Bridge" of Hafod (Fig. 37), Stothard has used the traditional pictorial convention of a looping, outlining pen or pencil line for rendering trees and foliage. Stothard modified the more rhythmic and calligraphic nature of this convention as developed by its most famous practitioner, Gainsborough. Stothard's soft, broken squiggles and the individual flecks of his pencil create a more agitated, intricate sense of surface detail.

As in his book illustrations, Stothard was never satisfied with exploiting the possibilities of only one style or technique but practiced several simultaneously. For example, the watercolors that Stothard executed on his tour in 1809 to the Lakes District and Scotland demonstrate his awareness of Turner's and Thomas Girtin's experiments. As in most of their drawings after 1800, Stothard used a horizontal composition in the majority of his drawings from this tour, such as a watercolor and pencil design inscribed "Grasmere Water— Dunmail or Raise Gap" (Fig. 38). This panoramic format amplifies the sense of breadth attained by Stothard's broad washes of watercolor.

A pencil drawing executed by Stothard "30 Nov. 1816" (Fig. 39) while on his journey to Yorkshire, Tadcaster, York, Lincoln, Ely, Beverley, and Dumfries reveals, however, the linear framework that underlies most of his landscape drawings. When developed into a watercolor design such as Stothard's *Farms in a Wooded landscape* (Fig. 40), which was probably executed on his trip to Derbyshire in 1824,[12] this linear underpinning was somewhat modified and softened by the watercolor washes. The gentleness with which Stothard's pencil touches the paper in tiny squiggles adds to the fresh, sparkling quality of this expansive, horizontal prospect. At the age of sixty-nine, Stothard produced this lyrical record of his per-

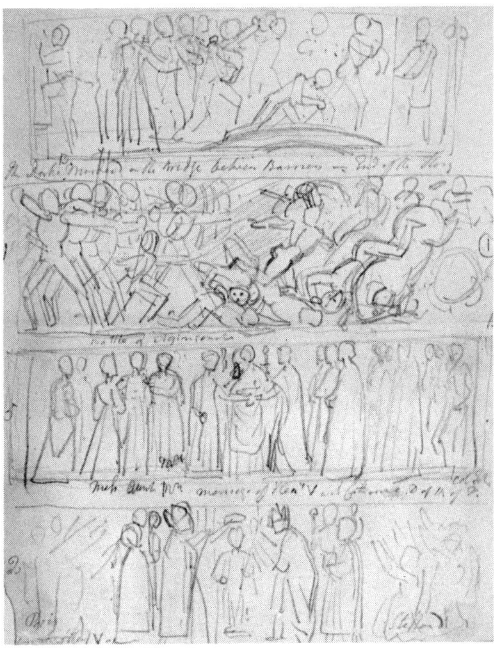

Fig. 34. George Cumberland, copy of Stothard's representations of scenes from Monstrelet for Johnes's Octagon Library, Hafod, pencil, 9 x 7¼".

sonal response to landscape. The sensitivity of Stothard's landscape technique may have influenced one of the masters of the landscape school, John Constable.[13]

In addition to reflecting his personal tastes, Stothard's increased interest in landscape reflects his astute awareness of the new importance of this subject matter after the turn of the century. Ever responsive to the prevailing tastes, he incorporated landscape into many of his book illustrations and oil paintings from this period. As a newspaper critic noted in 1818 of Stothard's painting *Fête Champêtre* for the Royal Academy exhibition, "Mr. Stothard is the only Academician who seems to think the landscape necessary in telling the story of the picture. How elegant the landscape is in a historical picture, everyone knows."[14]

In the early years of the nineteenth century, Stothard also sought out new sources of income in the diverse areas of silver, prints, and ephemera

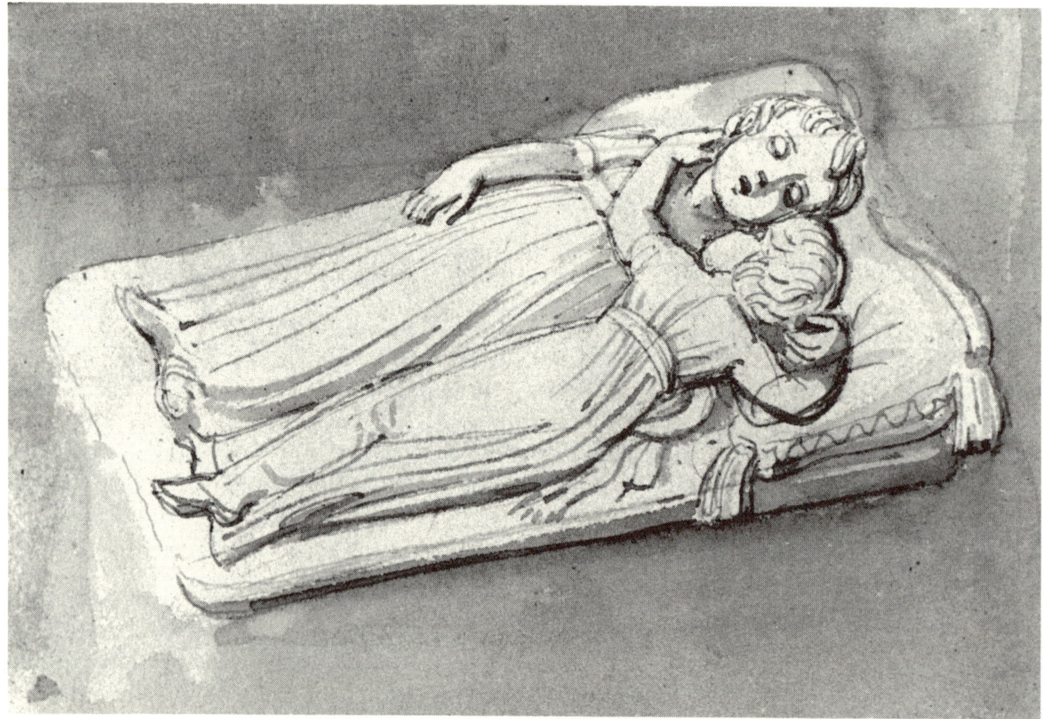

Fig. 35. Thomas Stothard, design for the funerary monument of the *Sleeping Children* executed by Francis Chantrey, pen and watercolor, 4⅝ x 5¼″, bound into an extra-illustrated edition of Bray's *Life of Stothard.*

such as the 1807 admission ticket to the Cambridge Musical Festival. These commercial activities were not, however, incompatible with his role as a respected Royal Academician. Stothard's reputation in the Academy had risen to such a height that he was elected as one of the two painters to represent the Academy when a committee was appointed in 1806 for the prestigious task of recommending to the Lords of the Treasury the proper places for the monuments of Lord Nelson, William Pitt, Captain Cook, and others in St. Paul's and Westminster Abbey. His involvement in Royal Academy business also led directly to another source of income. Stothard was appointed Deputy Librarian to the Royal Academy in December 1810 and full Librarian in 1812. In addition to his other myriad artistic ventures, this employment brought him an annual salary of £60.

In about 1810, Stothard began his profitable employment with the fashionable silversmiths Rundell and Bridge. In addition to his work for silver plate, he also designed for them a transparency for the jubilee of George III in 1810 and later executed transparencies for the "Temple of Concord" in the 1814 grand National Jubilee and for a fête given by the Prince Regent at Carlton House.[15]

Stothard's connections with the firm of Rundell and Bridge offer another opportunity for studying the mechanisms of patronage evolving during this period. Although neither Philip Rundell nor John Bridge had any silversmithing experience, they established a silver workshop applying the techniques so profitably developed by Wedgwood. Rundell and Bridge subcontracted the manufacture of their silver to two firms headed by Benjamin Smith and by Paul Storr, one of the most famous silversmiths of his

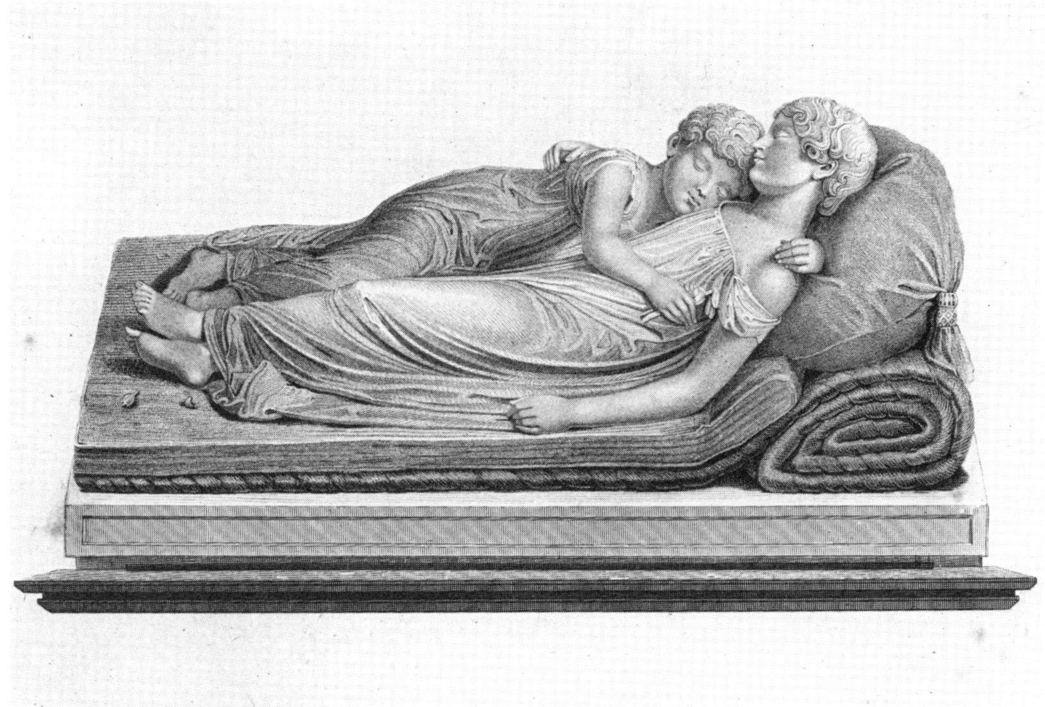

Fig. 36. Francis Chantrey, funerary monument of the *Sleeping Children* in Lichfield Cathedral (1817), engraved by W. Fry, image 8 x 3⅞".

day. Following Wedgwood's design policy, they employed some of the best artists to produce designs for their modelers. At various times, a number of Royal Academicians including Flaxman, Edward Hodges Baily (Flaxman's pupil), William Theed, Henry Howard (or his son Frank), C. R. Cockerell, and Stothard worked for the Rundell firm. Like Wedgwood, Rundell and Bridge made generous payments to their designers to assure a high quality of design.

Stothard spent as much, if not more, time and care in the preparation of his silverwork designs as he did for any major commission. For example, he made numerous preliminary studies for a large circular silver-gilt dish with the central design of the *Triumph of Bacchus and Ariadne* (Fig. 41). A pair of these dishes was executed by the workshop of Paul Storr in 1813. Another *Bacchus and Ariadne* dish of 1814, which also bears Paul Storr's maker's mark,

was bought by George IV for £497 7s. 7d. in 1815. Additional charges of £188 18s. were added for engraving the Royal Arms and applying gilding.[16]

Following the standard contemporary practice, Stothard looked to classical art for his prototypes. The central composition of *Bacchus and Ariadne* is derived from a similar design printed in Bartoli's *Gli Antichi Sepoleri* (Rome, 1727), a copy of which was in Stothard's possession at his death.[17] Many of Stothard's preliminary studies for this design exist, in addition to several copies of the final version. As usual, Stothard utilized a wide range of techniques to develop the design for the central group and bacchanalian border. The final design (Fig. 42) was executed in a variation of his silhouette technique, probably to produce a relief-like effect that could be easily imitated by the modelers.

Although the firms of Wedgwood and of Run-

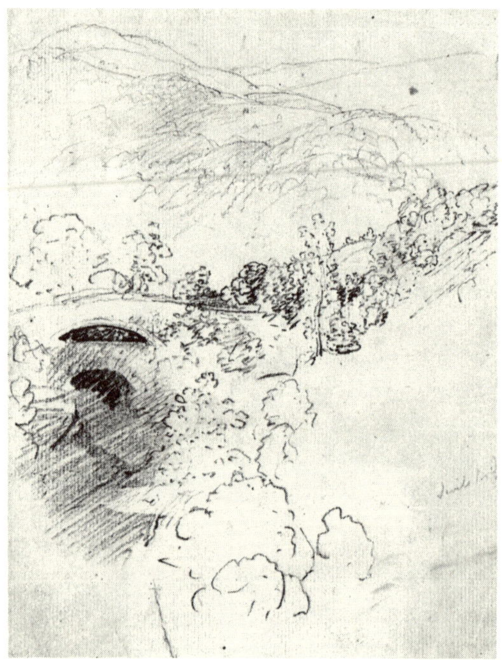

Fig. 37. Thomas Stothard, "The Devil's Bridge" of Hafod, 1805 or 1810, pencil, 8¼ x 6½".

dell and Bridge employed Stothard exclusively in the specialized role of a designer, the division of labor between the design of the work and its production was not as absolute as it would be later in the nineteenth century. For instance, a letter dated 13 June 1816 from Stothard to an unknown correspondent indicates his careful attention to the modeling of his design of *Bacchus and Ariadne* for the silver dish:

Sir, Mr. Talmash [Tollemach] has at various times modeled from my designs, particularly, the margin and center of a two handled dish for Rundel [*sic*] & Briggs [*sic*], the subject the Triumph of Bacchus and Ariadne, this he modeled both in Bas and Alto-Relief so as to satisfy me and do credit to himself as an artist.[18]

But as a designer whose function did not extend to the final production of the work, Stothard could execute designs for silver knife handles and decanter labels and then with easy facility turn

his attention to major silverwork commissions. Examples include his several projects to honor the Duke of Wellington. Stothard's commemorative projects celebrating this national hero were as various as a giant pair of silver Wellington candelabra (1816), the Waterloo Vase (1825), a Wellington medal, a Wellington monument, and the famous Wellington Shield (Fig. 43).[19] The Wellington Shield commission provides another valuable insight into Stothard's collaborative skills and market-conscious attitude.

Patriotic fervor was raised to such a high pitch in England by the victories of Wellington that all works of art dealing with the Duke were guaranteed a widespread audience; thus, the commemorative shield ordered by the Merchants of the City of London was an important commission for Stothard. When Green, Ward and Green, the silversmith firm that executed this commission, placed the shield on exhibition to the public, it drew the attention of many persons of rank and wealth. The public exposure it brought was a useful source for subsequent patronage. Engravings issued after the designs for the shield in 1820 proved to be an additional source of revenue for Stothard. The existence of a large number of copies by Stothard of his finished designs for this shield indicates that he anticipated yet another means of attaining a profitable market for these popular designs.

From the first Stothard seems to have realized the value of this commission for his future employment, for he was willing to submit a much lower bid than his fellow artists in order to obtain the initial commission. As Farington noted in his diary on 15 November 1814:

Westall called to inform me one of the Mr. Greens silversmiths on Ludgate Hill decidedly objected to his demand of 500 guineas for his design for the Wellington shield to be executed in silver presented by

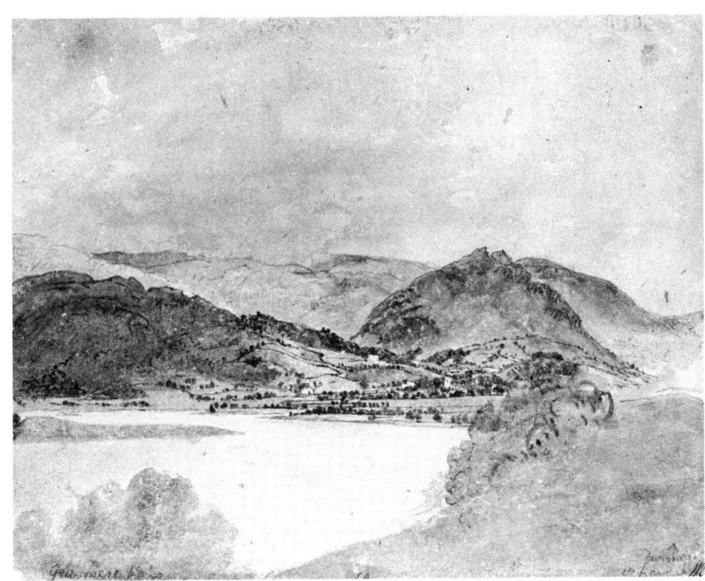

Fig. 38. Thomas Stothard, *Grasmere Water—Dunmail or Rise Gap*, 1809, pencil and watercolor, 7⅝ x 9⅞".

merchants who had subscribed 700 guineas; he said Smirke and Stothard had both made designs for them & that the former charged only 180 guineas & the latter whose design was preferred to all the rest, charged only 150 guineas. Westall replied that he had been occupied full two months on this subject & with such extraordinary application that it might justly be called the work of three months; —that he had charged it below what he could have got if otherwise employed; that he reckoned his time at Ten guineas a day in his ordinary practice, which would have made a much larger sum.

Bray relates that Stothard had "three weeks before him to study the history of the war, to make choice of his subjects, to execute all his designs, and to send them in to the committee." She also states, "It struck Stothard that the Shield of Achilles (executed some years before by Flaxman), in respect to arrangement of the compartments, having each a separate subject, would apply with propriety to the work in question."[20] His composition, which mirrors Flaxman's general arrangement, and a drawing by Stothard after Flaxman's *Shield of Achilles* (located in the Royal Academy Library) substantiate this claim. Stothard's subjects commence with the Battle of Assay,

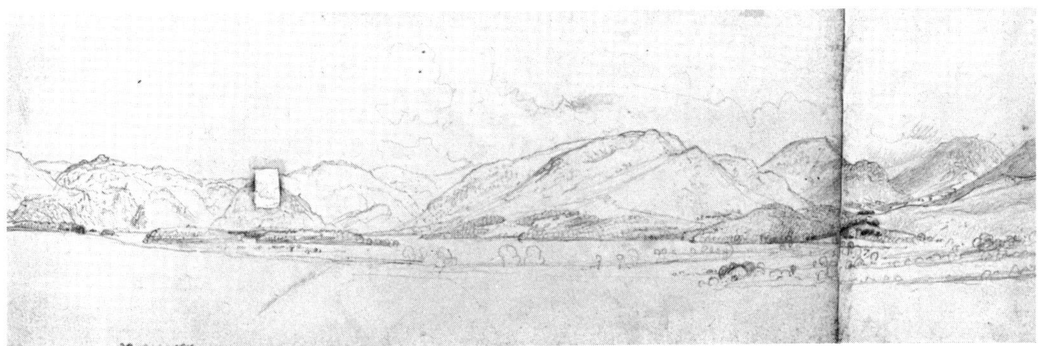

Fig. 39. Thomas Stothard, landscape study dated "30 Nov. 1816," pencil, 4¼ x 13".

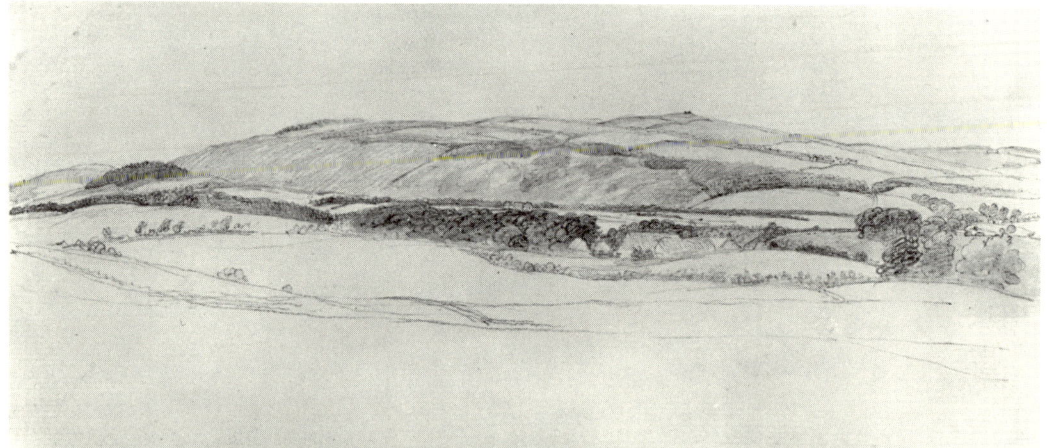

Fig. 40. Thomas Stothard, *Farms in a Wooded Landscape,* circa 1824, pencil and watercolor, 3¹⁵/₁₆ x 9″.

include the Duke's subsequent victories in the Peninsular War, and conclude with his receipt of the ducal coronet from the Prince Regent (Fig. 44). In the center of the shield, the Duke is depicted seated on horseback, surrounded by his generals, trampling on Tyranny and crowned by Victory.

So great was Stothard's concern for the success of this commission that when Tollemach, who was employed to make the model and execute the chasing, died suddenly, Stothard sculpted the models himself, much to the amazement of his contemporaries, for he was considered untrained in this field of art. Stothard also decided to execute the etchings after the shield, although this too was considered outside the area of his expertise. Evidently, the high level of design that resulted from the cooperative relationship between Stothard and the craftsmen who executed his other designs was in large part a result of Stothard's ability to understand and manipulate all of the various steps in the process of production.

Yet, as an artist whose primary responsibility did not extend to the final production of his craft, Stothard was able to make the transitions between the similar strictly "design" requirements of the various decorative arts. This increased specializa-

tion in the designer's function explains how Stothard was so easily able to adapt to the diverse commercial demands of various media.

For example, Stothard was employed by the printsellers producing reproductive prints throughout his career. Printsellers were quick to realize the profitability of catering to the lucrative commercial market for this low-cost substitute for paintings. By the end of the eighteenth century, the printseller-publisher had become a major source of patronage for British artists. Throughout his career, Stothard worked for the printsellers, executing paintings and drawings after which they issued single prints directed to the new mass audience for art. The subordinate role Stothard assumed in dealing with printsellers-publishers provides the proper perspective for a discussion of the controversy surrounding Stothard's painting of the *Canterbury Pilgrims,* which was commissioned by the engraver Robert Cromek in 1806.[21]

Canterbury Pilgrims (Fig. 45) brought Stothard great contemporary fame. The painting itself was first exhibited at Cromek's house in London, then shown throughout England and Scotland, drawing large crowds at the admission price of one shil-

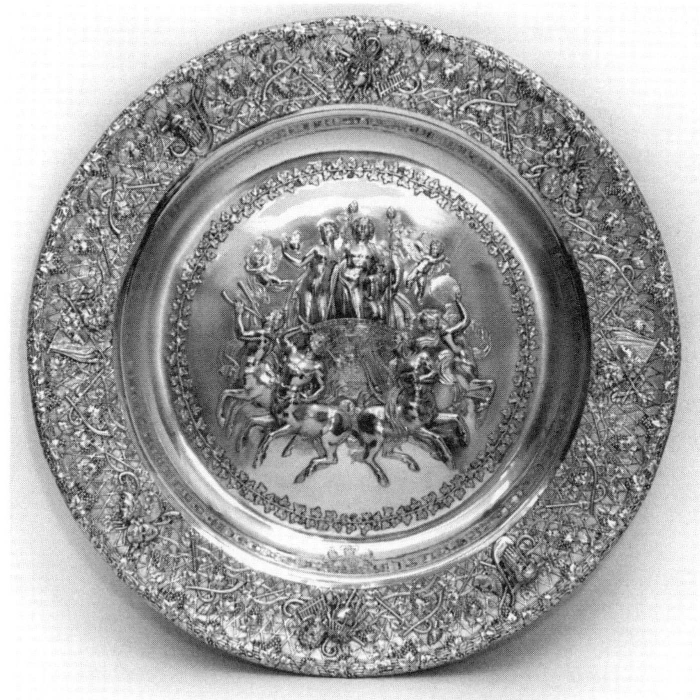

Fig. 41. *Triumph of Bacchus and Ariadne,* sideboard dish, silver gilt, 1814, 35″ diameter, executed by Paul Storr.

ling per person.[22] By May 1807, Cromek could claim that three thousand people had seen and praised it.[23] When the print finally appeared in 1817, after many delays caused by the death of a succession of its engravers, it too was enormously popular. In 1855 the cataloguer of the Vernon Collection in the National Gallery would declare, "Few, if any, engravings of that period, were so popular with the public."[24] The success of the painting and print demonstrates the ability of Stothard's art to reach a wide and profitable market.

In addition to its popularity with the general public, the painting for *Canterbury Pilgrims* was lavishly praised by many of Stothard's more famed contemporaries. Walter Scott proclaimed that it was "executed with the genius and spirit of a master, and all the rigid attention to costume that could be expected of the most severe antiquary."[25] Stothard's fellow Royal Academician John Hoppner wrote to Richard Cumberland on 30 May 1807:

In respect of the execution of the various parts of this pleasing design, it is not too much praise to say, that it is wholly free from that vice which the painters term *manner;* and it has this peculiarity besides, which I do not remember to have seen in any picture, ancient or modern, that it bears no mark of the period in which it was painted, but might very well pass for the work of some able artist of the time of Chaucer. This effect is not, I believe, the result of any association of ideas connected with the costume, but appears in a primitive simplicity, and the total absence of all affectation, either of colour or pencilling. Having attempted to describe a few of the beauties of this captivating performance, it remains only for me to mention one great defect—the picture is, notwithstanding appearances, A MODERN ONE. But, if you can divest yourself of the prejudice that exists against contemporary talent, you will see a work that would have done honour to any school at any period.[26]

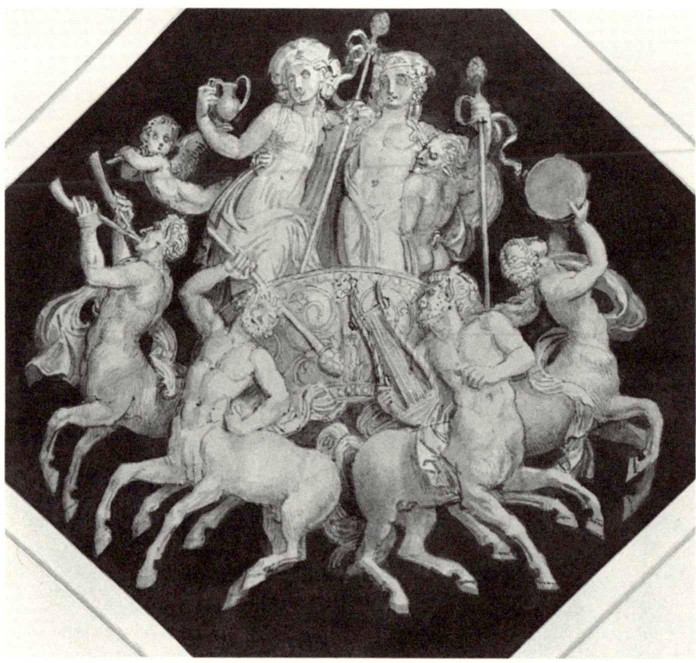

Fig. 42. Thomas Stothard, design of the *Triumph of Bacchus and Ariadne,* pen and wash, 6¼ x 7″.

An unidentified newspaper reviewer wrote in about 1807:

In a word, we do not hesitate to say, that the present picture [*Canterbury Pilgrims*] is by far the best that ever proceeded from the pencil of Mr. Stothard, and would have done honour to the most distinguished modern or ancient Artist . . . with so much truth and sprightliness, and in a manner so agreeable, that the Poet's humour may, with truth, be said to be revived in the Painter. . . . It is the particular merit of this Piece that the story is immediately brought home to the spectator; he becomes instantly one the groupe and sees them move before him, marked by their distinctive habits, characters, and sensations, in the same manner as Chaucer has drawn them—the idea of the Poet is impressed at the first view,—a humour unforced, agreeable and comic.[27]

One of the most profuse expressions of the contemporary opinion about this painting is found in a "Sonnet on Stothard's Painting of the Canterbury Pilgrims" by Enort, which was printed in the *European Magazine* in October 1821:

Methinks I hear their horses capering head,
    And now the merry group full blythe I see;
Genius, thou Sorcerer wild! by thee I'm led,
    And my heart leaps with heavenly ecstasy.
First comes the brawling Host, the rest close join,
    Pressing the greensward, Hark! they troup
        with glee,
Next Chaucer view—Behold the Bard divine!
    Lock'd in bright mental thought, how sweet
        looks he;
Oh! would I were a horseman by the side,
    Of you fair Nymph, prancing so courteously,
Or I should like with you blythe Friar to ride,
    His dewy eye full of rich roguery; —
Stothard! a peerless wreath thou here hast won,
    And Painting hails thee as her matchless son —[28]

In addition to the numerous prints issued after the painting,[29] Stothard was commissioned to execute three oil copies after the original, one of the same size for Samuel Rogers, one for Samuel Boddington, and another, larger copy for J. Benson of Doncaster.[30] He also made several water-

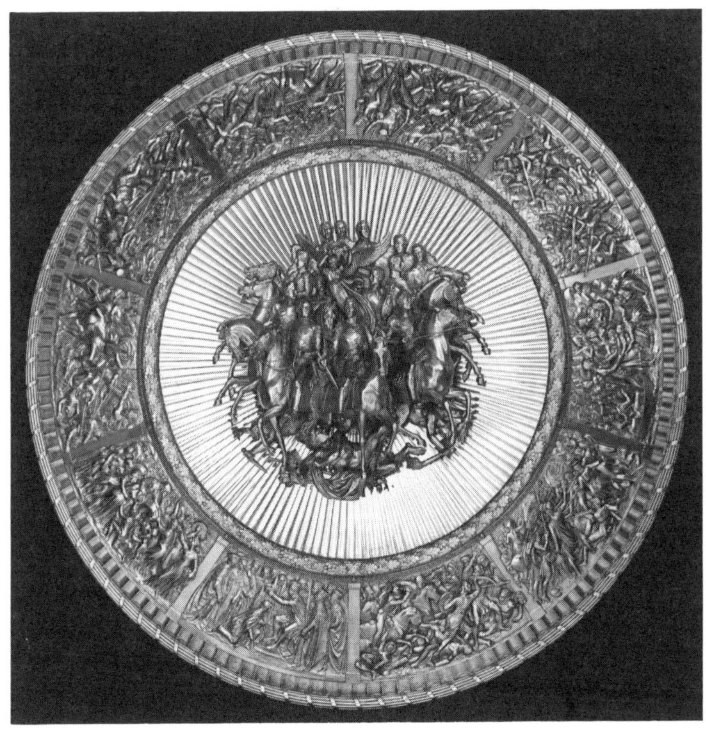

Fig. 43. *The Wellington Shield* ordered by the Merchants and Bankers of the City of London, designed in 1814, executed by Benjamin Smith, London hallmark, circa 1822, 40¹/₂″ diameter.

color versions.[31] By such means Stothard eventually found a way to exploit the profitable market for this image, for he never received more than £60 from Cromek for the original.[32]

It was Cromek who was responsible for the bitter quarrel between Stothard and Blake that ended their friendship. This controversy has been recounted in great detail in current Blake scholarship.[33] In brief, Blake claimed that Cromek commissioned from him a painting illustrating Chaucer's story of the pilgrimage to Canterbury (Fig. 46) and that after seeing his fresco sketch, Cromek withdrew the commission. According to Blake, Cromek then proceeded to commission from Stothard a similar painting based on what he had seen in Blake's sketch. Both Cromek and

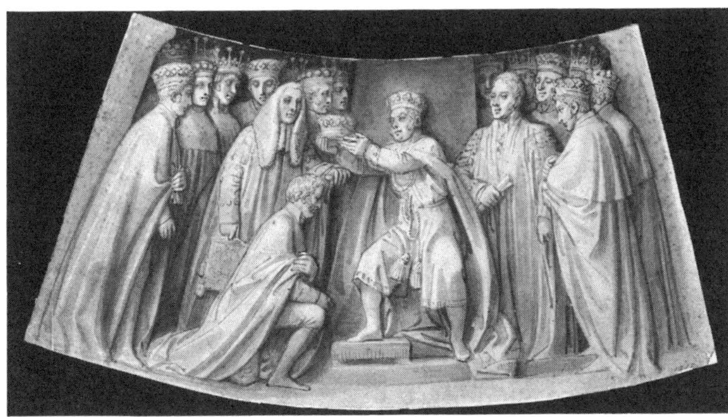

Fig. 44. Thomas Stothard, design of "Wellington's receipt of the ducal coronet from the Prince Regent" for the *Wellington Shield*, wash, 5³/₄ x 11¹/₄″.

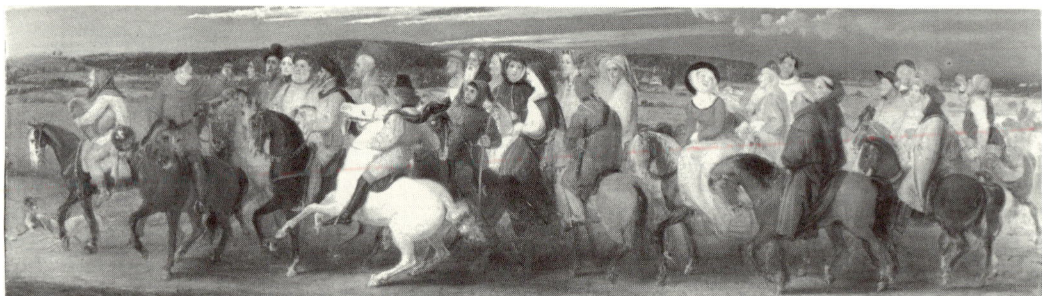

Fig. 45. Thomas Stothard, *The Pilgrimage to Canterbury*, oil, 12¹/₂ x 36¹/₂".

Stothard denied this accusation. Stothard's own account of his transactions with Cromek can be found in a letter written to a friend, probably Rev. Robert Markham:

I have to thank you for your kind offer of advancing a part, conjointly with other of my friends, who wish me well, as to the publication of the Canterbury Pilgrims. I certainly wish it completed on the score of my reputation, as well as on that of the family of poor Cromek [Cromek had recently died]. The sum the engraver requests is three hundred and thirty guineas, to be paid in three instalments; for this, he promised to complete it in fifteen months, from the time he begins it. Mrs. Cromek has (with a view to [Louis] Schiavonetti proceeding on it immediately) sold Blair's Grave for one hundred and twenty pounds. . . . The plate is in progress, and I think may procure more. . . . On maturer reflection, I am averse to enter into a responsibility for so large a sum as four hundred; nor, between ourselves, am I confident how clear Cromek has stood with the father of Mrs. C. Besides this, I must turn printer's devil, publisher, &c., &c.; and, for a time, quit my professional habits. But, if you please, I will request you to suspend this business to a future time—perhaps, when I see you in town, which I hope will be soon: at present I wish them to try their subscribers. When I undertook to paint the picture of the Canterbury Pilgrims, the price agreed was sixty pounds: the degree of finish was left to me at the conclusion of it. In the progress of the work, the subject and design appearing more important—worthy of more attention than either of us at first apprehended, Mr. Cromek himself made the following proposition: That, if I on my part would give one months' additional attention to the picture, over and above what was at first agreed, he would make the sum one hundred pounds. This additional forty was to be paid as soon as he could collect from his subscrib-

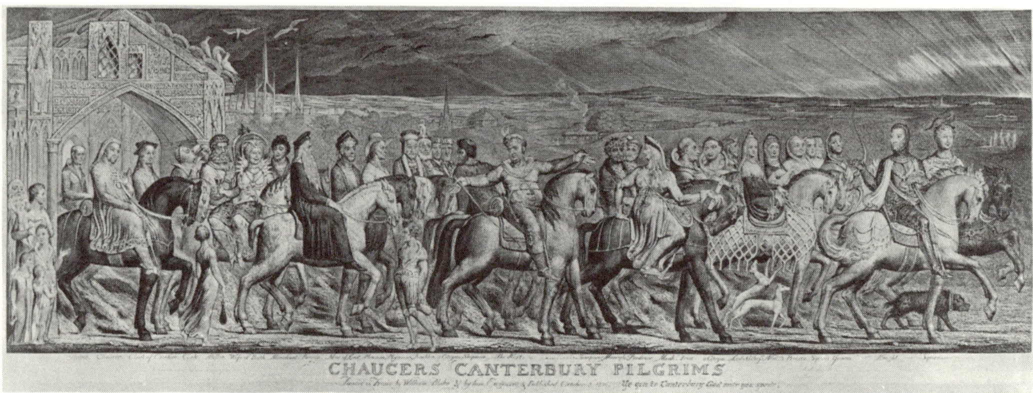

Fig. 46. William Blake, *Canterbury Pilgrims*, engraving, image 12 x 37".

ers. This he did not do; excusing himself on the score of the expense he was at in the advertising, &c., &c., He sold the picture to Mr. Hart Davis for three hundred pounds, or guineas. He then in like manner excused himself as he had done before; and as I received his plea of his success with the public with indulgence, and as the plate was in progress towards completion, deferred my demand till publication. This I have done in his alleged difficulties. Schiavonetti's [the engraver's] death following soon after, put a stop to the work; and from what succeeded soon after [Cromek's death], I had additional reason not to urge my demand on the widow.[34]

Evidently, both Stothard and Blake were pawns in Cromek's unscrupulous financial schemes, and Cromek's devious business practices unfortunately brought about a permanent breach in their long-standing friendship.[35]

In addition to his work in silverwork, book illustration, and separate print publications, Stothard continued to receive commissions from various men of station and influence. Among his friends and employers he could count William Beckford, Samuel Boddington, J. Benson of Doncaster, Rev. Thomas Streatfield, and Rev. Robert Markham, Archdeacon of York and Rector of Bolton Percy, Yorkshire. To satisfy the desires of these diverse patrons, Stothard performed a wide variety of artistic functions. The different projects commissioned by two of these patrons, Streatfield and Markham, further illustrate the range of Stothard's commercial activities.

As well as a curate, Thomas Streatfield was an avid genealogist, biographer, and amateur artist. With the considerable fortune he acquired from his first wife, he expended almost £3,000 on commissions for drawings and engravings for his projected publication of a history of Kent.[36] Surprisingly, none of Stothard's commissions for Streatfield can be directly connected with a history of Kent. Instead, Stothard executed a design

depicting one of Streatfield's ancestors receiving a knighthood after the Battle of Poirtiers.[37] Streatfield's associations with a knighthood received during the Hundred Years War made this period of history of particular significance to him.

This may explain why Streatfield also commissioned from Stothard a series of outline drawings of medieval historical subjects, now in the British Museum. The scenes that can be identified are: the "Battle of Poirtiers where Edward the Black Prince is taken prisoner by the King of France" (Fig. 47), "Sir Thomas Moore's Farewell to his Daughter, from Rogers' *Poems,*" and "The Bride of Tricimaine, by Sir Walter Scott."[38] A letter dated 1823 from Stothard to Streatfield suggests that Stothard was working on this private commission late in his career.[39]

Stothard, likewise, carried out several diverse commissions for Markham. In this relationship, Stothard was both the drawing master for Markham's daughter Georgiana and Markham's adviser on the remodeling of his house. A few drawings can be related to Stothard's suggestions for Markham's new picture gallery (Fig. 48).[40] In about 1813, Stothard wrote to Markham, "In answer to your fears you express that I may neglect the main business of the Gallery pray do them away & consider me as engaged heart & hand in your concern."[41] Another letter from Stothard that probably dates from this same period includes suggestions and sketches for an alternative model. References to additional commissions in these letters indicate that Stothard also executed several paintings that were to hang in this gallery.[42]

A critical piece of information about Stothard's working practices is contained in one of Stothard's letters to Markham. It reveals that Stothard consciously exploited the multipurpose function of his designs:

Cannot you recollect the design for the waiter [salver]

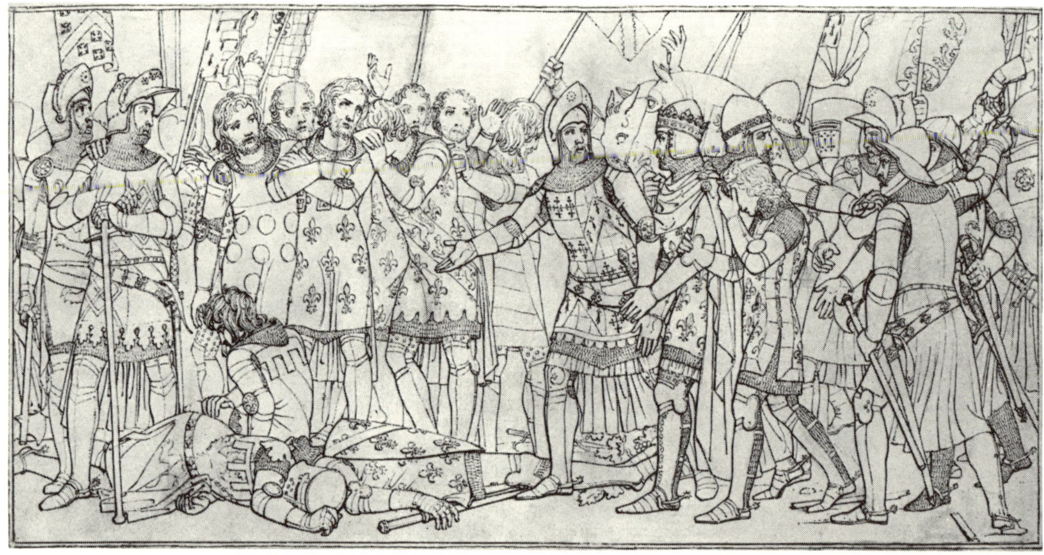

Fig. 47. Thomas Stothard, *Battle of Poirtiers Where Edward the Black Prince Is Taken Prisoner by the King of France,* pen, 7¹⁄₂ x 15¹⁄₂".

I did for Rundell & Bridge [probably *Bacchus and Ariadne,* Fig. 41]—it was from part of that composition perhaps [this will] assist your recollection, but if not, what I mentioned concirning [*sic*] it I have not forgot it don't imagine that I would abtrude [*sic*] this picture on you or that I have exchanged it solely with

that view. I have not & my sole motive is, as it is a favorite of mine, thinking it to be the same with you has induced me to say what I have on the business & I wish you should possess such pieces as I fancy I have been successful in tho I may be wrong & overrate what others may condemn, however as a venture I have

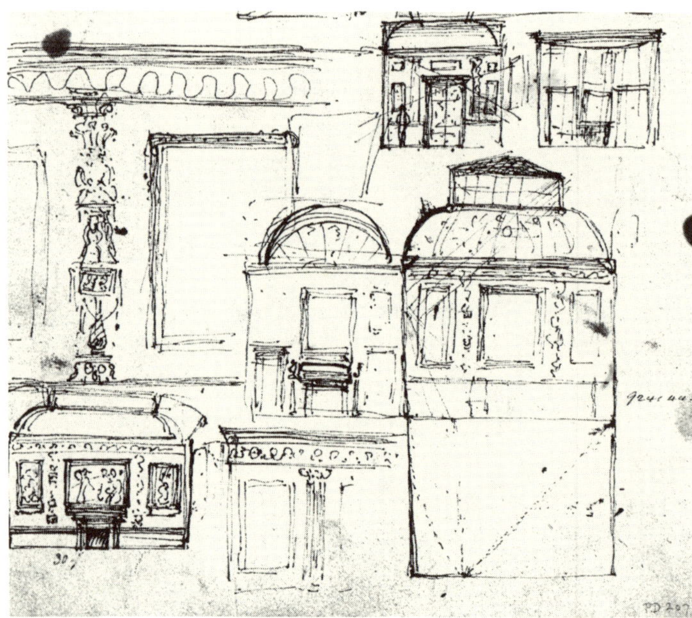

Fig. 48. Thomas Stothard, study for Markham's Picture Gallery, circa 1813, pen, 6¹⁄₂ x 8".

[probably "sent it to you," because he mentions crating it further along in the letter].[43]

Stothard discerned no impropriety in adopting a design produced for decorative silver to the format of a self-contained painting. His designs could be interchanged to suit either the whims of his private patrons or the requirements of the different commercial enterprises for which they were designed. This same practice was utilized by the manufacturers of art commodities. For example, the same components were used repeatedly for diverse products in the production of silver at the end of the eighteenth century and beginning of the nineteenth. Stothard time and time again adapted similar commercial practices to the production of his art in order to expand the market for his works.

5 INFLUENCE OF THE MARKET IN STOTHARD'S LAST YEARS

ALTHOUGH the first two decades of the nineteenth century were an active period in Stothard's career, he had enough spare time to begin writing his "Dictionary of the Lives of Painters." This document is based on sources that were readily available to Stothard after he became the Deputy Librarian of the Royal Academy in 1810.[1] The latter pages focus on Raphael's *Transfiguration,* a painting that overwhelmed Stothard on his trip to Paris in 1815. The feeble and shaky handwriting in this section also suggests a later date of composition, sometime after 1810.

Despite the enormous diversification of his activities during this period, Stothard evidently had the spare time to indulge in writing a book on painters of the past. This indicates that he was not fully employed at the time. A passage in a letter to Cumberland dated 24 May 1813, when Stothard was fifty-eight years old, may explain the cause for this situation:

[Speaking of their friend, the artist Edward Bird] he will I trust proceed with more composure in future and not by overexertion grown old too soon, as none but young men are to succeed, he has done himself justice in the six pictures now in the exhibition, and they have their admirers, but Wilkie's picture of Blindman buff has ever a crowd round it closely packed; and some of those in the rear, in vain struggling for a view, console themselves for the disappointment by looking at my Shakespeare subject, by which means I get admirers, as one theatre is filled by the overflow of the other. This you will say is but poor consolation, but so it is and I must be content so I console myself with the consciousness of having done what will not disgrace the best of my former productions, this is my secret satisfaction but for purchasers of high rank, Princes, Dukes down to right honeurables I am a perfect stranger to them in any shape even to commendation.[2]

In addition to this change in English artistic tastes, the overall economic situation was a cause of personal anxiety for Stothard. Following the end of the Napoleonic wars, England entered a period of economic depression. A low point in this postwar period of unemployment and misery came in the autumn of 1816, a crucial time in Stothard's financial situation. Stothard's work for the booksellers was affected by this economic depression. Between 1815 and 1820, very few publications appeared in England with illustrations by Stothard (see Appendix 2). After 1820, Stothard resumed his usual prolific rate of employment, supplying designs for several book publications per year. Stothard's unemployment during the postwar years probably reflects an unstable condition in the book industry in general.

The situation was aggravated by another new and unsettling experience for Stothard. As Farington noted in his diary on 13 April 1816, "Constable called. . . . He spoke of Stothard as being much mortified and disappointed. He sent 8 pictures [to the Royal Academy exhibition] some of which He was advised to withdraw. This had affected his spirits, causing a temporary despondence." Stothard seems to have been more than temporarily affected, for as late as December, an old friend, Robert Smirke, spoke of Stothard to Farington: "He mentioned several particulars of

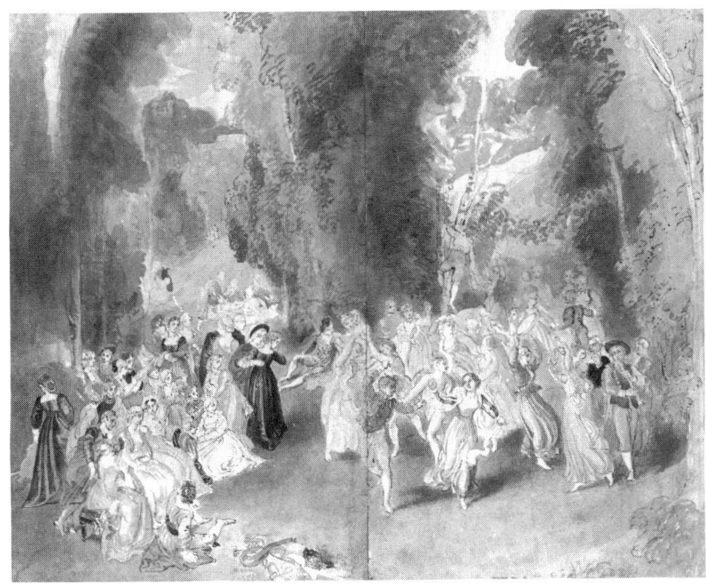

Fig. 49. Thomas Stothard, *Fête Champêtre,* pencil, pen and water-color, 15 x 19".

Stothard's hasty temper, and real want of that moderation of character which has been ascribed to him."

Stothard's lack of employment by the book-sellers made his failure at the 1816 Royal Academy exhibition a matter so deeply felt that he was spur-red on to a new development in his art. Watteau became his model. In 1817, Stothard sent his first painting based on a Watteau subject matter, *Sans Souci,* to the Royal Academy annual exhibition.[3] He continued in this mode for the rest of his career, executing various *Fête Champêtre* composi-tions (Fig. 49).[4] His choice of Watteau as a model may have followed from his direct exposure to French painting on his trip to the Louvre in 1815.[5] This new direction in Stothard's art found imme-diate favor with his contemporaries. Stothard did not initiate the Watteau revival in the early nine-teenth century in England, but he was certainly its most famous practitioner.[6] Once again, it demon-strates his ability to respond to prevailing market conditions.

Although Stothard's adoption of Watteau as a model in 1817 did not dramatically alter his style,

he did modify his oil technique. Stothard probably adapted from Watteau the idea of using white for both foreground and background objects. This in turn may have directed Turner's attention to the value of this technique. Turner told C. R. Leslie that he painted *Boccaccio Relating the Tale of the Birdcage* "in avowed imitation" of Stothard. While working on this painting during Varnish-ing Days prior to the opening of the 1828 Royal Academy exhibition, Turner said, "If I thought he liked my pictures half as well as I like his, I should be satisfied. He is the Giotto of England."[7] The success of Stothard's brightly painted pictures may also have encouraged Turner in his bold experi-ments with color.[8]

A newspaper review of the 1817 Royal Acad-emy exhibition explains the appeal of Stothard's new *fête galante* subjects to his contemporaries:

Contrasted with everything that is tremendous in Mr. Fuseli's genius, of everything terrible in and beyond nature, is Mr. Stothard's pencil. Fuseli paints at the command of the Furies, Stothard at the invitation of the Graces. The one dreams of dismal shades and Tar-

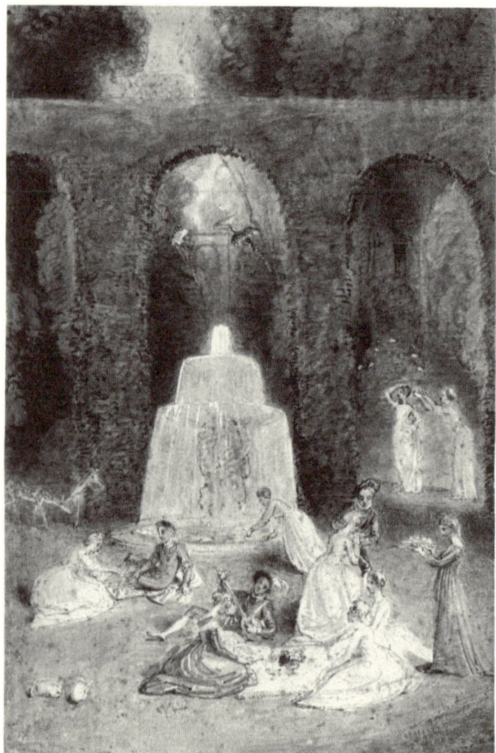

Fig. 50. Thomas Stothard, illustration to Boccaccio's *Decameron* (1825), watercolor, 4 x 6".

tarean horrors, and peoples his canvas with awful spectres and the foul committers of crime. The other looks at and delights in the sunshine of morals and of visible nature, thinks of the felicities of life, contemplates Elysium and feasts our eyes and our hearts with happy realities and ideal delights. Such is his celebrated picture of "the Chaucer's Canterbury Pilgrims," and such, in this Exhibition, are his too carelessly drawn, but well coloured and charmingly invented pictures . . . "Sans Souci," where groupes of elegant people are variously amusing themselves on a lawn, with fruits, conversation, music, rambling, reclining, and making love.[9]

The popularity of this subject matter encouraged Stothard to retain Watteau as his model for the remainder of his life. His greatest success in this mode came with his illustrations in both oil and watercolor to Boccaccio's *Decameron* (see Fig.

50). The oil versions were exhibited at the Royal Academy in 1819 and 1820, while the watercolors probably served as models for the book illustrations published by Pickering in 1825. What drew the attention and praise of Stothard's contemporaries was his treatment of the sentimental escapades of an elegant aristocratic society set in an arcadian retreat. The popular delight in his illustrations is captured in Charles Lamb's poem to Stothard, which was published in *The Athenaeum* on 21 December 1833:

To T. Stothard, Esq. on his illustrations of the Poems of Mr. Rogers.

Consummate Artist, whose undying name
With classic Rogers shall go down to fame,
Be this thy crowning work! In my young days
How often have I with a child's fond gaze
Pored on the pictured wonders thou hadst done:
Clarissa mournful, and prim Grandison!
All Fielding's, Smollett's heroes, rose to view;
I saw, and I believed the phantoms true
But, above all, that most romantic tale
Did o'er my raw credulity prevail,
Where Glums and Gawries wear mysterious things
That serve at once for jackets and for wings.
Age, that enfeebles other men's designs,
But heightens thine, and thy free draught refines.
In several ways distinct you make us feel
Graceful as Raphael, as Watteau genteel.
Your lights and shades, as Titianesque, we praise,
And warmly wish you Titian's length of days.

Or as a newspaper reviewer declared in 1827:

His "Fête Champêtre" [Fig. 49] combines all the elegancies of Boccaccio's delicious description of the country retreat of his noble Florentine cavaliers & ladies, with the very freshness of this cool meadow . . . the attitudes and action of the figures—the distant groves—the undulation of hill and dale—and the palazzo on the heights in the background—are true at once to nature and to poetry.[10]

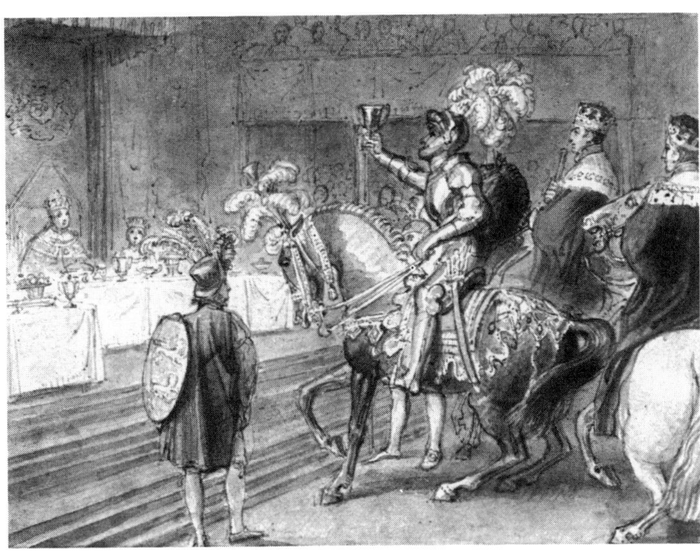

Fig. 51. Thomas Stothard, illustration for *The New Ladies Memorandum Book* (1822), pen and wash, 4½ x 3½".

Stothard's illustrations for various Watteau-esque projects exist in pen-and-ink outline drawings, finished watercolors, and oil paintings. As always, he exploited a variety of media to suit the different markets for his designs. Drawings and watercolors were probably submitted to the engravers due to the greater ease with which they could be transferred into engravings. Oil versions were most likely executed to gain further public exposure in exhibitions and for the purpose of an additional sale shortly after the assured success of the book illustrations. As in so many other instances, the variety of media used testifies to Stothard's adroit awareness of a profitable market.

For various reasons, there was, however, an overall change in Stothard's style in the last twenty years of his life. Increasingly, he tended to cover the page with intricate detailing, as seen in a pen-and-brown-wash illustration for *The New Ladies Memorandum Book* (Fig. 51) published in 1822. His pen work took on a new staccato rhythm. Rather than exploiting the decorative nature of simplified linear forms, Stothard now concentrated on the potential of minutiae to produce an interesting surface pattern.

Ever in search of a broader market for his art, Stothard may have deliberately altered his style in order to mimic Moritz Retzsch's popular engravings. In 1821 one of his patrons specifically requested drawings in the manner of this artist.[11] Retzsch's series of *Outlines* (Fig. 52) first began appearing in 1817. Following the publication of his *Outlines to Faust* in England in 1820, his work enjoyed great popularity for many years. The attraction of these outline engravings lay in their minute, decorative linear inventions and anecdotal incidents.

Other economic and technical considerations also encouraged Stothard to alter his style during the second decade of the nineteenth century. For example, the increased use of steel plates for engraving book illustrations around 1820 may have affected Stothard's style. Due to the hard nature of this medium, the engravers of steel plates required a more minute finish to drawings than that necessitated by earlier engraving techniques. Stothard inevitably responded to the demands of his engravers and often altered his style to adjust to their requirements, although the shaky and enfeebled nature of Stothard's handwriting in the

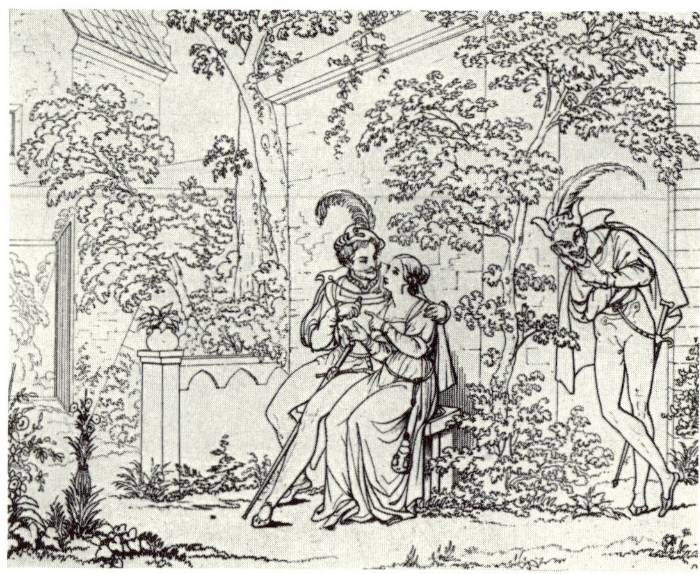

Fig. 52. Moritz Retzsch, illustration to *Faust* (English translation, 1839–1843), engraving, 3½ x 4½".

sections of his "Dictionary of the Lives of Painters" that were probably written during this decade indicates that the shift in his style was due, in part, to a loss of physical agility. Stothard was then in his sixties and perhaps limited in his ability to produce a firm and flowing pen line.

These slight changes in his style did not, however, alter the nature of his relation to his employers, as demonstrated by his association with George Thomson of Edinburgh, one of Stothard's new patrons during this period.[12] Stothard's connection with Thomson began in about 1815 and extended over the remainder of his life, although relatively few works were commissioned. Drafts of about fifty-five letters between Thomson and Stothard, now in the Boston Public Library and the National Library of Scotland, detail their working relationship. This lengthy correspondence, on the most part from Thomson to Stothard, spans the period from January 1815 to October 1833.[13]

Although Thomson (1757–1851) earned his livelihood as the principal clerk to the Board of Trustees for the Encouragement of Manufactures in Scotland, located in Edinburgh, he was an enthusiastic collector and publisher of Scottish national music.[14] Thomson, an amateur musician himself, also participated in the Edinburgh St. Cecilia concerts. His enthusiasm for music led him to become one of the organizers of the first Edinburgh music festival in 1815 and inspired him to publish his collection of national airs. He issued six volumes of Scottish songs between 1793 and 1841, three volumes of Welsh songs between 1809 and 1814, two volumes of Irish songs between 1814 and 1816, and in 1822 he published six volumes of a royal octavo edition compiled from all three collections.

Before publishing these national songs, Thomsom decided to commission introductory and concluding symphonies and accompaniments. In addition, he solicited new words for the verses, because he found many of the existing words repugnant to his prudish tastes. To carry out his rather eccentric scheme, Thomson applied to many famous poets and musicians, including Hayden, Beethoven, Burns, Scott, Moore, and Byron.[15]

This rather fastidious amateur publisher was a

constant "improver" and critic of the works he received from some of the most admired artists of his day. As his biographer J. Cathbert Hadden wrote in 1898: "In truth his criticisms are mainly of a niggling sort, many of them being wholly without justification, and springing either from a defective ear, a deficient imagination, or an exaggerated sense of propriety."[16]

Stothard's artistic dealings with Thomson must be viewed in the light of this patron's consistently troubled dealings with creative artists, for Thomson would seem to have played a larger role in their relationship than was usual for professional publishers. He often made trifling suggestions for improvements and additions to Stothard's illustrations. Stothard did not balk, however, at the frequently demeaning demands made by this parsimonious patron.

At the end of the eighteenth century, Thomson had commissioned about twenty designs for his Scottish airs from the Scottish artist David Allan. Although the designs were engraved, for some unknown reason he decided not to use Allan's illustrations.[17] Thomson's dissatisfaction may be discerned from a letter he wrote to Burns in 1794 in which he said, "In subjects of pastoral or humorous kind he is perhaps unrivaled by any living artist. He fails a little in giving beauty and grace to his females, and his colouring is sombre, otherwise his paintings and drawings would be in greater demand."[18] He later confessed to Stothard that, "in drawing and in pleasing contrast of light and shadow, Allan was careless and defective."[19]

In view of these criticisms, it is not surprising that Thomson turned to Stothard, whose art typified the eighteenth-century concept of grace and beauty and contained many decorative and pleasing effects. Stothard did not hesitate to revise and alter the work of a contemporary artist. Once again, this probably reflects a widespread contemporary practice that followed from the pressures of responding to an ever-changing art market.

A typical example of Stothard's cooperative and submissive attitude to the demands of this patron can be found in a letter he wrote on 31 January 1815 to Thomson:

I have sent you Strathallen's Lament altered with the license you gave me. I respect Allan much, & chiefly in the vivacity of his comic figures, in this sorrowful one I think he has failed somewhat; & to my thinking requires a little more dignity, for this purpose I have altered it.

Your Shepherd I have altered as you desired. Robin I have made taller, and altered the mouth of the Girl, etc., yet I cannot agree with you in liking her figure for this reason; she appears to me, too inanimate or upright for one flying from a shower, perhaps you may think otherwise, if so, you are at liberty to throw it into the fire.[20]

Stothard's dealings with Thomson in regard to another commission, a drawing of a Scottish musical dance entitled *Tullochgorum,* also demonstrate the subordinate role he played in this artist-publisher relationship. The first surviving letter in which the design to *Tullochgorum* is mentioned is dated 7 October 1821. Thomson wrote:

I feel much obliged to you also in your kind condescension in undertaking to do Allan's Designs in the manner of Retcsh's [*sic*] for me; because in no other way could they be rendered of use to my Collection of Songs; deficient as they are in good drawing, in female grace & in dignity whenever the character required it.

With respect to Tullochgorum (the dance), I beg that instead of doing it in outlines, you will have the goodness to give me a finished coloured drawing of it.[21]

In his letter of 24 November 1821, Thomson noted that he had not yet received from Stothard "a groupe of highland dancers designed by yourself, and incorporated with Allan's Fiddlers and

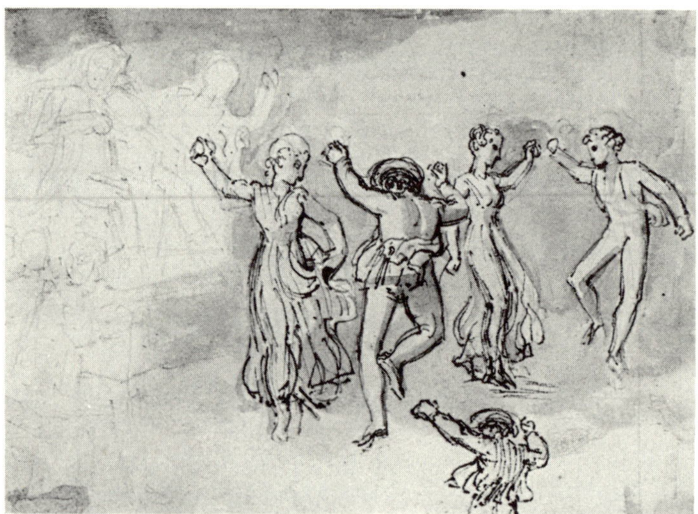

Fig. 53. Thomas Stothard,
illustration of *Tullochgorum* for
George Thomson, pencil, pen and
wash, 8 x 5¼″, bound into an
extra-illustrated Bray's *Life of
Stothard*.

Onlookers, in Tullochgorum; of which I gave you an Etching."[22] Stothard's designs for this subject in the Boston Public Library and the Henry E. Huntington Library and Art Gallery (see Fig. 53) indicate that, as directed by Thomson, he closely followed Allan's model.

Thomson was so enthusiastic about this subject that on 21 December 1821 he suggested that *Tullochgorum* would be a good subject for a painting and commissioned one of about sixteen by twenty-two inches from Stothard.[23] In a letter that probably dates from the summer of 1822, Stothard wrote in regard to this commission:

Dear Sir, In one of your letters you mentioned your wish to have the following subjects in colours and not in outline as I conceive . . . the 4th, the Highland Dance . . . you will now receive (when I received your proposition to have it painted in oil as an exchange for the Sleeping Lady you have sent me I had nearly compleated [*sic*] this drawing at the time I received it).[24]

Later in the letter Stothard quoted Thomson his different prices for outlines and colored drawings, then proceeded to thank Thomson for his

"friendly presant [*sic*] of happy ale," his frequent manner of recompense. On 18 August 1822, Thomson requested that this subject be done in the less expensive outline manner rather than in watercolor. He went on to state: "I scarce think that you should trouble yourself further with the coloured drawing of the Dance; since it has not succeeded. I imagine that the Engraver could have done a good Outline from a finish'd Drawing, but I now see that the finish'd Drawings are not available for that purpose."[25] And on 22 September 1822, he wrote to Stothard: "Instead of your taking any further trouble to improve the little coloured Drawing of Tullochgorum (the Dance), I would much rather you should favour me with a spirited Outline of the subject, making the four dancers entirely your own, without any regard to Allan's representation of them."[26]

On 26 October 1822, Thomson fired off another letter complaining, "I am completely at a stand and all my operations deranged by the want of your promised Outlines of Tullochgorum & Auld Robin Gray, each 5 inches broad by 3 ¼ high." At last, on 19 January 1823, Thomson noted: "I was duly favoured with your letter containing an Outline of the dancing group [*Tullochgorum*] & of Auld Robin Gray—which I liked very much." Although a drawing of *Tullochgorum* altered to Thomson's final specifications has not been located, it is likely that Stothard, once again, adjusted his artistic conceptions to suit the whims of this patron.[27]

In a manner typical of his parsimonious dealings with artists, Thomson wrote to Stothard on 19 January 1823: "You said you would charge me but three guineas for each Outline, and I proposed giving you 5 guineas along with the picture [by Stothard] I returned, in exchange for [a painting of] Auld Robin Gray."[28]

Over the next decades Thomson continually asked to return the paintings that he had bought from Stothard for new ones. The reasons were as whimsical as having moved to a new house where there was no suitable place to hang the old picture. Similarly, his criteria for commissioning a painting were such that if the composition did not fit into a twelve-inch-wide frame, Stothard was to leave out a figure. Thomson even sent paintings by amateur artists, such as his brother David, for Stothard to retouch. In one case he asked him to "put in a little groupe of boys in . . . [this] landscape. . . . I have always thought naked boys in the water most pleasing objects." Or Thomson requested Stothard to exchange *Apollo and Leucathae* for another painting, because "the nudity of Apollo & etc. makes it rather a bachelor's picture, & scarce fit for my walls." Stothard painted *Auld Robin Gray* in exchange for the *Apollo and Leucathae*.[29]

Thomson's requests for alterations to Stothard's illustrations often descended to the trifling and mundane. He complained that a youth's pants appeared too tight in one illustration, indicating the fashion of a smart town lad, rather than that of a Scottish shepherd, or that a figure was too "stout":

which might be cured in one of two ways, either by throwing part of the plaid across the body downward, which I conceive would impart more grace to him than he can have from the common breeches & gaiters —Or, . . . you might hide the lower half of his figure by means of the bank of flowers on which the sleeping Beauty is placed. I also venture to suggest a little more nudity about the neck and bosom of the Beauty because the whiteness of her lovely breast is in the song compared to the lily. —You know the roundness & firmness of those parts may be [unfortunately, the letter ends here].[30]

Stothard evidently had no trouble in assuming a submissive attitude when dealing with this patron, for he never refused any of Thomson's commissions.

Stothard's Scottish connections continued to expand during the first decades of the nineteenth century, climaxing in his receipt in 1821 of the major public commission to decorate the ceiling of the Advocates Library in Edinburgh. The equanimity of Stothard's last years was shattered, however, by the sudden death in 1821 of his beloved son Charles Alfred, a highly respected antiquarian draftsman. Stothard had lost his son Thomas in a shooting accident in 1801, and, on his return from Edinburgh in 1822, he found his third son Henry suffering from a paralytic stroke.

Stothard's personal sorrows continued to mount with the deaths of his wife, Rebecca, in 1824, and of his old friend Flaxman in 1826. George Cumberland reported to Francis Douce in a letter of 3 December 1824, "Gas lights indoors suffocate us, canals out of doors drown us—and steam boats threaten to boil us, scald us and annoy us with noise and tremor old Stothard says."[31] Grieved by his personal losses in his old age, Stothard shrank from the rapidly changing world around him. As he explained to Benjamin Robert Haydon in 1826 at the age of seventy-one, "I never read the papers, Mr. Haydon; they disturb my peace of thinking."[32]

Stothard continued to work until the final years of his life, in 1828–1830 receiving the important commission to design decorations for friezes in Buckingham Palace. Although deaf in his later years, Stothard staunchly supported the Royal Academy to the last, fulfilling his duties as Librarian, attending meetings and lectures, and serving as a member of the Council and as a Visitor to the Life Class. In 1833, Stothard was struck down by a cab, and about twelve to eighteen months later he died, on 27 April 1834, at the age of seventy-nine.

Numerous obituary notices attest to the warm regard in which he was held by his contemporaries. Leigh Hunt said of this beloved and respected artist, "an angel dwelt in that tottering house amidst the wintry bowers of white locks, warming it to the last with summer fancies."[33] Another eulogy confirms both Stothard's financial success and his continuing fame:

The late Stothard, RA, who was the "dulce decus," the grace and ornament of the English school of painting. In him was the true feeling of art. He is dead, and contrary to our expectations, but greatly to our satisfaction, has left £5,000, the surplus fruits of his labours, which according to their merits, well deserved a residue of double the amount. We do not say that "we shall not look upon his like again," but we shall be vastly glad to see one wearing his mantle.[34]

Stothard's works were avidly collected by his contemporaries and by admirers well into the nineteenth century. Caches of his drawings, prints, and paintings were amassed by Mrs. Flaxman, Robert Balmanno, Samuel Boddington, Robert Vernon, John Sheepshanks, Samuel Rogers, Thomas Lawrence, Francis Chantrey, Charles Heath, H. A. J. Munro of Novar, Benjamin Godfrey Windus, Isaac Watts, William Edward Frost, and others.[35]

Although critical, at times, of Stothard's drawing practices, John Ruskin's assessment of this artist typifies the esteem in which he was held for much of the nineteenth century:

The works of our own Stothard are examples of the operation of a mind singular in gentleness and purity, upon mere worldly subjects. It seems as if Stothard could not conceive wickedness, coarseness, or baseness. Every one of his figures looks as if it had been copied from some creature who had never harboured an unkind thought, nor permitted itself an ignoble action. With this intense love of mental purity is joined, in Stothard, a love of mere physical smoothness and softness; so that he lived in a universe of soft grass and stainless fountains, tender trees, and stones at which no foot would stumble.[36]

*   *   *

Stothard's life provides an invaluable example of an artist successfully involved in the production of a wide array of mass-produced art commodities as well as more traditional academic pursuits. He was able to accommodate these diverse demands because he functioned as a specialist. In this role, he could adapt his designs with great facility to a wide variety of markets, a factor that contributed significantly to his prolific employment and financial success. Stothard's market-conscious attitude to his work also encouraged him to adopt various industrial practices. He discerned no impropriety in adopting a design produced for silverwork or for book illustration to the format of a self-contained painting. His designs were interchangeable, satisfying the requirements of both his commercial employers and his private patrons. This did not adversely effect his work; for he was still able to master the diverse skills utilized in art production in the years around 1800. He was not cut off from the final execution of his artwork. Stothard's multifarious commercial activities mark, however, an important transitional stage in the transformation of the artist's function in an industrial society.

APPENDIX 1
Checklist of Stothard's Excursions

1777 Trip to Shrewsbury (mother's birthplace), then ten days in North Wales before the Society of Arts exhibition, where he showed two views of Wales; in September to Portsmouth to visit his friend Darcey (letter on a drawing in Nottingham Castle Museum).

1779 Sailing trip up the Medway River (drawing representing Allington Castle near Maidstone, Kent), probably in September when R.A. schools closed.

1781 Sailing trip with George Cumberland and Richard Collins (letter).

ca. 1781 Sailing trip with William Blake and Ogelby, arrested as French spies.

1799–1803 Summers painting murals at Burleigh House in Stamford, Northamptonshire.

1805 Drawing master to Col. Thomas Johnes of Hafod, Wales, after August 1 (attended R.A. meeting) and still there on September 14 (letter).

1809 To Scotland via the Lakes for nine weeks leaving the end of June, arriving in Leith on 7 July; then to Edinburgh; at the beginning of August to Dumfries; returning to London the beginning of September (see Davidson Cook, "Burns and Stothard").

1810 Drawing master to Johnes for three months in the summer after 26 July (Farington visited Stothard) and before 10 December (R.A. meeting).

1811 Possible trip to Hafod with Francis Chantrey to give advice to Johnes about a memorial for Mariamne, his daughter, who died on 4 July.

1812 Walked with Constable on 6 June through Putney, Wimbledon Common, Coombe Wood, and Richmond.

1813 Trip in October to Bristol, Chepstow, and the Wye (letter), probably on to Bath (dated drawing).

1815 Trip to Paris in September.

1816 Drawing master to Rev. Robert Markham, Bolton Perry, Yorkshire, for five weeks (letter), probably in October or November; traveled on to Tadcaster, York, Lincoln, Ely, Beverley, and Dumfries (dated drawings).

1818 Possible trip to the Lakes (dated drawing "Keswick, September 30, 1818").

1821 To Edinburgh; left by steamboat by 18 September (letter) and returned to London in late September, probably there for fourteen days (dated drawings).

1822 To Edinburgh; 24 May sailed up the coastline to Leith reaching Edinburgh on 30 May; returned to London the beginning of July (dated drawings and letters).

1824 To Derbyshire, trip down the Dovedale, etc. (see his journal in Anna Eliza Bray, *The Life of Thomas Stothard, R.A.*).

APPENDIX 2
Checklist of Books Illustrated by Stothard

ABBREVIATIONS

Balmanno: Robert Balmanno's collection of approximately 2,200 engravings after Stothard, located in the British Museum, London

Bennett MA thesis: Shelley M. Bennett, "Eighteenth-Century Book Illustration to Shakespeare: A Catalogue of the Turner Shakespeare in the Henry E. Huntington Collection," Master's thesis, University of California, Los Angeles, 1975

Bentley: G. E. Bentley, Jr., *Blake Books: annotated catalogues of William Blake's writings in illuminated printing, in conventional typography and in manuscripts . . .* (Oxford, 1977).

Bray: Anna Eliza Bray, *The Life of Thomas Stothard, R.A. with Personal Reminiscences* (London, 1851)

Boddington: Samuel Boddington's collection of approximately 2,500 engravings after Stothard, 12 vols., located in the Huntington Library, San Marino, California

Coxhead: A. C. Coxhead, *Thomas Stothard, R.A.: An Illustrated Monograph* (London, 1906)

Essick: Robert N. Essick, *The Separate Plates of William Blake: A Catalogue* (Princeton, 1983)

Essick/Easson: Robert N. Essick and Roger R. Easson, *William Blake: Book Illustrator: A Bibliography and Catalogue of the Commercial Engravings,* 2 vols. (American Blake Foundation, 1972, 1979)

Hammelmann: Hanns Hammelmann, *Book Illustrators in Eighteenth-Century England,* ed. and comp. T. S. R. Boase (New Haven and London, 1975)

Royal Academy: *Engravings from the Works of Thomas Stothard, R.A. . . . Collected by W. E. Frost, A. R. A.* (London, 1861), 12 volumes located in the Royal Academy of Art Library, London

UCLA: University Research Library, University of California, Los Angeles

Yale Center for British Art: Engravings after Stothard bound into numbered extra-illustrated editions of Anna Eliza Bray's *The Life of Thomas Stothard, R.A. with Personal Reminiscences* (London, 1851) located in Yale Center for British Art, New Haven

KEY

(?) following a date indicates the date of the following publications are in question

(?) preceding a publication indicates that publication is in question

sources have been listed in the order of their importance in establishing the verity of the entry; all entries have been searched in the Huntington Library and British Library, but only those copies located are included in this listing; later reprints have not been cited, except in a few notable instances

CHECKLIST

1778–1781

The Poets of Great Britain. Complete from Chaucer to Churchill. For John Bell. 42 illus. by Stothard (and perhaps 1 engraved but not used)

British Library (1066.b.1–42, c.1–2): 42 plates

Coxhead, pp. 82–89, and Hammelmann both list 42 illus. by Stothard: Chaucer (14 plates); Denham (1 plate); Donne (2 plates) [Coxhead, p. 84, and Bentley, p. 548, list another plate Stothard del.–Blake sc. as possibly a rejected plate for Donne in this ed.; Essick, pp. 236–37, suggests a date for this plate ca. 1780–1787]; King (2 plates); Fenton (1 plate); Lansdowne (1 plate); Garth (1 plate); Somerville (1 plate); Hughes (2 plates); Roscommon (1 plate); Tickell (1 plate); Cunningham (1 plate); Buckingham (1 plate); Watts (7 plates); Rowe (l plate); Pitt (1 plate); Pomfret (1 plate); Armstrong (1 plate); Akenside (2 plates)

Balmanno: 40 plates Stothard del.

Boddington, vol. 6, pp. 36–56

1779

Hervey, Frederic. *The Naval History of Great Britain.* For J. Bew. 2 illus. by Stothard

British Library (598.f.8–12): 2 frontispieces

Coxhead, p. 168, lists 1 Stothard del. and possibly 3 more; dates publication 1779, though plates bear 1780 date

Boddington, vol. 6, p. 68: 1 plate "1780"

Balmanno: 2 plates Stothard del. (identified in pencil and dated May and June 1779) and several more identified in pencil as by Stothard from 1780

(?) [unknown author, title, and publisher.] 1 illus. by Stothard

Essick, pp. 233–34, notes an early print in Balmanno identified in pencil as Stothard inv. Blake eng. 1779

The Stothard drawing for this illus. is in a private collection, England

1779(?)

Macpherson, James. *The Poems of Ossian. The Son of Fingal.* For R. Morison, Perth. 4 illus. by Stothard

British Library (11595.bbb.33) 1795 ed.: 4 plates

Coxhead, p. 167, lists 4 illus. probably published 1779, the date on the title page

Hammelmann: dates publication 1795

Balmanno: 4 prints Stothard del.

Boddington, vol. 4, p. 62: 1 plate

1780

Enfield, William. *The Speaker: or Miscellaneous Pieces selected from the Best English Writers.* For Joseph Johnson. 4 illus. by Stothard

Essick/Easson, pp. 8–10, lists 4 plates for the eds. of 1780, 1781, 1785, 1795, 1797, 1799 (re-engraved); 1801, 1805 (both re-engraved)

Coxhead, p. 169, lists 2 illus. plus some more; does not date but discusses with ca. 1782 publications

Boddington, vol. 4, p. 114: 3 plates; vol. 5, p. 46: plate identified in pencil for *The Speaker* 1795

Balmanno: plates dated 1780

1780(?)

Sime. *Military Science.* [unknown publisher.] 1 illus. by Stothard

Coxhead, p. 144, lists frontispiece by Stothard and dates it 1780

Hammelmann: frontispiece, dates publication 1781

Southwell, Henry. *The New Book of Martyrs.* For J. Cooke. 8 illus. by Stothard

British Library (4824.k.1) 1780[?] ed.: 8 plates

Coxhead, p. 171, lists 8 illus., dates ca. 1780–1785

Hammelmann: 8 illus., dates ca. 1780–1785

Boddington plates

1780–1785

The Town and Country Magazine. For John Harrison. 15(?) illus. by Stothard

Coxhead, p. 39, lists 15 illus. attributed to Stothard and possibly 3 more

Huntington Library (Reel 1672–679 Film 153E): 1780 vol. contains the 3 plates listed by Coxhead for this year—none bear the artist's name, but they are stylistically close to Stothard; in 1783 vol., 8 plates are close to Stothard; in 1784 vol., 1 plate is close to Stothard; in 1781 and 1782 vols., none are close to Stothard

British Library (P.P.5442.b): 1780 vol. contains the 3 plates listed by Coxhead for this year—none bears the artist's name, but they are stylistically close to Stothard; same is true of 1784 and 1785 vols.; 1781, 1782, 1783 vols. are missing

Hammelmann says that between 1780 and 1785 Stothard contributed at least 15 illus.

Balmanno: 4 plates (2 Stothard del.), frontispiece 1782

1780–1786

The Novelist's Magazine. For John Harrison. 244 illus. by Stothard

Huntington Library (148622) and British Library (P.P.5262.aa) 244 plates total: vol. I, 1 unsigned plate by Stothard to Fielding, *Joseph Andrew;* vol. II, 1 plate to Voltaire, *Zadig;* 4 plates to W. Combe, *Devil upon Two Sticks* [also in Coxhead, p. 61, and British Library P.P.5262.aa, though Hammelmann lists only 3 plates]; vol. III, 6 plates to Charles Morell, trans., *Tales of the Genii;* 12 plates to Fielding, *Tom Jones;* vol. IV, 10 plates to Le Sage, *Gil Blas;* 7 plates to Defoe, *Robinson Crusoe;* vol. V, 8 plates to Sterne, *Tristram Shandy;* 3 plates to M. Eneulette, *Chinese Tales;* 4 plates to Dodd, *The Sisters;* vol. VI, 11 plates to Smollett, *Peregrine Pickle;* 6 plates to M. Marmontel, *Moral Tales;* vol. VII, 6 plates to Chevalier de Mouny, *The Fortunate Country Maid;* 2 plates to Hugh Kelly, *Louisa Mildmay;* 2 plates to Langhorne, *Theodosius and Constantia;* 4 plates to Smollett, *Ferdinand Count Fathom* [Huntington Library missing 1 plate]; vol. VIII, 16 plates to Cervantes, *Don Quixote;* vol. IX, 2 plates to Sterne, *A Sentimental Journey;* 4 plates to Swift, *Gulliver's Travels;* 4 plates to Sarah Fielding, *David Simple;* 4 plates to Smollett, *Sir Launcelot Greaves;* 2 plates to Francis Ashmole, *A Peruvian Princess;* 2 plates to Fielding, *Jonathan Wild;* vols. X-XI, 28 plates to Richardson, *Sir Charles Grandison* (16 in vol. X; 12 in vol. XI); Vol. XII, 4 plates to Charlotte Lennox, *The Female Quixote;* 3 plates to Fielding, *A Journey from This World to the Next;* 4 plates to Kimber, *Life and Adventures of Joe*

Thompson; 6 plates to Paltock, *Adventures of Peter Wilkins;* vol. XIII, 8 plates to Eliza Haywood, *Betsy Thoughtless;* 6 plates to Ambrose Philips, *Persian Tales;* vols. XIV-XV, 28 plates to Richardson, *Clarissa Harlowe* (10 in vol. XIV; 18 in vol. XV); vol. XVI, 5 plates to Avellaneda, *A Continuation of Don Quixote;* 9 plates to Marivaux, *The Virtuous Orphan;* vol. XVII, 4 plates to La Mothe-Fénelon, *Telemachus;* 2 plates to Lady Susannah Fitzroy, *Henrietta, Countess Osenvor;* 6 plates to Eliza Haywood, *Jemmy and Jenny Jessamy* [1 plate missing in Huntington Library copy]; vol. XVIII, 10 plates to *The Arabian Nights*

Hammelmann lists 242 illus. by Stothard

Coxhead, pp. 61–74, also lists these novels and includes the Stothard illus. to *Joseph Andrews*

Balmanno: plate Dodd del. for *Joseph Andrew* dated 1779

1780–1797

The Lady's Magazine; or entertaining companion for the fair sex. For G. Robinson. 90(?) illus. by Stothard

Coxhead, pp. 42–50, lists 90 or more illus. attributed to Stothard bearing no artist's name

British Library (P.P.5141): no plates bear artist's name, but many are stylistically close to Stothard

Essick, p. 241, notes Stothard's receipt of 11 April 1795 for 2 drawings for *Lady's Magazine* (located in Princeton); see also Bentley, p. 292

Huntington Library (132125): incomplete

Boddington, vol. 2, p. 122 ff.; vol. 6, pp. 80 ff.

Balmanno: plates identified in pencil

Hammelmann: 90 plates

1781

The Lady's Poetical Magazine; or, Beauties of British Poetry. For John Harrison. 29 illus. by Stothard

Coxhead, pp. 33–36, lists 29 plates

Huntington Library (139554) missing vol. 4; vols. 1-3: 6 plates and headpiece in each plus repeated title-page illus. in each

Boddington, vol. 4, pp. 80–92: 26 plates

Hammelmann lists 24 plates

Royal Academy: advertisement for *Lady's Poetical Magazine* says it includes illus. by Stothard

Balmanno #191: associated with *The Lady's Magazine; or Beauties of British Poetry* for Harrison, vol. I, 1781

The London Magazine: or, Gentleman's Monthly Intelligencer. For R. Baldwin. 1 illus. by Stothard

Huntington Library (18390 and Reel 193–209 Film 8E)

vol. 1 (1781) frontispiece bears no artist's name, perhaps by Stothard

British Library (P.P.5437) 1781 vol. frontispiece bears no artist's name, perhaps by Stothard

Coxhead, p. 144, lists 1 illus.

Hammelmann lists frontispiece by Stothard

1781(?)

A new and complete universal history of the Holy Bible . . . by Edward Kimpton. For J. Cooke. 5 illus. by Stothard

British Library (L.16.d.3) 1785[?] ed.: 5 plates Stothard del.; 4 plates are duplicated in the 1785–1786(?) ed. of *The whole Genuine and complete Works of Flavius Josephus* by George Henry Maynard for J. Cooke (British Library 4517.dd.1) [see 1785–1786 entry for J. Cooke]

Essick, p. 238, dates this publication "1781?"; notes Stothard del. *The Battle of Ai*—plate is also in Josephus [see 1785–1786 entries]

Essick/Easson, pp. 21–28, notes that if the plate *The Return of the Jewish Spies from Canaan* (Stothard del.) is for Josephus [see 1785–1786 entries], then it is also for this ed., which has the same plates and was probably published first

Bentley, pp. 589–91, lists 1 illus. by Stothard that was engraved by Blake: *The Battle of Ai;* says the plates in this ed. were repeated in ed. of Josephus [see 1785–1786 entries]

1782

Bonnycastle, John. *An Introduction to Mensuration and Practical Geometry.* For Joseph Johnson. 1 illus. by Stothard

Essick/Easson, pp. 29–30, lists 1782, 1787, 1791 eds. with 1 plate attributed to Stothard

Bentley, pp. 534–35, lists 1 unsigned illus. attributed to Stothard (the Balmanno plate) and lists later eds.: 1787, 1791, 1794, 1798, 1802

Coxhead, p. 179, lists 1 plate

Balmanno #782: 1 plate

Knox, Vicesimus. *Essays Moral and Literary.* For Charles Dilly. 2 illus. by Stothard

British Library (629.c.9): 2 plates

Coxhead, p. 181, lists 2 illus. and notes 2 title vignettes implying they too are by Stothard

Boddington, vol. 7, p. 110: 1 plate

(?) *The Lady's Pocket Book.* For James Bodsley and Joseph Johnson. 2(?) illus. by Stothard

Bentley, pp. 591–92, accepts Gilchrist's statement that

Stothard del. 2 plates for this publication; 1 engraved
by Blake; notes the publication is untraced

Essick, pp. 239–41, notes that no copy of this publication
has ever been found, thus doubts the book exists

British Library (P.P.2469.c1.[1.]): only 1778 volume of
The Ladies' Complete Pocket Book (1769–?), no Stothard del.

Pinkerton, John. *Rimes.* For Charles Dilly. 1 illus. by Stothard

British Library (11632.b.42): 1 plate

Coxhead, p. 172: 1 plate

Hammelmann: 1 plate

(?) Priestley, Joseph. [unknown title and publisher.] 1 illus.
by Stothard perhaps published as a separate print

Jean H. Hagstrum, *William Blake: Poet and Painter,* p. 43,
notes print *Experimental Philosophy pushing aside the
Clouds of Darkness from the Garden of Science* for unspec-
ified work by Priestly located in Balmanno and in
Huntington Library Print Box 785

Coxhead, p. 170, lists 1 illus.

Balmanno #373: identified in pencil on print for
Priestley's works

Bray, p. 162

Boddington, vol. 3, p. 22: this plate is identified in pencil
as a frontispiece to a work on Perspective

Scott, John. *The Poetical Works.* For J. Buckland. 6 illus. by
Stothard

Huntington Library (68285): 6 plates

Coxhead, p. 145: 6 illus.

UCLA (PR3671 S37 A17): 6 plates

Hammelmann: 6 plates

Balmanno #920–25

Essick/Easson, pp. 38–39, lists 1782, 1786, 1795 eds.

Bentley, p. 611

Boddington, vol. 5, p. 22: 2 plates

Yale Center for British Art, Bray 2: illustration for this
publication identified in pencil: "An Arabian
Ecologue"

1782–1783

The British Magazine and Review; or Universal Miscellany. For
John Harrison. 14 illus. by Stothard

British Library (P.P.5433.h): 1 title-page vignette common to all three vols. and 13 illus.

Coxhead, p. 37, lists 1 title-page vignette common to all
three vols. plus 11 illus

Balmanno: 1 plate

Boddington, vol. 6, pp. 104–12: 16 plates

1782–1784

The European Magazine and London Review. For John Fielding [etc.]. 2(?) illus. by Stothard

Coxhead, p. 145, lists 2 illus. (1 to vol. 2; 1 to vol. 3)

Boddington, vol. 2, p. 50: identified in pencil for this
publication; vol. 3, pp. 128–30: 3 portrait illus.—2
with Stothard del.; 2 bear imprint "European Magazine 1782"

Hammelmann: frontispiece to vol. 2

Balmanno: 2 plates; only 1 bears artist's name

British Library (P.P.5459.2) 1782 vol. 2, 1 plate; vol. 4, 1
plate bears no artist's name

1782–1784(?)

Martyn, William Frederick. *The Geographical Magazine; or,
New System of Geography.* For John Harrison. 5 illus.
by Stothard

Huntington Library (149610) 1785–1793 ed., 5 plates: 4
in vol. 1 (dated 1785); 1 in vol. 2 (dated 1793)

Coxhead, p. 168, dates publication 1782 and lists 2 illus.

Boddington, vol. 3, pp. 12, 166 (1 plate with date "1782,"
identified in pencil for this publication); vol. 3, p. 28, 1
plate "For Harrison 1784"

Balmanno prints #500–501: 2 plates "Harrison 1784"

National Union Catalogue entry gives no publication
date

1782–1786

Lowndes's New English Theater. For T. and W. Lowndes
[etc.]. 6–10(?) illus. by Stothard

Coxhead, p. 173, lists 5 theatrical portraits; p. 176 lists 1
more

Boddington, vol. 2, contains 14 theatrical portraits, but
only 10 with Lowndes as publisher: p. 102 (4 plates
Stothard del.), p. 104 (4 plates Stothard del.); p. 106 (2
plates Stothard del.); p. 108 (4 plates Stothard del.)

Hammelmann: 2 plates

Bennett MA thesis: 2 plates for Shakespeare's *Plays* published by Lowndes as part of this series

Jane Shore. Tragedy, for T. and W. Lowndes [etc.], 1784,
including 1 Stothard del. theatrical portrait was
offered for sale at Zeitlin & Ver Brugge, Los Angeles

Balmanno plates

1783

Ariosto, Lodovico. *Orlando Furioso.* Translated by John
Hoole. For C. Bathurst [etc.]. 2 illus. by Stothard

Huntington Library (292845) 1783 ed.: 2 illus. by Stothard; same illus. included in the 1785 ed. for George

Nicol (344210), the 1791 ed. (105642) and the 1799 ed. for Otridge, Vernor & Hood, etc. (441517)

Bentley, pp. 512–13, says this is the 1st ed., reprinted in 1785, 1791, 1799

Essick/Easson, pp. 42–43, lists 1783, 1785, 1791, 1799 eds. with 2 Stothard del. plates

Coxhead, p. 160, lists 2 illus. for the 1799 ed.; probably the reissue for Vernor & Hood

Balmanno #1206–7: identified in pencil "For Vernor & Hood 1798"

Hammelmann lists only 1799 ed.: 2 plates

Boddington, vol. 3, p. 34

Fielding, John. *Origin, progress and present state of the Peerage of England, Scotland and Ireland.* For John Fielding. 1 illus. by Stothard

British Library (9905.a.10): 1 illus.

Coxhead, p. 170, lists 1 illus., dates 1783

Balmanno: 1 print Stothard del.

Ritson, Joseph. *A Select Collection of English Songs.* For Joseph Johnson. 17 illus. by Stothard

Huntington Library (108261) 1783 ed.: 1 full-page illus. Stothard del. and 16 vignettes (only 8 Stothard del.)

Coxhead, pp. 146–48, lists 17 illus.

Boddington, vol. 2, p. 41: frontispiece to vol. 1 and 12 vignettes

Balmanno: prints include 16 plates (9 Stothard del.)

Essick/Easson, pp. 45–46

1783–1787

Taylor, Charles. *The Picturesque Beauties of Shakespeare.* For Charles Taylor. 7 illus. by Stothard

Bennett MA thesis: 7 illus.

Coxhead, pp. 95–97, lists 7 illus.

Hammelmann: 7 illus.

Balmanno: 7 plates Stothard del.

1784

Holcroft, Thomas, ed. *The Wit's Magazine.* For Harrison and Co. 1 illus. by Stothard

Huntington Library (148541): 1 plate

Coxhead, p. 148, lists 1 plate

Hammelmann: 1 plate

Balmanno #501: identified in pencil

Bentley, pp. 634–35, and Essick, p. 251, both note that there are two different copperplates of this design

Essick/Easson, pp. 49–51

Huntington Library also has a proof in an extra-illustrated Bray, vol. V, pl. 11

Smollett, Tobias. *The Adventures of Peregrine Pickle.* For W. Strahan [etc.]. 4 illus. by Stothard

British Library (12611.d.8): 4 illus.

Hammelmann: 4 illus.

Coxhead, p. 64, lists only the illus. to *Peregrine Pickle* for the *Novelist's Magazine* [see 1780–1786 entry]

[unknown author and title.] For G. Robinson [etc.]. 4(?) illus. by Stothard

Coxhead, p. 172, lists 4 illus.

Boddington, vol. 4, p. 144: 1 plate "For W. Strahan, G. Robinson, T. Cadell, etc. 1784"

1785

[unknown author and title.] For Rivington. 6(?) illus. by Stothard

Coxhead, pp. 172–73, lists 6 illus.

Boddington, vol. 4, p. 142: 3 plates "For Rivington 1785"

(?) [Hancarville (Pierre François Hugues, called)]. *Recerches sur l'origine ... des Arts de la Grèce ...* For B. Appleyard. 1 illus. by Stothard

Marlborough Rare Books, Sept. 1983 cat. 102, no. 218, this ed.: "Plate 18 in Vol. I is a stipple engraving after Stothard by Charles Townley"

British Library (560.c.8): no Stothard plates

1785–1786(?)

Fenning, Daniel. *A New System of Geography.* For J. Johnson and G. and J. Wilkie. 1 illus. by Stothard

Balmanno: frontispiece *The Four Quarters of the World* (Blake & Trotter sculp.) identified in pencil for 1779 ed. for Fenning and Collyer

Bentley, pp. 554–56, says "no 1779 edition of Fenning and Collyer's book is known" and dates the ed. 1786 for J. Johnson

Essick/Easson, pp. 52–54, lists 1785–1786, 1787 eds.

Josephus, Flavius. *The whole Genuine and complete Works of Flavius Josephus . . . translated by George Henry Maynard.* For J. Cooke. 5 illus. by Stothard

British Library (4517.dd.1): 5 plates; 4 plates are duplicated in *A new and complete universal history of the Holy Bible . . . by Edward Kimpton.* For J. Cooke. Ca. 1785

Bentley, pp. 585–89, dates the publication ca. 1785–1786 and notes reprints in ca. 1795, ca. 1799, ca. 1800; says these eds. exhibit all the internal stigmata of works issued in parts in Kimpton's *History of the Bible* [see 1781 entry], where the plates were first used

Essick, p. 235, says Stothard del. plate *The Return of the*

Jewish Spies from Canaan is close in size and style to his plates for Kimpton's *Bible* [see 1781 entry]

Essick/Easson, pp. 21–26, notes six issues, ca. 1786–1800 of Maynard and 1781 of Kimpton

Coxhead, p. 173, lists 8 Old Testament illus.

Balmanno: 1 plate identified in pencil and dated 1786

Josephus, Flavius. *The Whole Works of Flavius Josephus . . . translated by Charles Clarke.* For the Proprietor and sold by J. Walker. 5 illus. by Stothard

British Library (L.20.f8): 4 illus. from Maynard ed. and 1 new plate dated 1786 Stothard del.

Balmanno #587–96: 4 plates identified in pencil as biblical subjects for Clarke, 1786; #594 (probably for this ed. of Josephus)

Coxhead, p. 173, lists 8 Old Testament illus.

1785–1787

Harrison's British Classics. For Harrison and Co. 16 illus. by Stothard

British Library (1456.g.3–10): 16 illus.

Coxhead, pp.78–79, lists 16 illus. and says they were reissued in 1795

Boddington, vol. 4, pp. 132–40: 16 plates

Hammelmann: 15 illus.

UCLA (PR1101/H24)

1785–1788

(?) *New London Magazine.* For A. Hogg. No(?) illus. by Stothard

Coxhead, p. 149, says no Stothard plates in the British Library copy of these years, but Balmanno includes 2 plates

New York Public Library vols. 1–2 for 1785 contain no Stothard plates

Huntington Library (Reels 950–952 Film 209[a]E): no Stothard plates

1786

(?) *Harrison's Fashionable Magazine; or Lady's and Gentleman's monthly recorder of new fashions.* For Harrison and Co. 3(?) illus. by Stothard

Coxhead, p. 49, lists 3 plates included in Balmanno

British Library (P.P.5141.c): front pages missing, no plates

Balmanno: prints of fashion designs with no artist's name

1786–1788

Rees, Abraham. *Cyclopaedia: or, an Universal Dictionary of Arts and Sciences.* For Rivington [etc.]. 1 illus. by Stothard

British Library ed.: frontispiece Stothard del.–Heath sc.

Boddington, vol. 3, p. 18: 1 plate

Balmanno #691: 1 plate Stothard del. for this publication, dated 1788

1787

Ruggle, Georgio. *Inoramus Comoedia.* For T. Payne and sons, William Ginger. 1 illus. by Stothard

New York Public Library ed.: 1 plate inscribed in pencil "Reynolds deferrd to Stothard on this"

British Library (685.g.26): 1 plate

1788

Hayley, William. *Triumphs of Temper.* For Thomas Cadell. 7 illus. by Stothard

Huntington Library (292930): 7 plates

Coxhead, p. 150, lists 7 illus.

Hammelmann: 7 plates; also lists 1793, 1796 eds.

Balmanno: prints dated 1787 and 1788

Boddington, vol. 6, pp. 76–77: 7 plates

Sargent, John. *The Mine; a dramatic poem.* For Thomas Cadell. 5 illus. by Stothard

British Library: the 1796 ed. (1344.c.55) contains the 1788 plates—3 plates Stothard del. and 2 bearing no artist's name, although probably by Stothard

Coxhead, p. 149, lists 5 illus.

Hammelmann: 5 illus.

Boddington, vol. 6, pp. 60–62: 5 plates

Balmanno: 5 plates identified in pencil

(?) [unknown title for a collection of plays] For Thomas Cadell. 1–6(?) illus. by Stothard

Coxhead, pp. 175–76, lists 6 plates

Balmanno #666–67: 2 illus. to Shakespeare; #669: 1 illus. to *Sigismunda*

Boddington, vol. 4, pp. 142: 1 plate "For Cadell 1788"

1788–1789(?)

Hume, David. *History of England.* For Thomas Cadell. 30 illus. by Stothard

Coxhead, p. 174, notes 30 illus.

Hammelmann notes "30 small designs beneath portraits of the kings and queens"

Boddington, vol. 4, pp. 2–16

National Union Catalogue 0609349: entry for 1790–1791 ed. for Cadell notes portraits

British Library Catalogue 9505.dd.6: entry for the 1789 ed. does not note publisher or plates

1788–1797

(?) Bunyan, John. *The Pilgrim's Progress.* For J. Thane. 16–17(?) illus. by Stothard [these large plates were probably issued as separate prints without text; a series of smaller plates may have been for a book]

Coxhead, pp. 176–78, lists 17 illus., says the plates bear dates from 1788 to 1797, but the book is dated 1789 and was republished in 1840

Huntington Library (113807) 1788–1797, for J. Thane, 16 plates: "proofs before the titles and before the plates were cut down" (no title page; thus not a book)

Hammelmann: 17 illus., dates publication 1789

Balmanno: plates for J. Thane 1788–1797

Boddington, vol. 2, pp. 150–64: 10 plates for Thane

1789

Smith, Charlotte. *Elegiac Sonnets.* For Thomas Cadell. 2 illus. by Stothard

Huntington Library (23330): 2 plates

Coxhead, p. 151, lists 2 illus.

Hammelmann: 2 illus.

Boddington, vol. 6, p. 66: 2 plates

Balmanno plates

(?) White, James. *Earl Strongbow: or, The history of Richard de Clare and the beautiful Geralda.* For T. Lowndes [etc.]. 1 illus. by Stothard

Coxhead, p. 178, lists 1 plate

Balmanno #716: 1 plate identified in pencil for this publication

New York Public Library: 1789 ed. for J. Dodsley has no plates

British Library (12611.b.7): 1789 ed. for J. Dodsley has no plates

1789(?)

Day, Thomas. *The history of Sanford and Merton.* For John Stockdale. 2 illus. by Stothard

British Library (12806.c.7) ed. dated 1795: 2 plates Stothard del. (bear dates 1786 and 1789)

Coxhead, pp. 178–79, lists 1 plate, discusses ca. 1789

Balmanno: 2 plates dated 1789

Boddington, vol. 3, p. 112: 2 plates identified in pencil for this publication, 1 bears date 1787

British Museum catalogue of drawings identifies Stothard drawings as for the 1789 ed. for Stockdale

1790

Defoe, Daniel. *The Life and Strange Surprising Adventures of Robinson Crusoe.* For John Stockdale. 14 illus. by Stothard

British Library (672.h.21,22): 14 plates Stothard del. (6 new plates were added to Cadell's ed. of 1820, see 1820 entry)

Huntington Library (436119): 14 plates Stothard del.

Coxhead, p. 75, lists 16 illus. for Stockdale ed. of 1790

Hammelmann: 16 illus.

Balmanno plates

The Literary Magazine and British Review. For the Proprietors and sold by C. Forster. 1 illus. by Stothard

British Library (439.d.1): 1 plate to vol. 4 only

Coxhead, p. 151, lists 1 illus. in 1790 (vol. 4), repeated in 1794 (vol. 12)

Balmanno: 1 plate Stothard del. 1790 for vol. 4

1790(?)

Raymond, George. *A New, Universal, and Impartial History of England.* For Charles Cooke. 1 illus. by Stothard

British Library (Cup.1247.pp.2) 1790[?]: 1 plate

Coxhead, p. 200, lists 1 plate, dates ca. 1803

Hammelmann lists 1 plate, dates 1786

1791

Arblay, Frances (Burney) d'. *Evelina; or, The History of a Young Ladies Entrance into the World.* For T. Lowndes. 1 illus. by Stothard

Coxhead, p. 181, lists 1 illus., discusses with 1791 publications

National Union Catalogue 0373310: entry for 1791 ed. for Lowndes notes frontispiece

Balmanno #815: for Evelina, Stothard del. "For Lowndes MDCCCI"

The Holy Bible. For Isaiah Thomas, Worcester, Mass. 3 illus. by Stothard

Huntington Library (437000): 3 plates

New York Public Library ed.: Stothard plates

1791(?)

The Holy Bible. For W. N. Gardiner [etc.] [see also 1791, 1793, and 1794 *Bible* entries]. 5(?) illus. by Stothard

Coxhead, p. 180, lists 5 plates for Gardiner [several of these designs are repeated in 1793 ed. for Zachariah Jackson, Dublin, and in 1794 ed. for James Reilly, Dublin: see separate entries]

Royal Academy plates of biblical subjects "For E. Harding 1791"; "For J. Good 1792"; "For W. N. Gardiner & J. Good 1791"

Boddington, vol. 3, p. 72: 2 plates of Adam and Eve in Paradise, identified in pencil for a folio Bible 1791 and 1792

[unknown title to a book of Psalms.] For Thomas Stockdale. 1 illus. by Stothard

    Balmanno #825: 1 plate identified as a frontispiece to the
 Psalms for Stockdale

    Coxhead, p. 180, lists the plate *They sing the song of Moses
 and the Lamb,* probably for a book of Psalms

[unknown title to a Prayer Book.] For E. Harding [see also
 1791, 1793, and 1794 *Bible* entries]. 12(?) illus. by
 Stothard

    Boddington, vol. 3, pp. 74–96: 12 plates identified in
 pencil "for Harding's Prayer book 1791 compleat"

    Balmanno #864–75: biblical subjects for E. Harding 1791

    Royal Academy plates of biblical subjects "For E. Hard-
 ing 1791"; "For J. Good 1792"; "For W. N. Gardiner
 & J. Good 1791"

1791–1797

Bell's British Theatre. For George Cawthorn. 20 illus. by
 Stothard

    Huntington Library (PR 1241 B4): 20 plates

    Coxhead, pp. 89–92, lists 20 plates

    Hammelmann: 19 plates; missed 1 illus. to J. Thomson,
 Edward and Eleanora, vol. 32

    Boddington, vol. 2, pp. 136–49

    Balmanno plates

1791–1798(?)

Montagu, Lady Mary Wortley. *Letters.* For C. Tomkins;
 Thomas Ladd(?). 2 illus. by Stothard

    Yale Center for British Art, Bray 1, vol. 2: 2 plates (1 for
 C. Tomkins 1791; 1 for Thos. Ladd 1798)

    Boddington, vol. 3, pp. 24, 26: 2 plates identified in pen-
 cil for this publication

1792

Goldsmith, Oliver. *The Vicar of Wakefield.* For E. Harding
 & J. Good. 6 illus. by Stothard

    Huntington Library (145309): 6 illus.

    British Library (12614.dd.17): 6 illus.

    Coxhead, p. 116, lists 6 illus.

    Hammelmann: 6 illus.

    Boddington, vol. 3, p. 154: 4 plates; vol. 7, p. 42: 2 plates

(?) Milton, John. *Paradise Lost.* For Edwards. 1 illus. by
 Stothard

    Coxhead, p. 104: 1 illus.

    Hammelmann: 1 illus.

Moseley, Walter Michael. *An Essay on Archery.* For J. Rob-
 son. 2 illus. by Stothard

    Huntington Library (245206): 1 plate Stothard del. and

    probably the title-page vignette, which bears no art-
 ist's name

    Coxhead, p. 182, list 2 plates

    Balmanno: 1 plate Stothard del.

Sterne, Laurence. *A Sentimental Journey.* For J. Good; and E.
 and S. Harding. 6 illus. by Stothard

    British Library (1301.i.11): 6 plates Stothard del.

    Boddington, vol. 3, pp. 116–18: 6 plates

    Coxhead, p. 82, lists 5 illus.

    Yale Center for British Art, Bray: 5 plates

    Balmanno plates

Tasso, Torquato. *Jerusalem Delivered . . . translated by John
 Hoole.* For J. Dodsley. 2 illus. by Stothard

    Huntington Library (433105): 2 illus.; (314858): 1797 ed.
 for J. Johnson, etc., including the 1792 ed. plates by
 Stothard with "Vernor & Hood" imprint on plate

    Coxhead, pp. 159–60, lists 2 illus. by Stothard, says Ver-
 nor & Hood published a 1798 ed. of Hoole's translation of Tasso's *Gerusalemme liberata*

    Hammelmann: 2 illus.

    Balmanno #31204–5: identified in pencil for this ed.,
 plates dated "1798"

1792–1796

(?) Milton, John. *Paradise Lost.* For Jeffreys [this may be a
 series of prints, not a book]. 13 illus. by Stothard

    Coxhead, pp. 103–4, lists 13 illus. and eds. of 1818 and
 1826

    British Museum: album of prints #20 "Thirteen Plates,
 The Subjects from Milton; Designed by Stothard, and
 Engraved by Bartolozzi. Price Five Guineas"; the
 plates bear Jeffrey's name and range in date from 1792
 to 1796

    Hammelmann: 13 illus.

    Balmanno: prints dated 1792, 1793

    Boddington, vol. 3, p. 106: 1 plate; vol. 8, p. 134: 1 plate;
 pp. 138–44: 4 plates, "Jeffreys 1792," identified in
 pencil as for Boydell's *Paradise Lost*

    Yale Center for British Art, Bray 1: prints dated 1792,
 1795; Bray 2, prints dated 1792

1793

Aesop. *The Fables.* For John Stockdale. 1 illus. by Stothard

    Huntington Library ed.: 1 frontispiece Stothard del.

    Coxhead, p. 205, says perhaps 1 or 2 illus. for Gay's
 Fables; however, Stockdale ed. of Gay's *Fables,* 1793,
 has plates based on earlier designs (1727, 1738)

Boddington, vol. 3, p. 134: 5 plates identified in pencil for Aesop's *Fables*

Cumberland, George. *Lewina, the maid of Snowdon.* For the author. 1 illus. by Stothard

G. E. Bentley, Jr., *A Bibliography of George Cumberland* (Garland, 1975), p. 7 and n. 1, notes, "Keynes says 'a letter' in his collection attributes the tailpiece on p. 32 to Stothard; a copy of the plate laid into George Cumberland Jr's *Bristol Beauties* of 1848 (BM) is inscribed in MS: 'By GC Sen.r & T. Stothard RA'"

(?) Goldsmith, Oliver. [Miscellaneous Works.] [unknown publisher.] 2(?) illus. by Stothard

Balmanno #928: "For J. Good 1793" and identified in pencil "Goldsmith's Miscellaneous work"; #911–13: plates "For A. Hamilton 1793"

Coxhead, p. 119, lists 6 illus. for Goldsmith's *Miscellaneous Works* ca. 1805, although he says an early impression of 1 plate bears the date 1793 and the whole may have been published originally in 1793

Coxhead, p. 117, lists 2 illus. for a 1793 ed. of *Vicar of Wakefield,* published again in 1797, perhaps included in this ed.

British Library (1568/6737): *The miscellaneous works* for A. Millar, W. Law, & R. Cater [1792], no plates; (11607.a.13): *Poetical Works* for T. Cadell [etc.]: no plates

Hunter, John. *An historical journal of the transactions at Port Jackson.* For J. Stockdale. 1 illus. by Stothard

Huntington Library (337262): 1 plate

Boddington, vol. 5, p. 24: 1 plate

Pollard, Robert. *The Peerage of Great Britain and Ireland.* For R. Pollard. 6 illus. by Stothard (and perhaps 1 engraved but not used)

British Library (138.e.10): 6 plates

Coxhead, pp. 185–86, lists 6 illus. and 1 engraved but not included

Hammelmann: 6 plates

Yale Center for British Art, Bray 2: plate identified in pencil

Thomson, James. *The Seasons.* For A. Hamilton. 3–10(?) illus. by Stothard

British Library (11656.g.9) and Huntington Library (21728) 1793 ed. for Hamilton: 3 plates "Stothard del." and 7 others very similar but with no artist's name

Coxhead, p. 109, lists 1 signed illus. by Stothard and possibly 7 others

Hammelmann: 1 illus. Stothard del., probably 7 others

Boddington, vol. 6, p. 94

The Universal Family Bible. [Edited by Benjamin Kennicott.] For Zachariah Jackson, Dublin [see also 1791 and 1794 *Bible* entries]. 7 illus. by Stothard

British Library ed.: 7 Stothard illus. (some are his designs for Macklin's *Bible*), but only 4 Stothard del.

1793–1794

Hayley, William. *A Philosophical . . . Essay on Old Maids.* For Thomas Cadell. 4 illus. by Stothard

Huntington Library (345673): 4 illus.

Coxhead, p. 151, notes 4 illus.

Hammelmann: 4 illus.

Boddington, vol. 6, p. 146: 4 plates

Balmanno plates

1793–1795

Hume, David. *Parson's Genuine Pocket ed. of Hume's History . . . with a continuation by Dr. T. Smollett.* [unknown publisher, probably Parson.] 2 illus. by Stothard

Coxhead, p. 175, lists 2 illus.

Hammelmann: 2 plates

Balmanno plates

1794

Church of England. *The Book of Common Prayer.* For J. Good and E. Harding. 10–12(?) illus. by Stothard

British Library (682.h.1): 10 illus.

Coxhead, p. 184, lists 12 illus., plates dated 1792 but published 1794

Hammelmann notes this publication but doesn't list number of plates

Boddington, vol. 3, pp. 74, 108 ff.

Yale Center for British Art, Bray 4

Edwards, Bryan. *The history, civil and commercial, of the British Colonies in the West Indies.* For John Stockdale. 1 illus. by Stothard

Huntington Library (432474): 1 plate

Hammelmann: 1 illus.

Langhorne, John. *The Fables of Flora.* For E. and S. Harding. 11 illus. by Stothard

Huntington Library (146490): 11 plates

Coxhead, pp. 112–13, lists 11 illus.

Hammelmann: 11 illus.

Boddington, vol. 3, pp. 148–52: 11 plates

Balmanno plates

Marmontel, Jean François. *Belisarius.* For E. Harding. 6 illus. by Stothard

British Library (1458.d.11) for E. Harding: 6 plates;
(12519.f.35) 1800 for Crosby and Letterman: 4 plates
reissued from the 1794 ed. for Harding

Coxhead, pp. 186–87, lists 6 illus. with 2 repeated in
another ed. in 1800 for Johnson or Heptinstall

Hammelmann: 6 illus. for Vernor and Hood

Balmanno: plates for Harding

Boddington, vol. 5, p. 110: 2 plates

Reilly's Doway Bible. [Published by the English College at
Doway.] For James Reilly, Dublin [see 1791 and 1793
Bible entries]. 4–8(?) illus. by Stothard

British Library (L.15.1): 4 illus. Stothard del. and 4 other
illus. close in style to Stothard

Rogers, Samuel. *Pleasures of Memory.* For Thomas Cadell. 2
illus. by Stothard

Huntington Library (425902): 2 illus.

Coxhead, p. 120, lists 2 Stothard del. illus. for 1794 and
1795 eds.; p. 122, for 1802 and 1802 eds.

Hammelmann: 2 illus.

Balmanno: plates dated 1793

Thomson, James. *The Seasons.* For John Stockdale. 13 illus.
by Stothard

Huntington Library (315468): 13 illus.

British Library (1465.b.2.[1.]): 13 illus.

Coxhead, p. 110, notes 13 illus.

Boddington, vol. 4, pp. 94–100: 13 plates

1795

Aikin, John. *A Description of the Country from thirty to forty
miles round Manchester.* For J. Stockdale. 2 illus. by
Stothard

Huntington Library (204522): 2 plates

Coxhead, pp. 197–98, lists 1 illus.

Boddington, vol. 3, p. 6: 1 plate

Balmanno: identified in pencil

Akenside, Mark. *The Pleasures of the Imagination.* For
T. Cadell, Jun. and W. Davies. 4 illus. by Stothard

Huntington Library (113850) 1795 ed.: 4 illus.

Coxhead, pp. 182–83, lists 4 illus., dates 1796

Boddington, vol. 5, p. 96

Balmanno: plates placed about 1803

Armstrong, John. *The Art of Preserving Health. A poem.* For
T. Cadell, Jun. and W. Davies. 4 illus. by Stothard

British Library (11631.b.3) 1795 ed. for Cadell & Davies: 4
Stothard plates dated "1794"

Boddington, vol. 5, p. 120: 4 plates dated "1794"

Yale Center for British Art, Bray 4: identified in pencil
with date 1794

Huntington Library (432402) 1796 ed.: 4 plates

Coxhead, p. 200, lists 4 illus., dates 1803

Balmanno: identified in pencil with date 1803

Fénelon, François de Salignac de la Mothe. *The adventures of
Telemachus, son of Ulysses.* For C. and G. Kearsley. 10
illus. by Stothard

Huntington Library (292917) and British Library
(87.I.12): 10 illus., title page dated 1795 but plates bear
dates from 1792 to 1794

Coxhead, p. 188, lists 10 illus., dates 1794

Boddington, vol. 6, pp. 4–22: 10 plates

Balmanno plates

Hammelmann: 1 plate, dates 1797

(?) *The Lady's New and Elegant Pocket Magazine.* For Hogg.
2–3(?) illus. by Stothard

Essick, p. 241, notes Stothard's receipt of 11 April 1795 for
2 drawings for *Lady's Magazine* (located in Princeton);
see also Bentley, p. 292

Coxhead, p. 189, lists 1 illus., possibly 1 or 2 others

Balmanno: plate dated 1795

Boddington, vol. 2, p. 60

(?) [unknown title to a magazine.] For G. Robinson. 3 illus.
by Stothard

Balmanno #1022–24: plates "For G.G. & J. Robinson
1795"

Coxhead, p. 40, lists 3 plates, perhaps for *Town and Country Magazine,* 1 for G. Robinson, 1784.

1795(?)

Falconer, William. *The Shipwreck.* For T. Cadell. 4 illus. by
Stothard

Coxhead, p. 152, lists 4 illus., plates dated 1795

National Union Catalogue 0020247: entry for 1796 ed.
for Cadell notes 4 plates dated 1 May 1795

Yale Center for British Art, Bray 4: plates identified in
pencil with date 1795

Boddington, vol. 5, p. 84: 4 plates identified in pencil for
1802 ed.

Hammelmann: 4 illus.

Balmanno #1318–21: identified in pencil for this
publication

1795–1801(?)

The Universal Magazine of Knowledge and Pleasure. For
W. Bent. 2–3(?) illus. by Stothard

Royal Academy: Stothard del. plate for *Universal Magazine,* "vol. CVIII For W. Bent 1801," and others that
bear no artist's name

Coxhead, p. 41, says a Balmanno plate is ascribed to 1795, but neither volume of this year contains this illus.; however the 100th vol. (1st half of 1797) has illus. by Stothard

Balmanno #1020: Stothard del. frontispiece to *Universal Magazine;* #1144: Stothard del. frontispiece to *Universal Magazine,* "Vol. L. For W. Bent, 1797"

Huntington Library (8631): no Stothard del. in vols. for 1794, 1795, 1797; Stothard del. frontispiece for 1801

1796

[Anonymous.] *Agatha; or, A Narrative of Recent Events. A Novel in three Volumes.* For C. Dilly [etc.]. 3 illus. by Stothard

Huntington Library (445255): 3 plates

Coxhead, pp. 152–53, lists 3 illus.

Boddington, vol. 6, p. 72: 3 plates

Balmanno #783–85: identified in pencil for this publication

Bunyan, John. *The Pilgrims Progress.* For T. Heptinstall. 3 illus. by Stothard

Huntington Library (268598) and British Library (4418.h.18) 1796 ed. for T. Heptinstall: 3 plates (different from the plates published in Thane ed. of 1789)

Coxhead, p. 190, lists 3 illus.

Boddington, vol. 5, pp. 8–10: 2 plates

[Dodsley, Robert.] *The Economy of Human Life.* For G. Sael, London. 4(?) illus. by Stothard

Coxhead, pp. 190–91, lists 4 illus.

Boddington, vol. 5, p. 52: 4 plates

British Library (8407.bb.4): only 1 illus.

Balmanno #1100–1102: "For G. Sael 1796"; #1154: identified in pencil for *Economy of Human Life,* frontispiece for G. Sael 1796

Green, Matthew. *The Spleen, and other Poems.* For T. Cadell, W. Davies. 3 illus. by Stothard

Huntington Library (349619): 3 plates

Coxhead, p. 182, about 3 illus., dates publication 1793

Balmanno #1103: identified in pencil for Green's *Poems* 1796

Boddington, vol. 6, p. 74: 3 plates

Johnson, Samuel. *The History of Rasselas, Prince of Abissinia.* For J. & E. Harding. 4 illus. by Stothard

New York Public Library 1796 ed.: 4 plates

Royal Academy: 4 plates Stothard del. to *Rasselas* "For J. & E. Harding 1796"

Balmanno #813–14: 2 large single prints to *Rasselas* for J. Harris 1791; separate plates, noted by Coxhead, p. 181

Boddington, vol. 5, p. 86: 2 plates

Pope, Alexander. *An Essay on Man.* For T. Cadell, Jun. and W. Davies. 4 illus. by Stothard

British Library (991.g.27.[1.]) 1796 ed.: 4 plates

Coxhead, p. 107, lists 4 illus., dates 1796

Huntington Library 1802 ed.: 4 plates

Hammelmann: 4 illus.

Boddington, vol. 5, p. 104: 4 plates

Balmanno: identified in pencil and dated 1797

Somerville, William. *The Chase, a poem.* For T. Cadell, Jun. and W. Davies. 6 illus. by Stothard

Huntington Library 1796 ed.: 6 plates

British Library (11633.b.50) 1800 ed.: 6 plates

Coxhead, p. 160, lists 6 illus., dates 1800

Boddington, vol. 5, p. 128: 6 plates identified in pencil with date 1796

Balmanno: plates dated 1796 and 1800

Townshend, Thomas. *Poems.* For Harding. 15 illus. by Stothard

Huntington Library (304142): 15 plates Stothard del.

Coxhead, p. 153, lists 15 illus. and 8 tailpieces that bear no artist's name

Hammelmann: 15 illus.

Boddington, vol. 3, pp. 140–42: 14 plates

Balmanno plates

1796–1826

The Royal Engagement Pocket Atlas. [unknown publisher.] 830–900(?) illus. by Stothard

Coxhead, pp. 53–54, lists 31 sets of illus. (none for 1814 and 1816)

Boddington, vols. 10–11: about 27–29 illus. for each set

Hammelmann lists from 1796–1800: 5 sets of illus.

Balmanno plates

1797

Collins, William. *Poetical Works.* For T. Cadell, Jun. and W. Davies. 4 illus. by Stothard

Huntington Library (405715): 4 illus.

Coxhead, p. 154, lists 4 illus.

Hammelmann: 4 illus.

Balmanno #1314–15: identified in pencil for this publication; #1166–7: "For Cadell & Davies 1797," probably for this publication

Boddington, vol. 5, p. 94: 2 plates

Gessner, Salomon. *The Death of Abel.* For T. Heptinstall. 7–8(?) illus. by Stothard

British Library (012251.i.2): 7 illus. (including 2 for *New Idylls*)

Coxhead, p. 155, lists 6 illus. for this ed. and 2 extra plates for another ed. of the same date and title, containing the *New Idylls*

Hammelmann: 6 illus.

Boddington, vol. 5, pp. 50–56: 7 plates

Balmanno plates

Gifford, William. *The Baviad, and Maeviad.* For J. Wright. 2 illus. by Stothard

Huntington Library (344107): 2 illus.

Coxhead, p. 193, lists 2 illus.

Balmanno #1159–60: "For J. Wright 1797 Baviad & Maviad"

Boddington, vol. 5, p. 116: 2 plates

(?) Goldsmith, Oliver. *The Deserted Village.* [unknown publisher.] 2(?) illus. by Stothard

Coxhead, p. 118, lists 2 illus. for *The Deserted Village* in a 1797 ed.

British Museum catalogue of drawings identifies Stothard drawings for a 1797 ed. of *The Deserted Village*

Boddington, vol. 5, p. 106: 1 plate identified in pencil "The Deserted Village in Lanes's[?] Beauties of Poets"

Gregory, Dr. John. *A father's Legacy to his Daughters.* For A. Strahan [etc.]. 4 illus. by Stothard

Huntington Library (70968): 4 illus.

Coxhead, pp. 192–93, lists 4 illus.

Balmanno #1165: identified in pencil for this publication

Boddington, vol. 5, p. 98: 4 plates

The Origin of Christianity. For T. Heptinstall. 1 illus. by Stothard

Balmanno #1149: Stothard del. frontispiece "The Origin of Christianity" "For T. Heptinstall 1797"

Royal Academy: Stothard del. frontispiece "The Origin of Christianity" "For T. Heptinstall 1797"

Park, Thomas. *Sonnets and other small poems.* For G. Sael. 2 illus. by Stothard

British Library (1465.f.32): 2 illus.

Coxhead, p. 193, lists 2 illus.

Balmanno #1161–62: "For G. Sael 1797" and identified in pencil for Park's *Sonnets*

Boddington, vol. 6, p. 100: 1 plate

Robertson, William. *The History of Scotland During the Reigns of Queen Mary and of King James VI.* For T. Cadell, Jun. and W. Davies. 9 illus. by Stothard

British Library (600.b.15): 9 plates dated 1798 and title page dated 1797

Coxhead, pp. 194–95, lists 9 plates dated 1798, although the title page is dated 1797

Boddington, vol. 5, pp. 72–82: 29 plates identified in pencil for Robertson's histories [see other entries]

Balmanno: plates dated 1799–1801

Yale Center for British Art, Bray 3

Staunton, Sir George, Bart. *An Historical account of the embassy to the Emperor of China.* For John Stockdale. 1–2(?) illus. by Stothard

British Library (10056.bb.15) 1797 ed.: frontispiece Stothard del.

Coxhead, p. 183, lists 2 illus., dates 1792

Yale Center for British Art, Bray 4: identified in pencil with date 1797

Boddington, vol. 3, p. 10: identified in pencil for this publication

Balmanno: identified in pencil

1797–1799(?)

[unknown biblical work.] For W. Button. 4 illus. by Stothard

Coxhead, p. 192, lists 4 illus. to a book on ecclesiastical history for Button, dates 1797

Balmanno #1009–12: biblical subjects "For W. Button 1797"; #1287: biblical subject Stothard del. "For W. Button 1799"

Royal Academy: biblical subjects "For W. Button 1797"

Boddington, vol. 5, p. 124: 4 plates identified in pencil for a *Dictionary of the Bible*

1798

Cowper, William. *Poems.* For J. Johnson. 10 illus. by Stothard

Huntington Library (120952) 1798 ed.: 10 illus.

Coxhead, pp. 158–59, lists 10 illus., says plates dated 1798 but published by Johnson in 1800

Boddington, vol. 7, pp. 64–68: 10 plates

Yale Center for British Art, Bray 2: 2 plates

Balmanno plates

Glover, Richard. *Leonidas, a Poem.* For Cadell, Du Roveray [etc.]. 4 illus. by Stothard

Huntington Library (145248), 1798 ed.: 4 plates; (247584) 1804 ed.: same 4 plates

British Library (11632.d.16) 1798 ed. for F. J. Du Roveray: 4 plates

Balmanno: plates dated 1798 for Du Roveray

Coxhead, p. 162, lists 4 illus. for the 1804 ed.

Yale Center for British Art, Bray 4

Boddington, vol. 7, p. 120: 4 plates

Pope, Alexander. *The Rape of the Lock.* For F. J. Du Roveray. 3 illus. by Stothard (and 1 illus. never published)

British Library (1163.b.40): 3 illus.

Huntington Library (133026): 4 illus., including 1 proof (never published)

Coxhead, p. 107, lists 4 illus.

Hammelmann: 3 illus.

Boddington, vol. 3, p. 160: 3 plates

Balmanno plates

Shenstone, William. *The Poetical Works.* For T. Cadell, Jun. & W. Davies. 6(?) illus. by Stothard

Boddington, vol. 5, pp. 66–68: 6 plates

Coxhead, p. 194, lists at least 4 illus.

Balmanno #1220–26: 5 plates identified in pencil for this ed.

Sterne, Laurence. *The Works.* For Johnson [etc.]. 9 illus. by Stothard

Huntington Library (472594): 9 plates

Coxhead, pp. 80–81, lists 9 illus.

Hammelmann: 9 illus.

Balmanno plates

Boddington, vol. 5, pp. 34–36: 9 plates

Young, Edward. *The Night Thoughts.* For T. Heptinstall. 9 illus. by Stothard

Huntington Library (140385): 9 illus.

Coxhead, p. 157, lists 9 illus.

Hammelmann: 8 illus.

Boddington, vol. 5, pp. 3–7: 9 plates

1798–1800

Shakespeare, William. *Plays.* For E. Harding. 8 illus. by Stothard

Bennett MA thesis: 8 illus.

Coxhead, p. 96, lists 8 illus.

Hammelmann: 8 illus.

Balmanno #1185–92: "For Harding 1798"

Boddington, vol. 7, pp. 96–100: 7 plates

1799

The Cabinet of the Arts. A series of engravings by English artists, from original designs. [unknown publisher.][no text, plates bound together.] 1–2(?) illus. by Stothard

British Library (1401.i.25): 1 Stothard del.

Coxhead, p. 38, lists 2 plates, 1 a reissue of a 1782–1783 *British Magazine* plate

Milton, John. [unknown title to a work including *L'Alle-gro, Il Penseroso,* and *Comus.*] [unknown publisher.] 3 illus. by Stothard

Coxhead, p. 105, lists 3 plates to *L'Allegro, Il Penseroso,* and *Comus*

Balmanno: identified in pencil 1799

British Museum: Stothard drawings in sketchbook 200*c.2 identified in pencil for this ed. and dated 1799

Boddington, vol. 5, p. 102: 3 plates

Shakespeare, William. *Seven Ages of Man Illustrated.* For W. Bromley [a series of plates, not an ed.]

Coxhead, p. 96, says published in folio a series of illus. with an illustrated title

Balmanno #1205

1799(?)

(?) Robertson, William. *The History of the Reign of the Emperor Charles V.* Cadell & Davies. 12 illus. by Stothard

Coxhead, pp. 194–95, lists 12 illus., dates 1799

1800

Garnett, Thomas. *A lecture on the preservation of health.* For T. Cadell, Jun. and W. Davies. 1 illus. by Stothard

British Library (7383.aa.30): 1 illus.

Boddington, vol. 5, p. 92: 1 plate identified in pencil for this publication

Mackenzie, Henry. *The Man of Feeling.* For T. Cadell. 4 illus. by Stothard

New York Public Library 1800 ed.: 4 plates

Coxhead, pp. 196–97, lists 4 illus.

Balmanno #1312–13: possibly for this publication, Stothard del. "For Cadell & Davies 1800"

Boddington, vol. 5, p. 118: 2 plates

Yale Center for British Art, Bray 3: identified in pencil

Metastasio, Abbe Pietro. *Dramas and Other Poems.* Translated from the Italian by John Hoole. For Otridge and Sons [etc.]. 3 illus. by Stothard

Huntington Library (69885) 1800 ed.: 3 plates

Boddington, vol. 4, p. 70: 3 plates "Stothard del. 1800 For Cadell & Davies"

(?) [unknown author]. *The Indian Sportsman.* For John Debrett. 1–2(?) illus. by Stothard

Coxhead, p. 196, lists 2 illus., dates 1800

Balmanno #1305: Stothard del. plate perhaps for this ed., placed ca. 1800

1800–1801

(?) Robertson, William. *A History of America.* For T. Cadell, Jun. and W. Davies. 12 illus. by Stothard

Coxhead, pp. 194–96, lists 12 illus.

1800–1816

The Holy Bible. For Thomas Macklin. 5 illus. by Stothard
Coxhead, p. 180, lists 5 illus.
Huntington Library (112962): 4 plates [1 missing]
Balmanno plates

1801

Bowles, William Lisle. *Sonnets and other Poems.* For T.
Cadell, Jun. and W. Davies [etc.]. 1 illus. by Stothard
British Library (238.g.19[1.]) vol. I: 1800 ed. with no
Stothard del.; vol. II: title page dated 1801, 1 plate
Coxhead, p. 198, lists 1 illus., dates 1800
Yale Center for British Art, Bray 1: plate identified in
pencil with date 1801
Cervantes Saavedra, Miguel de. *The life and exploits of the
ingenious gentleman Don Quixote de la Mancha.* For
William Millar. 7 illus. by Stothard
Huntington Library (441445): 7 illus.
Coxhead, p. 197, lists 7 illus.
Boddington, vol. 7, pp. 72–74: 7 plates
Balmanno plates
*The Field of Mars: being an alphabetical digestion of the principal
naval and military engagements.* For G. & J. Robinson. 1
illus. by Stothard
British Library (9009.m.5): 1 plate
Coxhead, p. 198, lists 1 plate
Macneill, Hector. *The Poetical Works.* For T. N. Longman
and O. Rees [etc.]. 8 illus. by Stothard
Huntington Library (404622): 8 illus.
Coxhead, p. 161, lists 8 illus.
Boddington, vol. 5, p. 142: 6 plates identified in pencil
with date 1806
Balmanno: identified in pencil
Penn, John. *Poems.* For J. Hatchard. 1 illus. by Stothard
Huntington Library (442736): 1 plate
Coxhead, p. 198, lists 1 plate
Balmanno #1578: Stothard del. identified in pencil for
this publication
Rogers, Samuel. *Pleasures of Memory.* For Thomas Cadell. 15
illus. by Stothard
Coxhead, p. 121, lists 15 illus. for 1801 ed.
Boddington, vol. 7, pp. 122–26: 15 plates identified in
pencil for 1801 ed.

1802

Gessner, Salomon. *The Works.* For T. Cadell, Jun. and W.
Davies. 16 illus. by Stothard

British Library (12251.bb.8): 16 illus.
Coxhead, pp. 155–56, lists 16 illus.
Boddington, vol. 5, pp. 58–64: 16 plates
Balmanno plates
(?) Pope, Alexander. *Essay on Criticism.* For F. J. Du Roveray
[part of Du Roveray's *Classics*? see 1804 and 1805
entries]. 1 illus. by Stothard
Coxhead, p. 108, lists 1 illus. for Du Roveray's *Poets* of
1802
Boddington, vol. 7, pp. 114–18: 9 plates identified in pen-
cil for Du Roveray's *Classics:* Pope's *Works*, includes
Homer subjects, and Pope's *Miscellaneous Works*,
includes *Essay on Man, St. Cecelia, Rape of the Lock,
Elegy to the Memory of an Unfortunate Lady*, and the
Traveller plates
Shakespeare, William. *Dramatic works . . . revised by George
Steevens.* For John and Josiah Boydell [etc.]. 2 illus. by
Stothard
Bennett MA thesis: 2 illus.
Coxhead, p. 94, lists 2 illus.
Spenser, Edmund. *Faerie Queene* [part of a collection of
works?]. For Heath & Kearsley. 12 illus. by Stothard
Coxhead, pp. 92–93, lists 12 illus. to Spenser's *Faerie
Queene*
Boddington, vol. 7, pp. 54–58: 12 plates
Balmanno #1383: "Faery Queene For Heath & Kearsley
1802"
British Museum catalogue of drawings identifies Stoth-
ard drawings for Heath's 1802 ed. of Spenser

1802–1804

Shakespeare, William. *A new edition of Shakespeare's Plays.*
For Heath & Robinson. 22 illus. by Stothard
Bennett MA thesis: 22 plates—see Huntington Library
(406915), 1807 Stockdale publication of "Heath's ed."
British Library (644.m.6,7): 20 plates; missing 2 to
Winter's Tale
Coxhead, pp. 96–98, says most of the full-page and title-
page illus. to each play are by Stothard, dates 1803
Balmanno #1416 ff.
Boddington, vol. 6, pp. 64–98

1803

(?) Raymond, George Frederick. *A new, universal and impartial history of England.* For Cooke. 1(?) illus. by Stothard
Coxhead, p. 200, lists 1 plate, dates ca. 1803

National Union Catalogue 0081719: ed. dated ca. 1785 for Cooke, notes plates

(?) [unknown title to a collection of plays and unknown publisher.] 13(?) illus. by Stothard

Coxhead, p. 201, lists illus. of scenes from various plays, dates ca. 1803: John Home, *Douglas, A Tragedy* (1 plate); *A Bold Stroke for a Wife* (1 plate); Walpole, *Mysterious Mother* (1 plate); pp. 98–99, several illus. for Shakespeare

Balmanno #1672–84: Stothard del. plates identified in pencil to various plays, including *King John, Pericles,* and Walpole, *Mysterious Mother,* placed ca. 1804

Boddington, vol. 7, pp. 84–98: 13 plates in same format illustrating various plays: some to Shakespeare, 3 plates identified in pencil for *Douglas;* p. 88: 2 plates in different format identified in pencil for the *Gamester;* p. 88: 2 plates in different format identified in pencil for *Richard III* and *Macbeth*

1803–1804

Bell's British Classics. For John Sharpe. 7 illus. by Stothard

Coxhead, pp. 76–77, lists: *Tatler* (2 plates), *Spectator* (5 plates); pp. 77–78 lists an 1808 ed. in 1 volume of the *Spectator* published by Sharpe and others that includes another rendering of 1 of the 1803–1804 plates

Boddington, vol. 5, pp. 138–40: 6 plates identified in pencil; vol. 9, p. 36: 1 plate identified in pencil for the *Spectator,* 1803–1804; vol. 4, p. 144: 2 plates identified in pencil for the *Tatler;* vol. 8, pp. 88–90: 8 plates identified in pencil for Sharpe's *Spectator*

Balmanno #1463–67, 1469: 6 plates Stothard del. for *Spectator* and *Tatler* "For John Sharpe 1803/1804"

1804

Pope, Alexander. *The Poetical Works.* For F. J. Du Roveray [part of Du Roveray's *Classics?*]. 7 illus. by Stothard

Huntington Library (134287): 7 illus.

Coxhead, p. 108, lists 7 illus.

Boddington, vol. 7, pp. 114–18: 9 plates identified in pencil for Du Roveray's *Classics:* Pope's *Works,* includes Homer subjects, and Pope's *Miscellaneous Works,* includes *Essay on Man, St. Cecelia, Rape of the Lock, Elegy to the Memory of an Unfortunate Lady,* and the *Traveller* plates

1805

Homer. *The Iliad. Translated by A. Pope.* For F. J. Du Roveray [part of Du Roveray's *Classics?*]. 6 illus. by Stothard

British Library (1348.b.16–27): 6 plates

Huntington Library (143633): 6 plates; (321473): 1810 ed. for J. Johnson [etc.] a reissue of the 5 plates for the 1805–1806 ed. for Du Roveray's 1805 ed. (his imprint on the plates)

Coxhead, pp. 162–63, lists 5 plates and says these designs were used again for Johnson's ed. of Cowper's translation in 4 vols. (1810); in Tegg's later publication of the plates without text; and all 6 plates on a reduced scale in an ed. of Homer by Du Roveray in 12 vols. in 1805

Boddington, vol. 7, pp. 114–18: 9 plates identified in pencil for Du Roveray's *Classics:* Pope's *Works,* includes Homer subjects, and Pope's *Miscellaneous Works,* includes *Essay on Man, St. Cecelia, Rape of the Lock, Elegy to the Memory of an Unfortunate Lady,* and the *Traveller* plates; 4 Homer plates also included in vol. 8, pp. 94, 130

Balmanno 1805 plates

1805(?)

Milton, John. *The Poetical Works.* For W. Suttaby [etc.]. 1 illus. by Stothard

British Library (11626.a.31,32) 1806 ed. for Suttaby: 1 illus.

Coxhead, p. 104, lists 1 illus. for an 1806 ed. of *The Poetical Works* for Suttaby

National Union Catalogue 0604374: 1805 ed. for Suttaby [etc.] notes plate

Milton, John. *The Poetical Works.* For John Sharpe. 3 illus. by Stothard

Coxhead, p. 104, lists 3 illus. for an 1805 ed. of Milton's *Poems* and notes proof impressions in British Museum

Royal Academy: 1 plate Stothard del. and 2 others "The Poetical Works of John Milton. For John Sharpe 1810" [probably a reissue of 1805 ed.]

Balmanno #1536–38: illus. to Milton, placed ca. 1805–1807

1806

Dryden, John. *Fables from Boccaccio and Chaucer.* For T. Cadell, Jun. and W. Davies. 8 illus. by Stothard

Huntington Library (446409): 8 illus.

Coxhead, pp. 201–2, lists 8 illus.

Balmanno #1510–17 "For Cadell & Davis 1805" [probably for this ed.]

Boddington, vol. 8, pp. 120–22: 8 plates

(?) Goldsmith, Oliver. [Miscellaneous Works.] [unknown publisher.] 6(?) illus. by Stothard

Boddington, vol. 7, pp. 76–78: 5 plates identified in pencil for *Citizen of the World* 1806

National Union Catalogue 0296003: 1806 ed. of *The Works* for J. Johnson [etc.] notes plates

Coxhead, p. 119, lists 6 illus. for Goldsmith's *Miscellaneous Works*, ca. 1805, although he says an early impression of 1 plate bears the date 1793 and the whole may have been published originally in 1793 [see the 1793 entry]

Balmanno #1504–9: Stothard del. identified in pencil for Goldsmith

Hume, David. *The history of England*. For R. Bowyer. 17 illus. by Stothard

Huntington Library (128912) 1806 ed.: 17 plates

Coxhead, pp. 164–65, lists 13 illus., dates 1805

Boddington, vol. 6, pp. 106–22: 8 plates dated 1796–1805 Balmanno plates

Shakespeare, William. *Plays . . . edited by Manley Wood, A.M.* For George Kearsley. 16 illus. by Stothard

Bennett MA thesis: 16 illus.

Coxhead, p. 99, lists 16 illus.

Balmanno #1667 ff.

1806–1808(?)

Inchbald, Elizabeth. *The British Theatre*. For Longman [etc.] 5(?) illus. by Stothard

New York Public Library ed. contains George Lillo's *The Fatal Curiosity* (1807) with 1 illus. by Stothard and Lillo's *George Barnwell; a tragedy* (1807) with 1 illus. by Stothard; both promptbooks are bound together with other plays as Mrs. Elizabeth Inchbald's *The British Theatre* 1808 for Longman [etc.]: these promptbooks were probably published separately, then later bound together as a book that was reissued several times (1824 ed. in New York Public Library)

British Library (1507/316 [7]): George Lillo's *The Fatal Curiosity* (1807) with 1 illus. by Stothard; (1507/315 [5]): George Lillo's *George Barnwell; a tragedy* (1807) with 1 illus. by Stothard; plate dated 1806; (1507/317 [4]): Edward Moore of Abingdon's *The Gamester* (1807) with 1 illus. by Stothard

Coxhead, p. 202, lists 4 illus. to *George Barnwell, Rule a Wife and Have a Wife, The Gamester,* and an unknown play, published by Longmans in 1806, and on p. 209 lists 1 illus. for Longmans in 1817, *Fatal Curiosity* for Lillo's *Tragedy,* which he says is similar in format to those published in 1806

1807

Fielding, John. *Tom Jones*. For Hunt, Reynell and Chopple. 1 illus. by Stothard

Balmanno #1561: "Tom Jones," "Stothard pinxt," "For Hunt, Reynell and Chopple 1807"

Coxhead, p. 202, lists 1 plate

National Union Catalogue 0127433: 1807 ed. for J. Hunt, notes plates

(?) Pope, Alexander. [unknown title.] For W. Suttaby. 1(?) illus. by Stothard

Coxhead, p. 108, lists 1 illus. to Pope's *Essay on Man* in a miniature ed. [of Du Roveray's 1805 *Poets*?]

Shakespeare, William. *Plays*. For Longman [etc.]. 4 illus. by Stothard

Bennett MA thesis: 4 illus. for Longman, printed by James Ballantyne & Co., Edinburgh

National Union Catalogue 0454383: this ed.

1807–1815(?)

A selection of Irish melodies . . . by Sir John Stevenson. For J. Power, Dublin. 1(?) illus. by Stothard

Huntington Library (303857) has no publication date, 8 numbers bound together for J. Power; "Advertisement" to 1st number contains date 1807, 6th number "Advertisement" date 1815, 1 plate Stothard del.

Balmanno #1542: identified in pencil frontispiece to a Music "For W. Miller 1807," for this publication?

1808

Defoe, Daniel. *Robinson Crusoe*. For W. Suttaby [etc., probably including J. Walker]. 2 illus. by Stothard

Balmanno #1554–55: "For Suttaby 1808"

Royal Academy: plates "For Suttaby 1808"

Coxhead, p. 76, lists 2 illus.

National Union Catalogue lists only 1808 ed. for J. Walker [etc.] with 2 plates

Boddington, vol. 8, p. 4: 2 plates

Goldsmith, Oliver. *The Vicar of Wakefield*. For W. Suttaby [etc.]. 2 illus. by Stothard

British Library (12638.a.68): 2 illus.

Coxhead, p. 117, lists 2 illus.

Balmanno #1556–57: "For Suttaby 1808"

The Works of the British Poets, Collated with the Best Editions: By Thomas Park, F.S.A. For J. Sharpe Printed by Charles Whittingham and sold by W. Suttaby. 5 illus. by Stothard

British Library (1066.c.13–44; 1066.d.1–16): Jago (1 plate), Thomson (1 plate), Watts (2 plates), Hill (1 plate), Philips (1 plate); plates are dated 1805 but title page bears date 1808

Coxhead, p. 203, lists Jago's *Poems* (1 plate), pp. 110–11 lists Thomson's *Seasons* (1 plate), Philips (1 plate), Hill (1 plate), Watts (2 plates), dates 1807

Balmanno #1543: Stothard del. identified in pencil for Jago's *Poems*, 1808

Boddington, vol. 8, p. 82: 4 plates identified in pencil for Sharpe's *Poets* and 1 plate for Jago's *Poems*

1809

Cervantes Saavedra, Miguel de. *The life and exploits of the ingenious gentleman Don Quixote de la Mancha.* For John Sharpe. 8 illus. by Stothard

Coxhead, p. 204, lists 8 plates

Balmanno #1566–78: "For John Sharpe 1809"

National Union Catalogue lists this 1809 ed. for Sharpe, notes plates

Boddington, vol. 8, p. 76: 5 plates; p. 78: 6 plates in different format

Franklin, Benjamin. *The Works.* For W. Suttaby [etc.] [part of Suttaby's *Miniature Library*]. 2 illus. by Stothard

British Library (12206.aaa.1): 2 illus.

Coxhead, p. 204, lists 2 illus.

Balmanno #1576–77: "For Suttaby 1809"

Le Sage, Alain René. *History and Adventures of Gil Blas of Santillane.* For John Sharpe. 8 illus. by Stothard

British Library (C.134.a.8): 8 illus.

Coxhead, p. 204, lists 8 illus.

Balmanno #1558–65: "For John Sharpe 1809" for this ed.

Boddington, vol. 8, pp. 72–74: 4 plates identified in pencil for Sharpe's *Classics*

The Panorama of Wit. For John Sharpe. 1 illus. by Stothard

Coxhead, p. 205, lists 1 plate

National Union Catalogue 0062461: entry for this ed. notes title-page plate

[unknown title to a hymnbook.] For John Sharpe. 1 illus. by Stothard

Coxhead, p. 205, lists 1 plate to a hymnbook for the Foundling Hospital, discusses ca. 1809

Boddington, vol. 8, p. 100: 1 plate "Cradle Hymn Stothard del. For Sharpe 1809"

1809(?)

Gay, John. *Poetical Works.* For Suttaby [etc.]. 1 illus. by Stothard

Coxhead, p. 205, lists 1 illus. for Suttaby's series; no date given but discusses ca. 1809

British Museum catalogue of drawings identifies Stothard drawing for this edition

1810

Cromek, Robert Hartley. *Remains of Nithsdale and Galloway song.* For T. Cadell and W. Davies. 1 illus. by Stothard

Coxhead, pp. 163, 205, lists 1 plate

Huntington Library (121132): 1 plate with no artist's name but in style of Stothard

Rogers, Samuel. *The Pleasures of Memory, with other Poems.* For T. Cadell and W. Davies. 34 illus. by Stothard

Huntington Library (104489): 34 woodcuts

British Library (11645.bbb.32): 34 woodcuts

Coxhead, pp. 122–27, lists 34 woodcuts by Clennell after Stothard for the 1810 ed. and later eds. of 1812 (with additions, total 63 plates), 1814 (with additions, total 59 plates), 1816 (with additions, total 64 plates), 1820 (with additions, total 44 plates), 1822 (with additions total 49 plates)

Balmanno plates

Spenser, Edmund. *Poetical Works.* For John Sharpe. 4 illus. by Stothard

Coxhead, p. 93, lists 4 plates (3 are new designs)

Balmanno #1583–86: Stothard del. "For John Sharpe 1810 Spenser"

National Union Catalogue 0813091: entry for this ed. notes plates

British Museum drawings catalogue identifies Stothard drawings for this ed.

Boddington, vol. 7, p. 52: 3 plates identified in pencil for Spenser 1810, 2 imprinted "Stothard del. For Sharpe 1810"

1810–1812(?)

Knox, Vicesimus. *Elegant Extracts from the Most Eminent British Poets.* For John Sharpe. 5(?) illus. by Stothard

Coxhead, p. 205, lists 5 plates

Balmanno #1588 ff.: Stothard del. "Elegant Extracts from the Most Eminent British Poets 1812 For John Sharpe," also dated 1810 and 1811

Boddington, vol. 4, p. 68: 1 plate identified in pencil for *Elegant Extracts*; vol. 9, p. 112: 2 plates imprinted "Elegant Extracts from the Most Eminent British Poets Sharpe 1811" and "1812"

1811

More, Hannah. *The Search after Happiness.* For Johnson and Warner, Philadelphia [probably a reprint of Stothard's illus. from an earlier, untraced English ed.]. 1 illus. by Stothard

Huntington Library (141760): 1 plate

New York Public Library ed.: 1 plate

Spencer, William Robert. *Poems.* For T. Cadell and W. Davies. 1 illus. by Stothard

Huntington Library (215466): 1 plate

Coxhead, p. 206, lists 1 plate

1811–1813

The Holy Bible. [Samuel Clarke, ed. unknown publisher.] 1–2(?) illus. by Stothard

Bentley, in correspondence, notes that the ed. in British Library contains 1 plate Stothard del. and 1 plate in style of Stothard

1812

Addison, Joseph, Sir Richard Steele, and others. *The Spectator.* For Suttaby [etc.] 8 illus. by Stothard

Coxhead, p. 78, lists 8 plates for Suttaby's *Miniature Library*

Balmanno #1616 ff.: Stothard del. "Spectator For Suttaby 1812"

National Union Catalogue 0802029: entry for this ed., notes plates

Richardson, Samuel. *The history of Sir Charles Grandison.* For Sharpe [etc.]. 1 illus. by Stothard

British Library (12613.h.19): frontispiece

Coxhead, p. 206, lists 1 plate

Shenstone, William. *Poetical Works.* For Suttaby [etc.]. 2(?) illus. by Stothard

Coxhead, p. 206, lists 2 illus. for Suttaby's *Miniature Library*

Balmanno #1629: Stothard del. "Poetical Works of William Shenstone For Suttaby [etc.] 1812"

Royal Academy: Stothard del. "Poetical Works of William Shenstone For Suttaby [etc.] 1812"

1812(?)

Richardson, Samuel. *The history of Sir Charles Grandison.* For Suttaby & Co. 7 illus. by Stothard

Royal Academy: 7 plates to this publication Stothard del. "For Suttaby," "1812"

Balmanno #601–7: 7 plates to this publication Stothard del. "For Suttaby & Co.," placed ca. 1810

Coxhead, p. 206, lists 7 plates, discusses ca. 1811

1813

Scott, Walter. *Rokeby, a Poem.* For Longman [etc.]. 7 illus. by Stothard

Huntington Library (120381): 1 plate Stothard del. and 6 proof impressions bearing no artist's name but by Stothard

Coxhead, p. 137, lists 7 illus. for Ballantyne's ed.

Balmanno #1634–40: 7 plates "Rokeby For Longman [etc.] 1813"

Boddington, vol. 7, pp. 4–6: 7 plates

Yale Center for British Art, Bray #3

(?) Young, Edward. *The Works.* For R. C. and J. Rivington. (?) illus. by Stothard

Howes' *Sale Cat. 227, 1985,* #398: this ed., notes plates by Stothard

National Union Catalogue 0025256: entry for this ed. notes plates

1814

(?) Akenside, Mark. *The Pleasures of Imagination.* For Suttaby. 1(?) illus. by Stothard

Coxhead, p. 183, notes 1 illus. for Suttaby

1814(?)

Burns, Robert. *Poetical Works.* For T. Cadell and W. Davies. 12 illus. by Stothard

Coxhead, pp. 114–15, lists 12 illus.

Boddington, vol. 8, pp. 110–12, 116–18: 12 plates

Balmanno #1641–52: proof plates to this ed., "Stothard del. For Cadell & Davies 1814"

1814–1818(?)

Wayland's Ladies Annual Present or Pocket Companion. For Suttaby. 1–2(?) illus. by Stothard

Coxhead, p. 207, notes 1 or 2 plates for Wayland's *Ladies' Annual Present or Pocket Companion* for Suttaby 1814 (1 plate: *The Indian Jugglers*); p. 100 says 2 Shakespeare illus. of Falstaff in the Buck-basket and Jacques and the stag possibly in Wayland's *Ladies' Present,* dates about 1818 [see 1818 Shakespeare entry]

Balmanno #1653–54: Stothard del. "*Wayland's Ladies Annual Present or Pocket Companion* for Suttaby 1814" (1 plate: *The Indian Jugglers*)

Boddington, vol. 6, p. 38: 1 plate "1817" but does not bear imprint "Stothard del."

1815(?)

Byron, George Gordon Noel. *The Works.* For John Murray. 12 illus. by Stothard

Huntington Library (428942) 1815 ed. is the earliest ed. that includes the 12 Stothard del. plates

National Union Catalogue 1022013: 1815 ed. for Murray is the earliest ed. that notes plates

Coxhead, p. 139, lists 12 illus. of 1813 and 1814

Balmanno #1660 ff.: 12 proof plates to Byron "For John Murray 1814"

Boddington, vol. 8, pp. 124–28: 12 plates [and 1 to *Zuleikal* for Longman & Co. that differs from the *Zuleikal* plate for Murray: no eds. for Longman listed in National Union Catalogue]

British Library (11604.f.25): 1815 ed. with no illus., but card catalogue notes "previously published separately between 1812 and 1818 with collective title pages bearing the date 1815 prefixed to each vol."; (239.f.39–46) 1818 ed. for Murray: 12 plates

Hammelmann says plates first published in 1818 for Murray

1816(?)

Milton, John. *Paradise Lost, a poem.* For John Sharpe. 1 illus. by Stothard

British Library (11626.aaa.26) 1817 ed.: 1 illus. with plate dated 1816

National Union Catalogue 0605254: 1816 ed. for Sharpe, notes plate

Coxhead, pp. 103–4, 208, lists 1 illus., says published by Sharpe in 1816 and reissued in 1822

Huntington Library (230570): 1821 ed. with reissue of plate dated 1816

Boddington, vol. 9, pp. 48, 82: 1 plate illustrating Milton dictating to his daughters

British Museum catalogue of drawings identifies Stothard drawing for Pickering's *Milton* (n.d.)

1816–1817

The Family Bible. [William Gurney, ed. Unknown publisher.] 14 illus. by Stothard

Bentley, in correspondence, notes that this ed. in British Library contains 14 illus. Stothard del.

1818

(?) Goldsmith, Oliver. *Deserted Village.* For Suttaby. 1(?) illus. by Stothard

Coxhead, p. 118, lists 1 illus.

1818(?)

Shakespeare, William. *The Beauties of Shakespeare.* For J. Walker [etc.] 2 illus. by Stothard

Royal Academy plates "*The Beauties of Shakespeare* for J. Walker [etc.]": illus. of Falstaff in the Buck-basket

and Jacques and the stag [see 1814–1818 entry for *Wayland's Ladies Annual* for Coxhead]

National Union Catalogue 0465609: 1818 ed. for J. Walker, notes only frontispiece plate (portrait); 0465602: ca. 1800 ed. of this title for C. Kearsley [etc., including J. Walker] notes only engraved title page with vignette

Balmanno #1693–94

Boddington, vol. 9, p. 22: 1 plate of Jacques and the stag

1818–1825(?)

[Thomson, George.] *A Select Collection of Original Scottish Airs.* For G. Thomson. 14(?) illus. by Stothard

Royal Academy plates for "*Select Melodies of Scotland*": 1 with imprint "G. Thomson 1825"; about 14 total

National Union Catalogue 0186778: entry dated ca. 1817–1818 notes that a later ed. of this collection is entitled *Select Melodies of Scotland*

Huntington Library (371818): no publication date, preface dated 1803, 1 plate

Coxhead, p. 179, lists 2 plates to "Auld Robin Gray," probably for this publication

Balmanno #1916: Thomson subject, Stothard del. proof plate dated "1823"; #1917 may be for this publication

The Stothard/Thomson correspondence in the Boston Public Library and National Library, Scotland, dates from 1813 to 1833

T. Crouther Gordon, *David Allen of Alloa, 1794-1796,* says this work was published in 1818

Boddington, vol. 5, pp. 26–28: 4 plates identified in pencil for *Scottish Songs;* vol. 5, p. 141: 2 plates with Scottish subjects; vol. 8, p. 108: 1 plate, misattributed to Burns; vol. 9, p. 124: 2 plates identified in pencil as lithographs by T. Stothard Jun.r for *Scottish Songs,* 1838, vol. 5, p. 126

1818–1826(?)

A Selection of Popular National Airs . . . by Sir John Stevenson [and others]. For J. Power, Dublin. 12(?) illus. by Stothard

Coxhead, pp. 165–66, lists 12 illus. published from 1818 to 1826

Balmanno #1697–98: "*A Selection of Popular National Airs . . . by Stevenson* For Powers 1818," 1 plate Stothard del.; #1699–1702: "*A Selection of Popular National Airs . . . by Bishop* For Powers 1820"; #1703–7: "*A Selection of Popular National Airs . . . by Bishop* For Powers 1822"

Huntington Library (303857), *A selection of Irish melodies*

. . . by Sir John Stevenson, for J. Power, Dublin, ca. 1808–1821: 8 numbers bound together, the 7th has Stothard title-page illus.

1820

Defoe, Daniel. *The Life and Strange Surprising Adventures of Robinson Crusoe.* For T. Cadell and W. Davies. 20 illus. by Stothard

Huntington Library (122045): 20 illus., including 6 new plates and 14 plates from the 1790 ed. reengraved in reverse

British Library (12612.g.17): 14 plates and 6 new plates

Boddington, vol. 8, pp. 6–44: 20 plates

Coxhead, pp. 75–76, says Cadell's ed. of 1820 has the 16 illus. from the 1790 ed. for Stockdale and 5 others

Balmanno plates

Ripps, A. *Narrative of Captain Cook's Three Voyages.* For Thomas Tegg [perhaps issued as part of a collection, see 1820–1827 entry]. 2 illus. by Stothard

Coxhead, p. 209, lists 2 illus.

Balmanno #1804–5: Stothard del. "*Narrative of Capt. Cook's Three Voyages* by A. Ripps For R. Jennings [etc.] Printed by Whittingham 1820"

Boddington, vol. 9, p. 50: 2 plates identified in pencil as *Cook's Voyages*

Scott, Walter. *Tales of My Landlord.* For Rodwell & Martin [perhaps published as part of a collection of Scott works]. 13–16(?) illus. by Stothard

Boddington, vol. 7, pp. 7–38: 16 plates identified in pencil for Scott novels, including *Kenilworth, A Legend of Montrose, The Heart of Mid-Lothian, Monastery, Old Mortality, The Black Dwarf, Guy Mannering, Ivanhoe*

Royal Academy: 16 plates "For Rodwell & Martin 1820" for this ed.

Coxhead, pp. 137–38, lists 13 illus. for this ed., including *Old Mortality, The Black Dwarf, The Heart of Midlothian, The Bride of Lammermoor, A Legend of Montrose, The Monastery, Kenilworth*

Balmanno #1791–1803: "For Rodwell & Martin 1820"

1820–1827

(?) [unknown title to a collection of various authors: *Novelists Library, Pocket Novelist,* or *Chiswick's Classics.* Printed by Whittingham at the Chiswick Press, perhaps for Thomas Tegg. Also listed as separate entries.]

Coxhead, pp. 209–11, says eds. of the classics, ancient and modern, began to be issued by Chiswick Press in 1820 and lists A. Ripps's *Narrative of Capt. Cook's Three Voy-*

ages (1820), 2 plates; Sterne's "Maria" from *Sentimental Journey* (1821), 1 plate; Bacon's *Essays, Moral, Economical, and Political* (1822), 1 plate; *Franklin, the Whistle* (1822), 1 plate; *The Book of Utility* (1822), 1 plate; *Vocal Lyre, a Collection of Songs* (1822), 1 plate; Blair's *Grave* (1823), 1 plate; Walpole's *Castle of Otranto* (1823), 1 plate; Clara Reeve's *Old English Baron* (1823), 1 plate; Pope's *Essay on Man* (1823), 1 plate; Richard Johnson's *Seven Champions of Christendom* (1823), 2 plates; p. 105, lists from Chiswick Press: Milton's *Paradise Lost & Regained* (1823), 2 plates; Pope's *Essay on Man* (1823), 1 plate; pp. 157–58, Young's *Night Thoughts* (1825), 1 plate; p. 159, Cowper's *Poems* (1825), 1 plate; p. 102, Shakespeare's *Plays* (1827), several plates; p. 211, lists a series of authors issued by Tegg in 1825 including Lord Chesterfield (1825), about 6 plates; also for Tegg: p. 216, *A Cookery Book* (1825), 1 plate, and an unknown book of stories (1826), 1 plate of *The Dwarf and the Peacock;* p. 217, *A Dictionary of Science* (1826), 1 plate, and Goldsmith's *History of Rome* (1826), 1 plate

Boddington, vol. 9, pp. 106–10: plates identified in pencil as frontispieces to works published by Tegg

Balmanno plates

1821

[Fordyce, William.] *Mavor's The English Spelling-Book.* For Longman, Rees, Orme, Brown, and Green. 1 illus. by Stothard

Coxhead, p. 212, lists frontispiece, dates 1821

Balmanno #1811: Stothard del. "*Mavor's The English Spelling-Book* 1821"

British Library (12982.aa.59) 1826 ed.: 1 plate bears no artist's name but is in style of Stothard; imprint date on plate 1821

Yale Center for British Art, Bray 2: frontispiece dated 1838

(?) Huish, Robert. *Memoirs of George III.* [unknown publisher.] 2 illus. by Stothard

Coxhead, p. 212, lists 2 illus.

Boddington, vol. 4, p. 126: 2 plates illustrating events in the life of George III, no publication noted

Ritson, Joseph, ed. *The Cadeldonian Muse: A chronological Selection of Scottish Poetry.* For Robert Triphook. 14 illus. by Stothard

Huntington Library (132817) 1821 ed.: text states this publication is a companion work to Ritson's *Select Collection of English Songs* (1783) ready for publication in 1785, but partly consumed in a fire and abandoned;

35 years afterward it was resuscitated by Robert Trip hook and published in the original design; the illus. are attributed to Stothard on the title page; 14 illus.

Coxhead, p. 148, repeats this information; lists 14 illus.

(?) Sterne, Laurence. *A Sentimental Journey.* For R. Jennings [etc.] [perhaps issued as part of a collection, see 1820–1827 entry]. 1 illus. by Stothard

Coxhead, p. 82, lists 1 illus. for "Maria," part of *A Sentimental Journey* for Chiswick Press in 1821 [see 1822 entry]

National Union Catalogue 0918306: entry for 1821 ed. of *A Sentimental Journey* for R. Jennings [etc.] printed by Whittingham [Chiswick Press], notes engraved title page

1822

Bacon, Francis. *Essays, Moral, Economical, and Political.* For R. Jennings [etc., including Thomas Tegg] [perhaps issued as part of a collection, see 1820–1827 entry]. 1 illus. by Stothard

Balmanno #1868: Stothard del. "Bacon's *Essays, Moral, Economical, and Political* for R. Jennings [etc.] Printed by Whittingham 1822"

Coxhead, p. 209, lists 1 plate for Chiswick Press

National Union Catalogue: 1822 ed. by Whittingham, notes added title-page vignette

Boddington, vol. 9, p. 110: 1 plate identified in pencil for Bacon's essays 1822 for Tegg

The New Ladies Memorandum Book. For Baldwin [etc.]. 1 illus. by Stothard

Boddington, vol. 6, p. 38: 1 plate "1822"

Royal Academy print

Tegg, Thomas. *Book of Utility, or repository of usefull information, connected with the moral, intellectual, and physical condition of man.* For Thomas Tegg [perhaps issued as part of a collection, see 1820–1827 entry]. 1 illus. by Stothard

British Library (1136.g.6): 1 plate

Coxhead, p. 210, lists 1 illus.

The Vocal Lyre, a Collection of Songs. For R. Jennings [etc.] [perhaps issued as part of a collection, see 1820–1827 entry]. 1 illus. by Stothard

Balmanno #1869: Stothard del. "*The Vocal Lyre, a Collection of Songs* For R. Jennings [etc.] Printed by Whittingham 1822"

Coxhead, p. 209, lists 1 plate for Chiswick Press

Boddington, vol. 9, p. 112: 1 plate identified in pencil for *Collection of Songs* 1822

British Museum: drawings catalogue identifies a Stothard drawing for a song by T. Moore published in 1822 [perhaps for this publication]

(?) [unknown author.] *Franklin, the Whistle.* For Chiswick Press [perhaps issued as part of a collection, see 1820–1827 entry]. 1 illus. by Stothard

Coxhead, pp. 209–10, lists 1 plate

[unknown author.] *Maria, a tale.* For W. Wright. 1 illus. by Stothard

Coxhead, p. 213, lists 1 plate to *Maria, a tale,* perhaps for Wright; gives no date but discusses ca. 1822 [see 1821 entry]

Balmanno: plate identified in pencil for this ed.

Boddington, vol. 5, p. 144: 1 plate "*Maria.* Stothard del. For W. Wright. 1822"

1822–1823(?)

Southey, Robert. *Poems.* For J. Arliss. 8 illus. by Stothard

Coxhead, p. 212, lists 8 illus.

Balmanno #1855–62: Stothard del. "Southey For J. Arliss 1822/1823"

Boddington, vol. 9, pp. 16–18: 7 plates identified in pencil with date 1823

Yale Center for British Art, Bray 4

1823

Blair, Robert. *The Grave.* For Thomas Tegg [etc.] [perhaps issued as part of a collection, see 1820–1827 entry]. 1 illus. by Stothard

British Library (11646.ppp.21): 1 illus.

Balmanno #1907: Stothard del. "For Thomas Tegg 1823"

Royal Academy: Stothard del. "For Thomas Tegg 1823"

Coxhead, p. 210, lists 1 plate for Chiswick Press

Milton, John. *Paradise Lost. A Poem.* For Thomas Tegg [etc.] [perhaps issued as part of a collection including *Paradise Regained,* see 1820–1827 entry]. 2 illus. by Stothard

Royal Academy: 2 plates Stothard del. "*Paradise Lost. A Poem* For Thomas Tegg," no date

Boddington, vol. 9, p. 108: 1 plate identified in pencil for *Paradise Lost,* 1823, for Tegg

Coxhead, p. 105, lists 2 plates for 1823 ed. of *Paradise Lost* and *Paradise Regained* for Tegg

National Union Catalogue 0606723: 1823 ed. for Tegg [etc.], notes added title page engraved with vignette, bound with his *Paradise Lost* (1829)

Pope, Alexander. *Essay on Man.* For Thomas Tegg [etc.]

[perhaps issued as part of a collection, see 1820–1827 entry] 1 illus. by Stothard

    Boddington, vol. 9, p. 110: 1 plate identified in pencil for Pope's *Essay on Man,* 1823, for Tegg

    Coxhead, p. 109, lists 1 plate for Chiswick Press

Reeve, Clara. *The Old English Baron.* For Thomas Tegg [etc.] [perhaps issued as part of a collection, see 1820–1827 entry]. 1 illus. by Stothard

    British Library (12603.a.15): 1 illus.

    Balmanno #1908: Stothard del. "For Thomas Tegg 1823"

    Coxhead, p. 201, lists 1 plate

Walpole, Horace. *The Castle of Otranto.* For R. Jennings [etc., including Thomas Tegg] [perhaps issued as part of a collection, see 1820–1827 entry]. 1 illus. by Stothard

    Boddington, vol. 9, p. 110: 1 plate identified in pencil for *Castle of Otranto,* 1823, for Tegg

    National Union Catalogue 0050753: 1823 ed. for R. Jennings [etc.] printed by Whittingham, notes Stothard del. title-page vignette

    Coxhead, p. 210, lists 1 plate

1823(?)

Coxe, Peter. *The Social Day: A Poem.* For James Carpenter and son. 3 illus. by Stothard

    British Library (L.R.408.c.14) 1823 ed.: 3 illus.

    Coxhead, pp. 213–14, lists 3 illus., discusses ca. 1822–1823

    Yale Center for British Art, Bray 3: identified in pencil with date 1822

    Boddington, vol. 7, p. 106: 3 plates identified in pencil with date 1798

Johnson, Richard. *The renowned History of Seven Champions of Christendome.* For Rivington [etc.] [perhaps issued as part of a collection, see 1820–1827 entry]. 2 illus. by Stothard

    Boddington, vol. 9, p. 88: 2 plates identified in pencil for *Seven Champions of Christendom*

    Balmanno #1911–12: identified in pencil for *Seven Champions of Christendom,* placed ca. 1823

    Coxhead, p. 210, lists 2 plates possibly for Chiswick Press

    National Union Catalogue 0217811: 1824 ed. for Rivington, notes frontispiece

1823–1825

Shakespeare, William. *The Plays.* For William Pickering. 26 illus. by Stothard

    Bennett MA thesis: 26 illus. (many are reprints of illus. for the 1803 Heath ed. of Shakespeare but recut and on a reduced scale)

    Huntington Library (232166, 132541, 150578, 113375)

    British Museum catalogue of drawings identifies Stothard drawings for Heath's Shakespeare reduced for Pickering's Shakespeare of 1823

    Coxhead, pp. 100–101, lists 26 plates, many repeats of 1803 Heath ed. of Shakespeare, dates publication 1825

    Balmanno #1982 ff.: total about 26 plates "For Pickering 1826"

1824

Burns, Robert. *The Songs, Chiefly in the Scottish Dialect.* For John Sharpe. 1 illus. by Stothard

    British Library (11622.aaa.11): 1 plate

    Coxhead, p. 115, lists 1 plate and possibly another

    Balmanno #1943: plate for this ed. dated 1824

Catullus, Caius Valerius. *Catullus, Tibullus et Propertius.* For G. Pickering. 1 illus. by Stothard

    British Library (c.o.g.3.[2]): 1 plate

    Coxhead, p. 214, lists 1 plate

    Balmanno #1945: for this ed.

Doddridge, Philip. *The Rise and Progress of Religion in the Soul.* [For Dove's *English Classics*?] 2 illus. by Stothard

    Boddington, vol. 9, p. 88: 2 plates "Doddridge's Rise and Progress of Religion in the Soul For the Proprietors of the English Classics 1824 Stothard del."

    Balmanno #1946–47: identified in pencil for Doddridge

    Coxhead, p. 216, lists 1 plate for Dove's *English Classics,* gives no date but discusses ca. 1824

Horatius Flaccus, Quintus [Horace]. [unknown title, perhaps *The Odes, Satires, and Epistles.*] For William Pickering. 1 illus. by Stothard

    Coxhead, p. 214, lists 1 plate

    One print in private collection, U.S.

    National Union Catalogue 0521005: 1844 ed. of *The Odes, Satires, and Epistles* for Pickering, 1 plate noted

Irving, Washington. *Tales of a Traveller.* For J. Murray. 6 illus. by Stothard

    Huntington Library (386379): 6 plates

    Coxhead, pp. 215–16, lists 6 illus., says that 4 appear again in the *The Pledge of Friendship* 1827

    Balmanno: identified in pencil with date 1824

    Boddington, vol. 9, pp. 12–14: 6 plates identified in pencil for *Tales of a Traveller*

(?) Moore, Thomas. *Irish Melodies.* For G. Robinson. 6–8(?) illus. by Stothard

Balmanno #1967–72: Stothard del. "*Irish Melodies* For
G. Robinson 1824," illus. identified in pencil "never
published"

Boddington, vol. 9, pp. 4–6: 8 plates identified in pencil
for Moore's *Melodies* 1824

Coxhead, p. 166, lists 6 illus.

Yale Center for British Art, Bray 3: identified in pencil
with date 1824; Bray 4: identified in pencil with date
1824

[Procter, Bryan Waller.] *Effigies poeticae; or, Portraits of the
British Poets.* For James Carpenter and Son. 1 illus. by
Stothard

British Library (c.5.e.16,17) 1824 ed.: 1 plate

Coxhead, p. 216, lists 1 plate

Balmanno plate

Boddington, vol. 9, p. 36: 1 plate identified in pencil with
date 1820

Yale Center for British Art, Bray

Scott, Walter. *Ivanhoe; a romance.* For Hurst, Robinson and
Co. 2 illus. by Stothard

Balmanno #1942–43: Stothard del. "*Ivanhoe* For Hurst,
Robinson & Co. 1824"

Coxhead, p. 138, lists 2 illus. for Hurst

Boddington, vol. 7, p. 738: plates illustrating *Ivanhoe*
included with others illustrating Scott's *Tales of My
Landlord* for Rodwell & Martin [see 1820 entry]

Tegg, Thomas. *Gems of Lyric Poetry and Gems of Devotional
Poetry.* For Thomas Tegg [perhaps two separate pub-
lications]. 2 illus. by Stothard

Balmanno #1953: Stothard del. "*Gems of Lyric Poetry* For
Tegg 1824"; #1955: Stothard del. "*Gems of Devotional
Poetry* For Tegg 1824"

Boddington, vol. 9, p. 106: 1 plate "*Gems of Lyric Poetry*
Stothard del."

Coxhead, p. 211, lists two plates

Watts, Alaric Alexander. *Poetical Sketches.* For Hurst,
Robinson & Co. 2 illus. by Stothard

British Library (11642.aaa.24): 2 illus.

Coxhead, p. 215, lists 2 illus.

Zimmerman, Johann Georg. *Solitude Considered with Respect
to its Influences Upon the Mind and the Heart.* For
T. Griffiths. 3 illus. by Stothard

Balmanno #1939–41: Stothard del. "*Solitude Considered
. . . by Zimmerman* for T. Griffiths 1824"

Boddington, vol. 7, p. 44: 3 plates

Coxhead, p. 214, lists 3 illus.

National Union Catalogue: 1825 ed. for Griffiths, notes
frontispiece

1825

La Belle Assemblee or Court and Fashionable Magazine. Sup-
plementary Number to Vol. 1. For George B. Whittaker [etc.]. 1 illus. by Stothard

Boddington, vol. 5, p. 70: 1 plate for this publication
"Stothard del." "MDCCCXXV"

Boccaccio, Giovanni. *Decamerone.* For William Pickering.
10 illus. by Stothard

British Library (12470.d.29): 10 illus.

Coxhead, pp. 141–42, lists 10 illus. for Pickering

Balmanno: plates to the *Decamerone* "For R. Jennings,"
identified in pencil with date 1828; also plates "For
Longman [etc.] 1830" [these are later reprints]

Boddington, vol. 9, pp. 138–42: 10 plates for this ed.; pp.
142–44: reprints for later eds.

Chesterfield, Philip Dormer Stanhope, 4th earl of. *Letters,
written by the Earl of Chesterfield to his son.* For Thomas
Tegg [etc.] [perhaps issued as part of a collection, see
1820–1827 entry]. 6(?) illus. by Stothard

Coxhead, p. 211, suggests about 6 illus. for Tegg

Balmanno #2030: Stothard del. "For Tegg 1825," identified in pencil for Lord Chesterfield

National Union Catalogue lists 1823 ed. printed for
Whittingham's *Cabinet Library* with added engraved
title page dated 1825; lists 1827 ed. of *Letters, written by
the Earl of Chesterfield to his son* for Tegg, notes plates

Cowper, William. *Poems.* For Thomas Tegg [etc., possibly
including C. & J. Rivington] [perhaps issued as part of
a collection, see 1820–1827 entry]. 1 illus. by Stothard

Balmanno #2027: Stothard del. "For Tegg 1825," identified in pencil for Cowper

Coxhead, p. 159, lists 1 plate

National Union Catalogue lists 1824 ed. for Tegg, notes
added title pages as part of Park's *Works of the British
Poets;* lists 1825 ed. for C. & J. Rivington [etc.], notes
plates

Mason, John. *Self-Knowledge. A Treatise.* For Thomas Tegg
[etc.]. 1 illus. by Stothard

British Library (8408.a.7): 1 illus.

Royal Academy: Stothard del. 1 illus.

Terentius Afer, Publius [Terence]. *Triphook & Lephard Publii
Terentii Afri comoediae sex, adfidem ed.is Zeunianae accurate recensitae.* For Harding. 2 illus. by Stothard

British Library (011388.a.6): 2 illus.

Coxhead, p. 216, lists 2 illus.

Balmanno #2020–21: for this ed.

Walton, Izaak. *The complete Angler; or Contemplative Man's Recreation.* For William Pickering. 2 illus. by Stothard

Huntington Library (132929): 2 plates

Boddington, vol. 3, p. 168: 2 plates

Coxhead, p. 142, lists 1 or 2 plates

Young, Edward. *The Complaint: or, Night Thoughts.* For Thomas Tegg [perhaps issued as part of a collection, see 1820–1827 entry]. 1 illus. by Stothard

Boddington, vol. 9, p. 108: 1 plate identified in pencil for Young's *Night Thoughts,* 1824, for Tegg

National Union Catalogue 0025436: 1824 ed. printed by Whittingham (for Whittingham's *Cabinet Library*), notes engraved title page

Coxhead, pp. 157–58, lists 1 plate

(?) [unknown title to a cookery book.] For Thomas Tegg. 1 illus. by Stothard

Balmanno #2634: Stothard del. "For Tegg 1825," identified in pencil for a cookery book

Coxhead, p. 217, lists 1 plate

1825(?)

[unknown title to book of *Arabian Nights.* unknown publisher.] 2–3(?) illus. by Stothard

Coxhead, p. 211, says perhaps 2 illus. dates ca. 1825

Boddington, vol. 8, p. 80: 6 plates identified in pencil for *Arabian Nights:* 3 in one format and 3 in a different format

1825–1827

Oxberry, William. *Dramatic Biography and histrionic anecdotes.* For G. Virtue. 3(?) illus. by Stothard

Huntington Library (220277) 1825–1827 ed. and British Library (P.P.5114.b): no Stothard del., but 3 plates close to his style

Coxhead, p. 102, lists 3 or 4 illus. attributed to Stothard, dates 1826

1825–1832

Friendship's Offering, A Literary Album and Annual Remembrancer. For Smith, Edler & Co. 3(?) illus. by Stothard

Coxhead, p. 55, lists 1 plate for 1825 and 1 for 1826

Huntington Library (14491) missing 1825 vol.; 1826 vol.: no Stothard del.; 1830 vol.: 1 plate; 1832 vol.: 1 plate

British Library (P.P.6605) also missing 1825 vol.

1826

Goldsmith, Oliver. *The History of Rome.* For Thomas Tegg. 1 illus. by Stothard

British Library (586.a.27): 1 plate

Royal Academy: 1 plate Stothard del. for this ed.

Boddington, vol. 9, p. 108: 1 plate

[unknown title to a book of stories.] For Thomas Tegg [perhaps issued as part of a collection, see 1820–1827 entry]. 1 illus. by Stothard

Balmanno #2033: Stothard del. "The Dwarf and the Peacock For Tegg 1826"

Boddington, vol. 9, p. 62: 1 plate "The Dwarf and the Peacock For Tegg 1826"

Coxhead, p. 217, lists 1 illus. to "The Dwarf and the Peacock"

[unknown title to a dictionary of science.] For Thomas Tegg [perhaps issued as part of a collection, see 1820–1827 entry]. 1 illus. by Stothard

Coxhead, p. 218, lists 1 illus.

Balmanno #2073: Stothard del. "For Tegg 1826," identified in pencil for a dictionary of science

Yale Center for British Art, Bray 2: identified in pencil

1826–1828

Shakespeare, William. *Plays.* For Hurst, Robinson & Co. & R. Jennings. 2 illus. by Stothard

Bennett MA thesis: 2 plates

Coxhead, p. 102, lists 2 plates

Balmanno #2074–75: dated "1826"

Boddington, vol. 7, p. 102: 2 plates Stothard del. "1826" and "1827"

1827

The Amulet or Christian and Literary Remembrancer. For W. Baynes and Son [etc.]. 1 illus. by Stothard

Huntington Library (111208): 1 plate

Coxhead, p. 55, lists 1 plate

Shakespeare, William. *The Dramatic Works.* For Thomas Tegg [perhaps issued as part of a collection, see 1820–1827 entry]. 1 illus. by Stothard

British Library (11763.bb.6): 1 plate

Coxhead, p. 102, says probably several plates, dates the publication 1826

Walton, Izaak. *The complete Angler; or Contemplative Man's Recreation.* For William Pickering. 1(?) illus. by Stothard

Huntington Library (69935): 1 plate, differs from plates for 1825 ed.

Coxhead, p. 142, says that 1 or 2 plates were published in a miniature ed. within 2 or 3 years of the 1825 ed.; p.

218 lists 3 plates from the *Complete Angler* for Pickering's miniature books

Boddington, vol. 9, p. 102: 1 plate identified in pencil for Walton's *Angler*

Walton, Izaak. *The Lives of Donne, Wotton, Hooker, Herbert and Sanderson.* For William Pickering. 1 illus. by Stothard

Huntington Library (151059): 1 plate

1827–1828

The Pledge of Friendship [for 1826-1828]. For W. Marshall. 7(?) illus. by Stothard

British Library (P.P.6565): no Stothard del. in 1826; 1827 missing (but probably 4 plates as Coxhead notes); 1828 has 3 illus.

Coxhead, p. 55, lists 4 illus. for 1827

1828

The Forget-Me-Not; a Christmas and new year's present [for 1824-1847]. For R. Ackermann. 1(?) illus. by Stothard

British Library (P.P.6595): 1 plate for 1828

Coxhead, p. 56, lists 2 plates for 1828

Watts, Alaric A., ed. *The Literary Souvenir; or, Cabinet of Poetry and Romance.* For Longman, Rees, Orme, Brown, & Green. 3 illus. by Stothard

British Library (P.P.6655): 1 plate for 1828, 1 for 1831, 1 for 1832

Coxhead, p. 58, lists 1 plate for 1828, 1 for 1831, and 1 for 1832

Boddington, vol. 8, p. 58: 1 plate, *A Conversation,* identified in pencil for 1828

1828(?)

Specimens of Lyrical, Descriptive & Narrative Poets. For Oliver of Edinburgh. 2 illus. by Stothard

Balmanno #1123–24: "*Specimens of Lyrical, Descriptive & Narrative Poets* For Oliver of Edinburgh," identified in pencil with date 1828

Coxhead, p. 218, lists 2 illus. for this miniature book without publication date, but belonging to 1828

1828–1830

The Bijou; or Annual of Literature and The Arts [for 1828-30]. For William Pickering. 7–9(?) illus. by Stothard

Huntington Library (112527): 5 illus. for 1828, 2 illus. for 1830

Coxhead, p. 56, lists 7 plates and 1 unsigned for 1828; 1 (*Christabel*) for 1829; 1 for 1830

Balmanno #2127: Stothard del. "Christabel For William Pickering 1828"

Boddington, vol. 9, p. 60: 1 plate "1828"; vol. 9, p. 144: 1 plate identified in pencil as *San Souci* for the *Bijou* 1828

1828–1836

The Keepsake [for 1828-1839]. For Hurst, Chance, & Co. 7 illus. by Stothard

Coxhead, pp. 57–58, lists 3 plates for 1828; 1 for 1829; 1 for 1834; 1 for 1835; 1 for 1836

Huntington Library (111444): 3 plates for 1828, 1 for 1829, 1 for 1834

British Library (P.P.6670): 1 plate for 1836

Balmanno #2183: Stothard del. identified in pencil for the *Keepsake,* but "For Moon, Boys and Graves 1834"

Boddington, vol. 9, p. 64: 1 plate "For Moon, Boys and Graves 1834"

1829

The Juvenile Keepsake [for 1826-1830]. For Hurst, Chance, and Co. 1 illus. by Stothard

Coxhead, p. 58, lists 1 plate

British Library (P.P.6765): no Stothard del. plates, but 1 plate is missing from this ed.

Pope, Alexander. *The Rape of the Lock, and other poems.* For John Sharpe. 1 illus. by Stothard

British Library (11609.aa.31,32) 1829 ed.: 1 plate

Coxhead, p. 109, lists 1 plate (a reduction of the 1804 plate), dates 1828

1829(?)

Scott, Walter. *Guy Mannering.* For R. Jennings [etc.] 1 illus. by Stothard

Coxhead, p. 138, lists 1 plate

Balmanno: print to *Guy Mannering* for Jennings, identified in pencil with date 1830

Boddington, vol. 7, p. 738: plate illustrating *Guy Mannering* included with others illustrating Scott's *Tales of My Landlord* for Rodwell & Martin [see 1820 entry]

Stewart, Alexander. *Stories for the History of Scotland.* For Oliver & Boyd, Edinburgh. 2 illus. by Stothard

British Library (600.c.7) 1829 ed.: 2 plates

Coxhead, p. 218, lists 2 illus., dates ca. 1828

Balmanno #2125–26: "Stewart's *Stories for the History of Scotland* For Oliver & Boyd, Edinburgh," identified in pencil with date 1828

1830

The alphabet engraved in wood from designs by Thomas Stothard. W. Pickering. 1–10(?) illus. by Stothard

Newberry Library, Wing Collection catalogue lists this ed.

Boddington, vol. 12, p. 30: 1 woodcut print of alphabets A-Z; vol. 12, p. 30: 10 woodcut prints of the alphabet, for "Whittingham" [perhaps for another ed.]

Rogers, Samuel. *Italy, a poem.* For T. Cadell. 20 illus. by Stothard

Huntington Library (22342): 20 illus.

Coxhead, pp. 131–32, lists 20 illus. and 2 more attributed to Stothard

Boddington, vol. 12, pp. 36–94: 61 plates for *Poems* and *Italy*

Thomson, James. *The Seasons and Castle of Indolence.* For William Pickering. 4(?) illus. by Stothard

Coxhead, p. 111, lists 4 illus.

Boddington, vol. 7, p. 108: 2 plates, 1 identified in pencil as "Lavinia" for Thompson's *Seasons*

1832

Watts, Isaac. *Songs, Divine and Moral, for the Use of Children.* For Charles Tilt. 6 illus. by Stothard

A copy of this ed. is in a private collection, U.S.: 6 illus.

A copy of this ed. in the Victoria and Albert Museum is hand-colored by Constable

Boddington, vol. 12, p. 8: 5 plates identified in pencil for Watts's *Hymns*

The Winter's Wreath [for 1828-1832]. For Whittaker, Treacher [etc.]. 1 illus. by Stothard

British Library (P.P.6805): 1 plate for 1832

Coxhead, p. 58, lists 1 plate for 1832

1834

Rogers, Samuel. *Poems.* For T. Cadell; E. Moxon. 35 illus. by Stothard

Huntington Library (22341): 35 plates, including *A Convent Gate* (p. 134); (22784) 1834 ed. for T. Cadell; E. Moxon: 35 plates

British Library (c.108.c.1) 1834 ed. for T. Cadell; E. Moxon: 35 illus.

Coxhead, pp. 133–34, lists 34 illus. to the 1834 ed.; p. 134 says another ed. of *Poems* published by Moxon in 1838 with the same illus. but differently arranged and with the addition of 1 plate, *A Convent Gate* [National Union Catalogue 0376863: this 1838 ed. is the first published just by Moxon]

Balmanno plates

Boddington, vol. 9, pp. 19–20: 4 plates; vol. 12, pp. 36–94: 61 plates for *Poems* and *Italy*

1835

Cunningham, Peter. *Songs of England and Scotland.* For James Cochrane & Co. 1 illus. by Stothard

Huntington Library (PR1187 C76): 1 plate

Coxhead, p. 116, lists 1 plate

Boddington, vol. 12, p. 18: 1 plate identified in pencil for this ed.

Balmanno: 1 plate for this ed.

1836

Chambers' Spelling Book. For W. & R. Chambers. 1 illus. by Stothard

Royal Academy: Stothard del. "Chambers' Spelling Book For R. Chambers 1836," 1 plate

Boddington, vol. 9, p. 74: 1 plate "Chambers' Spelling Book Stothard del.," identified in pencil with date 1839

Coxhead, p. 219, lists 1 plate to *Chambers' Spelling Book*

Walton, Izaak. *The complete Angler; or Contemplative Man's Recreation.* For William Pickering. 29 illus. by Stothard

British Library (556.f.10,11): 29 illus.

Coxhead, p. 143, lists about 22 illus.

Watts, Alaric, ed. *The Cabinet of Modern Art.* For Whittaker & Co. 2(?) illus. by Stothard

A copy of this ed. is in a private collection, U.S.: 2 illus.

Boddington, vol. 9, p. 42: 3 plates "Stothard pinx," identified in pencil with date 1837

1838

Rogers, Samuel. *Italy, a poem.* For Edward Moxon. 21 illus. by Stothard

Huntington Library (265012 and 234972): 1838 ed. for Edward Moxon: 21 illus.

Rogers, Samuel. *Poems.* For Edward Moxon. 35 illus. by Stothard

Coxhead, p. 134, lists 35 illus. [see 1834 entry]

1839

The New Sporting Magazine. For Baldwin & Cradock [etc., including R. Ackermann]. 1 illus. by Stothard

Boddington, vol. 9, p. 120: 1 plate "Stothard pinxt 1837 The New Sporting Magazine For R. Ackermann"

National Union Catalogue 0166121: entry for this magazine (1831–) for Baldwin & Cradock [etc.]

Rogers, Samuel. *Italy, a poem.* For Edward Moxon. 26 illus. by Stothard

A copy of this ed. is in a private collection, U.S.: with "wood-engraved vignettes throughout by J.

Thompson & Clennell after Stothard, Landseer and others . . . printed by Whittingham"; 26 plates Stothard del.

Coxhead, p. 135, says Moxon published a small ed. of *Italy* in 1839 with 26 illus. from the 1816 ed. of the *Poems* and in 1849 published another *Italy* with some of the Clennell vignettes

Rogers, Samuel. *Poems.* For Edward Moxon. 49 illus. by Stothard

A copy of this ed. is in a private collection, U.S.: with Clennell wood-engraving after Stothard; 49 plates Stothard del.

1867

Bell, Robert, ed. *Art and Song. A series of original . . . engravings from masterpieces of art of the nineteenth century accompanied by a selection of the choicest poems in the English language.* For Bell & Daldy. 1–4 (?) illus. by Stothard

British Library (11651.k.1) 1867 ed.: 1 plate; also eds. for J. S. Virtue and H. Virtue in 1892 and 1900

Coxhead, pp. 163–66, lists 4 illus. for an ed. for Virtue; says the book was published after Stothard's death

NOTES

NOTES TO PREFACE

1. Letter of 27 March 1828 from Lawrence to Rev. Edward Bury, located in the Royal Academy Library Anderson Collection (AND 28/119).

2. Extract from the *Journal* of Leigh Hunt (1784–1859), located in Stothard Album c. 102* no. 55, Department of Prints and Drawings, British Museum.

3. Edward Dayes, *The Works of the late Edward Dayes, containing Professional Sketches of Modern Artists,* ed. E. W. Brayley, p. 351.

4. Stothard's manuscript notes for his projected "Dictionary of the Lives of Painters" survive in the extra-illustrated edition of Anna Eliza Bray's *The Life of Thomas Stothard, R.A. with Personal Reminiscences* in the Wiggins Collection, Boston Public Library.

NOTES TO CHAPTER 1: FORMATIVE YEARS

1. Anonymous Review of *The Life of Thomas Stothard* by Anna Eliza Bray, *Gentleman's Magazine,* 1852, p. 146.

2. Ibid.

3. W. B. Adams, *English Pleasure Carriages* (1837), cited by E. P. Thompson, *The Making of the English Working Class,* p. 262.

4. Bray, *Life of Stothard,* p. 6.

5. Ibid., p. 3.

6. Cited by Norma Perry, "John Vansommer of Spitalfields: Huguenot, Silk-designer, and Correspondent of Voltaire," p. 301n.

7. All information on Vansommer is based on Perry's article. Bray, *Life of Stothard,* pp. 7–8, says that Stothard served a full seven-year term of apprenticeship. Later sources report that he gave up the last year of his apprenticeship due to a decline in the silk trade; see *The Cromolithograph,* 26 September 1868, p. 374.

8. British Library Add MSS 36, 521 f. 586.

9. Cumberland presented nineteen copies of *Thoughts on Outline* to his friends, including Stothard and Blake; G. E. Bentley, Jr., *Blake Records,* p. 55. Cumberland's correspondence with his brother is now in the British Library.

10. British Library Add MSS 36, 492 f. 188.

11. Cumberland dedicated an ode to Horne Tooke in 1810 and etched his portrait; Sir Geoffrey Keynes, "George Cumberland 1754–1848," p. 46.

12. British Library Add MSS 36, 492 f. 104.

13. Ibid., f. 346.

14. This letter is in the Nottingham City Art Gallery and Museum.

15. This sketch is in the Victoria and Albert Museum.

16. There is no record of what this painting looked like.

17. Entry on 7 December 1795 in Joseph Farington's *Diary* (1793–1821), Royal Archives at Windsor (typescript in the British Library).

18. Article dated 28 April 1834 pasted into the William T. Whitley, *Scrapbooks of Printed Material on British Artists,* Department of Prints and Drawings, British Museum.

19. William T. Whitley, *Art in England 1800-1820,* p. 275.

20. Cited by S. C. Hall, ed., *The National Gallery; Comprising the Pictures Known as the Vernon Collection,* entry 6.

21. One of the volumes, *Le Pitture Antiche d'Ercolane,* from this nine-volume set was in Stothard's possession at his death. It is listed in the third day of the sale of his works at Christie, Manson and Christie: *A Catalogue of the Remaining Portion of the Finished Pictures . . . by . . . Stothard . . . which will be sold by auction on Wednesday, March 25, 1835.*

22. Wolf Mankowitz, *Wedgwood,* caption to pl. 98.

23. Two versions exist of his embarkation on this profession; one is related by Bray and most subsequent writers and the other by a few sources such as Stothard's lifelong friend Samuel Boddington and John Pye (*Patronage of British Art,* p. 247n.). The anonymous reviewer of Bray's *Life of Stothard* in 1852 notes both versions (p. 147). Bray says that, while Stothard was an apprentice, he occupied his leisure time with making designs from Homer, Spenser, and the poets. These sketches were noticed by one of Mrs. Vansommer's customers, Mr. Harrison the publisher. Harrison was so pleased with what he saw that he gave Stothard a novel to read and requested that he illustrate those subjects that struck his fancy. When Harrison returned at the end of the week, Stothard presented him with three designs that Harrison paid a half-guinea for. Bray declares this first success as a book illustrator decided Stothard on his future career, although he did not gain regular employment in book illustration for several years. The other version of the story is related by Boddington in a note pasted above a print dated December 1779 for *Joseph Andrews,* from the *Novelist's Magazine,* designed by Daniel Dodd, and engraved by James Heath. This note is located in a vast collection of Stothard prints compiled by Boddington and now residing in the Henry E. Huntington Library. It reads, "Mr. Corbold [Corbould] who was a pupil of Stothard's, says that Stothard at the request of Heath improved the drawing for this print by Dodd, No. 1 in the Novelist's Magazine (for

doing which Heath gave him five shillings) that Harrison the publisher of the Novelist's Magazine employed him afterwards for many years."

24. Richard D. Altick, *The English Common Reader: A Social History of the Mass Reading Public, 1800-1900*, pp. 49–52; Charles Knight, *Shadows of the Old Booksellers*, pp. 278–80 from the Appendix, which is a reprint of an article by Knight originally published in *The Printing Machine* periodical (1834).

25. Altick, *English Common Reader*, pp. 53–55, 267; G. E. Bentley, Jr., and Martin K. Nurmi, *A Blake Bibliography*, p. 141; based on his investigation of the *Novelist's Magazine*, Bentley estimates that in a number there were about five sheets or gatherings, with about one plate to a gathering; the sheets were issued at sixpence apiece.

26. Knight, *Shadows*, p. 249.

27. *Press Cuttings from English Newspapers on Matters of Artistic Interest 1686-1835*, p. 586.

28. In the early years of the eighteenth century, the three-dimensional character of the patterns was accentuated by such devices as the *point rentrés*, which John Vansommer introduced into England about 1732. As in French furniture, silver, porcelain, and most examples of decorative art of this period, the plastic predilections of the earlier Baroque style were not entirely eliminated from the ornate, curvilinear rococo patterns. By the 1760s, these rhythmic, compounded curves took on a more two-dimensional character. By the time of Stothard's apprenticeship as a Spitalfields silk designer, meanders were constricted and stripes had gained in importance. Wreaths, garlands with medallions, and trophies of musical instruments prevailed in the much simpler and lighter patterns; see Peter Thornton, *Baroque and Rococo Silks*, pp. 130–31.

NOTES TO CHAPTER 2: ENTRY INTO THE ART WORLD

1. Although Stothard did not win any of the coveted silver and gold medals or traveling scholarships awarded by the Academy, he was the only student of the thirty-two young artists who entered with him in 1777 to receive the highest distinctions bestowed by the Royal Academy, election to the rank of Associate and then full Royal Academician. During his student days, Stothard was influenced by the various Visitors to the Life Drawings Class, in particular James Barry, who was elected Visitor for 1779, 1780, 1781, 1782, 1783, and often thereafter. In 1782 Barry was appointed Professor of Painting for the Academy. Although Barry did not commence his lectures on art until 1784, Stothard was probably thoroughly familiar with both Barry's theory and practice from his days as a student.

2. Only portrait *drawings* survive.

3. British Library Add MSS 36, 492 f. 104.

4. The drawing identified in Stothard's handwriting as "Allington Castle 1779" is in the Dennis Oppé collection, England; Allington Castle is near the Medway River in Maidstone, Kent.

5. Letter in the British Library Add MS 39, 168 f. 88.

6. The existing drawing dated 1779 indicates this excursion probably took place in September 1779. Bentley also surmises that this expedition took place between the summer of 1779, when Blake was free of his apprenticeship, and 1783, the end of the war with France. Bentley, however, reasons that since Blake and Stothard seem to enjoy a bachelor's freedom at the time of their trip, the most probable date is 1780 or 1781 (Blake married in August 1782 and Stothard in 1783) and the most likely month is September when the Royal Academy was closed; *Blake Records*, pp. 19–20.

7. Bray, *Life of Stothard*, p. 21.

8. The earliest date at which Flaxman may have met Stothard was December 1779, the date of the first print of the *Novelist's Magazine*.

9. Stothard was among the Academicians who voted for Barry's expulsion from the Royal Academy in 1799.

10. David V. Erdman, *Blake: Prophet Against Empire; A Poet's Interpretation of the History of His Own Times*, p. 38, cites Godwin's *Diary*.

11. In 1792 Flaxman wrote to his father from Rome inquiring after Stothard, Blake, and Barry; cited by David Irwin, *John Flaxman, 1755-1826: Sculptor, Illustrator, Designer*, p. 53.

12. See Flaxman's letters in the British Library (BM Add MSS 39,780–39, 792) and the Fitzwilliam Museum, Cambridge (Flaxman MSS).

13. It is probable that Stothard was an early purchaser of Blake's *Songs of Innocence*. His copy of *The Book of Thel* is now in the Beinecke Library, Yale University. See David Bindman, *Blake as an Artist*, p. 65; on p. 27 Bindman notes that Blake produced five plates in 1780, two of which were after designs by Stothard, and that he had made as many as thirty-three engravings after Stothard by 1785.

14. Cited by Erdman, *Prophet Against Empire*, p. 110, without footnoting his source.

15. Anonymous review, *Gentleman's Magazine*, 1852, p. 146.

16. Frederick Cummings and Allen Staley, *Romantic Art in Britain, Painting and Drawings 17600-1860*, p. 146. Cummings says that Romney introduced Flaxman to the Mathews; Iolo Williams, "An Identification of Some Early Drawings by John Flaxman," p. 249, says that Flaxman introduced Stothard to Mrs. Mathew.

17. G. E. Bentley, Jr., "A. S. Mathew, Patron of Blake and Flaxman," pp. 171, 168.

18. Erdman, *Prophet Against Empire*, p. 93, n. 7 ff., says that Priestley was probably a member of the Mathew circle. The print (#373) in the Balmanno collection of Stothard prints in the British Museum is identified in pencil "for Priestley's works." Although a pencil note on the print (vol.

3, p. 22) in the Boddington collection of Stothard prints in the Huntington Library identifies it as a frontispiece to a work on perspective, the edition has yet to be located; see Bray, *Life of Stothard*, p. 162.

19. Letter located in the Flaxman MSS, Fitzwilliam Museum.

20. All of Hayley's writings stressed this chief attribute of the doctrine of sensibility. Hayley was such a devoted disciple of this doctrine that in 1786 he suggested that his friend George Romney entitle one of his many portraits of Emma Hamilton the *Personification of Sensibility* (Evelyn Morchard Bishop, *Blake's Hayley*, p. 95). His first success as a poet of these finer feelings followed the publication in 1780 of the *Triumphs of Temper* expounding the sentimental message that if a young woman wants to secure a husband, the chief quality she requires is a good temper. Very likely, it was Hayley himself who advised his publisher, Thomas Cadell, to commission from Stothard the designs for the 1788 illustrated edition of the *Triumphs of Temper* and for his 1794 edition of *A Philosophical Essay on Old Maids*.

21. Both odes were published in the newspapers in 1776; William Hayley, *The Life of George Romney, Esq.*, p. 63.

22. Farington, *Dairy*, entries on 25 January, 12 and 18 February, 4 and 18 March, and 1 April.

23. Letter no. 1 located in the extra-illustrated edition of Bray's *Life of Stothard*, Wiggins Collection, Prints and Drawings Department, Boston Public Library; internal evidence indicates that the manuscript material and drawings contained in the four-volume edition at Boston were compiled by Bray herself.

24. Erdman, *Prophet Against Empire*, p. 161, n. 38.

25. British Library Add MSS 36, 518 f. 23.

26. Henry Crabb Robinson, *Henry Crabb Robinson on Books and Their Writers*, ed. Edith T. Morley, an 1809 entry.

27. Bray, *Life of Stothard*, appendix.

28. Copies of receipts in the Anderson Collection (AND/9/36), Royal Academy Library.

29. Letter no. 2 located in the extra-illustrated edition of Bray's *Life of Stothard*, Boston Public Library.

30. Both the 1809 citations are included in the Thomson Correspondence, MSS 1654 f. 73, National Library of Scotland.

31. Letter from Stothard to Rev. Markham (?), probably written in 1813, located in the extra-illustrated edition of Bray's *Life of Stothard*, Boston Public Library.

32. Letter from Stothard to Thomson dated by internal evidence to 1822, located in the extra-illustrated edition of Bray's *Life of Stothard*, Boston Public Library.

33. Letter from Thomson to Stothard dated November 1824, Thomson Correspondence MSS, National Library of Scotland.

34. *Press Cuttings*, p. 1709.

35. Article pasted into the copy of Whitley, *Scrapbooks of Printed Material on British Artists*, Department of Prints and Drawings, British Museum.

36. For example, Stothard based several of his works on Raphael. Many of Raphael's compositions would have been known to him from the cartoons hanging in Windsor Castle or through prints after Raphael by his Mannerist followers. Of particular importance to Stothard was the collection of engravings after Raphael's Vatican Loggia designs that were known as *Raphael's Bible*. A copy was in Stothard's possession at his death (Christie, Manson and Christie, *Catalogue of the Remaining Portion*). Stothard's illustration of *Experimental Philosophy pushing aside the Clouds . . .* for Priestley is based on Raphael's *Divine Creation* from the Vatican Loggia (noted by Jean Hagstrum, *William Blake: Poet and Painter*, p. 43). Bray relates that Stothard advised daily copying in outline from Raphael and recommended *Raphael's Bible* as a useful source (*Life of Stothard*, p. 64). In his commissions for Bowyer's Historical Gallery of the late 1780s and 1790s (which were so important in advancing his reputation as a history painter worthy of notice by the Royal Academy), Stothard closely imitated Raphael. For example, Stothard's *Joseph's Dream* is based on Raphael's depiction of the same subject in the Vatican Loggia. Likewise, when he received the major commission in 1821 to paint the ceiling of the Advocates' Library in Edinburgh, Stothard turned to Raphael's *Parnassus* as a source for his depiction of the famous figures of Scottish culture.

Stothard also studied early Italian painting. A copy of Thomas Patch's engravings after Ghiberti was in his possession at his death and is listed in Christie, Manson and Christie, *Catalogue of the Remaining Portion*. His art was influential in forming a new appreciation of early Italian painting in the early nineteenth century. When William Hilton was viewing the Giottos in the Arena Chapel and Lady Callcott was confronted with a Botticelli, both were reminded of Stothard; see Francis Haskell, *Rediscoveries in Art*, pp. 50, 53. Similarly, C. R. Leslie called Stothard "the Giotto of England" in his *Recollections* (1860). And John Ruskin referred to him as the "Fra Angelico of England" (cited by Selby Whittingham, "What You Will; or some notes regarding the influence of Watteau on Turner and other British Artists," p. 8).

Many drawings by Stothard after medieval art survive, for example an album of studies in the Bodleian Library, Oxford University, of medieval costume and monastic orders. Bray related that Stothard thought the study of Gothic art so useful that he recommended it to his son Charles and even drew models for him to copy. Charles became a famous antiquarian draftsman and before his early death in 1822 published such works as *Monumental Effigies of Great Britain*; see *Life of Stothard*, p. 79.

Farington notes in his diary two discussions on the subject of Church decoration that included Stothard. On 10 February 1979, Farington "Called on Flaxman. He, Opie and Stothard drank tea at Romney's yesterday, and had much conversation on the subject of decorating Churches, all were on fire at the proposal." On 24 May 1811, Farington dined with Stothard, Woodforde, Heath, Bone, and Flaxman: "We talked of the restoration of the outside of the Henry VII Chapel at Westminster Abbey now carrying on. Stothard and Flaxman thought it a very proper work, the latter however depreciating doing anything in the inside of the Abbey. Flaxman spoke strongly against the alterations made in Salisbury Cathedral under the direction of Wyatt."

37. Stothard's illustration of *Boadicea Inspiring the Britons against the Romans* was probably for George Raymond's *History of England*, which was published about 1786 or earlier.

38. Letter no. 2 in the extra-illustrated edition of Bray's *Life of Stothard*, Boston Public Library. This letter would seem to have been written by Stothard in the summer of 1822 due to its reference to commissions that Thomson remarks on in his dated letters in the National Library of Scotland.

39. G. E. Bentley, Jr., "Notes on the Early Editions of Flaxman's Classical Designs," pp. 289, 293; there also may be size considerations here.

40. Letter no. 1, from Stothard to Thomson, in the extra-illustrated edition of Bray's *Life of Stothard*, Boston Public Library; from internal evidence this letter probably dates after September 1822 and before February 1823.

41. During the second half of the eighteenth century, there was an indigenous development within English engraving processes toward more tonal effects. Experimentations with the engraving techniques of mezzotint, aquatint, and stipple culminated at the end of the eighteenth century in the invention of lithography, which was rapidly popularized in the nineteenth century. In most book illustrations executed at the end of the century, the engraver's preference for tonal effects that stressed the surface and texture of the print took precedence over most other considerations.

42. Letter from Flaxman to Hayley, no. 26, Flaxman MSS, Fitzwilliam Museum.

43. Letter from Flaxman to Hayley, no. 28, Flaxman MSS, Fitzwilliam Museum.

44. Letter from Flaxman to Hayley, no. 31, Flaxman MSS, Fitzwilliam Museum.

45. British Library Add MSS 36, 519 I, f. 388 and f. 356: "Stothard a woodcut—He draws them in pencil on the block for the engravers."

46. Thomson Correspondence MSS, National Library of Scotland.

47. Stothard revealed to George Thomson in a letter of about 1822 quoted later in the text that his usual price for a vignette was £5; letter no. 2 in the extra-illustrated edition of Bray's *Life of Stothard*, Boston Public Library.

Notes to Chapter 3: Elevation in Status as an Artist

1. *Press Cuttings*, p. 418.

2. *Press Cuttings*, p. 574.

3. British Library Add MSS 36, 496 f. 97.

4. Experts could also be duped: in 1797, Stothard, along with Joseph Farington, John Opie, Hyacinthe Rigaud, Richard Westall, Smirke, and John Hoppner, believed the claims of a young woman named Provis that she had discovered the lost secret of Titian's coloring, which she sold to them for 10 guineas each. This "secret" was soon made public by Richard Cosway's discovery of the original treaties from which Miss Provis had taken her knowledge; Farington, *Diary*, and Ada Earland, *John Opie and His Circle*, pp. 120–21.

5. A letter from Shelley to Cumberland that can be dated to 1789/90 on the basis of internal evidence reports about Stothard: "He studies close—has 3 children"; British Library Add MSS 36, 516 f. 259.

6. John Williams (pseudonym of Anthony Pasquin), review of Stothard's *The Interview between Henry VIII and the Emperor Charles V* in the 1794 Royal Academy exhibit, in *Memoirs of the Royal Academicians*, p. 6.

7. P. W. Clayden, *The Early Life of Samuel Rogers*, p. 262.

8. Adele M. Holcomb, "A Neglected Classical Phase of Turner's Art: His Vignettes to Rogers' *Italy*," p. 406, n. 3.

9. The article on Rogers's house in *The Anthenaeum* (29 December 1855) is cited by Frank Herrmann, *The English as Collectors: A Documentary Chestomathy*, p. 254.

10. Stothard's illustrations appeared in at least nine editions of *The Pleasures of Memory*; cited by Holcomb, "Turner's Art," p. 406, n. 6; see also *Dictionary of National Biography* entry on Rogers.

11. Holcomb, "Turner's Art," p. 407, no. 14, and P. W. Clayden, *Rogers and His Contemporaries*, 2:6, both cite a memorandum by Rogers: "Paid Turner £147, paid Stothard £189, paid for embellishment £2,016"; Clayden inferred that this was for *Italy*. Turner was originally to have been paid £50 per drawing, but Rogers paid £5 apiece for the loan of them. Holcomb says that Turner accepted this arrangement because he was anxious for the success of the publication due to his admiration of Rogers.

12. Rev. John Mitford, "Recollections 1847–56," vol. 7, British Library Add MSS 32, 567 f. 110.

13. Holcomb, "Turner's Art," pp. 407, 408; Holcomb says that in the discussions between Walter Scott and the publisher Thomas Cadell all issues concerned the selection of subjects, although Scott allowed Turner was "unquestionably the best judge of everything belonging to art." She says that evidently this wasn't the case with Rogers. There are other examples that indicate that Rogers followed the customary practice. For instance, the Dowager Countess Spencer had supervised Flaxman's designs for Homer's *Odyssey* and demanded alterations of certain plates; see Sarah Symmons, "The Spirit of Despair: Patronage, Primitivism and the Art of John Flaxman," p. 647. Allen M. Sammuels, "Rudolph Ackermann and the English Dance of Death," has suggested that the publisher Ackermann

was often the guiding force in the creation of his numerous publications. For example, in the case of his tremendously popular *Dr. Syntax* tours (1812–1821), he was the intermediary in the collaboration between Thomas Rowlandson, the illustrator, and William Combe, the writer.

14. British Library Add MSS 32, 566 f. 41.

15. Clayden, *Rogers and His Contemporaries*, 2:6, identified this vignette as the *Fountain*. This note is located in his copy of Rogers's *Italy*, now in the Victoria and Albert Museum.

16. The choice of engravers and of the engraving process was often as crucial to the ultimate success of the finished book illustration as was the choice of illustrator. Indeed, the engravers for most publications often were paid as much, if not more, for their efforts than the draftsmen; see Sven Bruntjen, "John Boydell (1719–1804); A Study of Art Patronage and Publishing in Georgian London." For example, William Finden and his school of steel engravers received 40 to 50 guineas apiece for their work on Rogers's *Italy* and *Poems*, while Turner was paid merely £5 apiece for the loan of his drawings; see Percy Muir, *Victorian Illustrated Books*, p. 72. On p. 83, Muir notes that the prints were prepared in two batches dated September 1829 and January 1830 and that there is evidence on some of the prepublication proofs that they were in "hand" in 1827. Also, in a letter from Turner to the publishers Hurst and Robinson noted by Thornbury, *Turner*, 2:250–51, Turner estimates the time required to engrave a steel plate at two years.

17. Italics mine. This article was published by Pickering and was printed in part in the *New Monthly Magazine* (October 1825). Both are included with no further identification in the Robert Balmanno *Scrapbook of Printed Material on Thomas Stothard*, No. NN 6.18, Department of Prints and Drawings, British Museum.

18. There are three relationships that are most likely to exist between an artist and author in book illustration. In a few cases, the artist and author may be the same person, as with Blake and his composite art form. This is the rarest and of course most notable situation. The second relationship, a collaboration between artist and author, occurs in a few instances, for example, in Rowlandson's and Combe's creation of the illustrations and text for the *Dr. Syntax* tours (1812–1821). In the third type of relation, the artist visualizes situations described in preexisting texts. In this role, the artist, with or without guidance from the publisher, acts as an interpreter or critic in his choice of particular episodes to illustrate and in his attitude toward the text. Most of Stothard's illustrations fall within this category.

19. As a corollary of this admiration for the woman-child of innocent simplicity, the role of the child was sentimentalized and likewise found fertile ground for expression in Stothard's art. Undoubtedly, Stothard's notable mannerism of drawing many of his figures with large, blank eyes may be traced to his desire to appeal to this taste for childlike

innocence. Stothard could have found precedent for this trick in earlier art. Hogarth offered an explanation for this phenomenon in *The Analysis of Beauty*, p. 143: "But there is another very extraordinary circumstance (perhaps never taken notice of before in this light), which nature hath given us to distinguish one age from another by: which is, that tho' every feature grows larger and longer, till the whole person has done growing, the sight of the eye still keeps its original size; I mean the pupil, with its iris or ring; for the diameter of this circle continues still the same, and so becomes a fixt measure by which we, as it were, insensibly compare the daily perceiv'd growings of the other parts of the face, and thereby determine a young person's age."

20. Dayes, *Works*, p. 351.

21. *Press Cuttings*, p. 565.

22. A copy of this poem by Leigh Hunt, printed in both English and French, is included in the *Royal Academy Collection of Engravings by Thomas Stothard, R.A.*, collected by W. E. Frost, A.R.A. (London, 1861), in the Royal Academy Library.

23. Letter no. 16 in a collection of sixteen letters from Flaxman to Hayley (1786–1814), Flaxman MSS, Fitzwilliam Museum.

24. Another example of Stothard's sentimental interpretation is found in his illustration of *Reu Primrose Lecturing to His Fellow Prisoners* (1792 edition), which set the precedent for illustrating one of the prison scenes from *The Vicar of Wakefield*. This precedent was followed by Henry Courbould in the 1797–1799 Cooke edition and by Richard Westall in the 1819 Sharpe edition.

25. Farington, *Diary*, 7 March 1805, notes that Stothard has received this commission.

26. The present location of this painting is unknown.

27. David Irwin, *English Neoclassical Art: Studies in Inspiration and Taste*, p. 36; David and Francia Irwin, *Scottish Painters at Home and Abroad, 1700–1900*, p. 115; Dorothy Moulton Mayer, *Angelica Kauffman, R.A. (1741–1807)*, pl. 41. In addition, Flaxman's representation of the *Meeting of Hector and Andromache* appeared in the second London edition (printed in 1805) of his illustrations to the *Iliad;* thus, Flaxman was probably working on this new illustration during the same period that Stothard was designing his painting for Hope and his illustration for Du Roveray (1805), which will be discussed in the following paragraphs in the text. Both Stothard's and Flaxman's studies for this subject reflect a similar interest in a variety of moments in Homer's narrative. As Robert Wark noted, "Flaxman clearly considered the possibility of a family group with Hector and Andromache holding their infant son, an episode about 100 lines later in the poem than the lines he finally illustrated" (*Drawings by John Flaxman in the Huntington Collection*, pp. 25–26). Flaxman's family group is strikingly similar to Stothard's illustration for Du Roveray.

28. *The Iliad of Homer*, trans. Richmond Lattimore (Chi-

cago & London: University of Chicago Press, 1961), book 6, lines 466–70.

29. Ibid., lines 470–74.

Notes to Chapter 4: Additional Sources of Income

1. *The Romantic Movement* (London: The Tate Gallery, 1959), p. 214.

2. George Phillips, *Rudiments of Curvilinear Design* (ca. 1839), p. 49. I would like to thank Sir Ernst Gombrich for calling this citation to my attention.

3. This same period witnessed one of the greatest alterations of the English countryside. While towns and cities were expanding, the transportation revolution was opening up the countryside to the effects of industrial revolution. The Enclosure Acts and agricultural revolution were beginning to reorganize the physical features of the countryside. Undoubtedly, the growth of interest in landscape in the late eighteenth and early nineteenth centuries was partially the result of a desire to find in nature an escape from this crushing advance of civilization; see John Barrell, *The Dark Side of the Landscape: The Rural Poor in English Painting, 1730-1840* and *The Idea of Landscape and the Sense of Place (1730-1840): An Approach to the Poetry of John Clare*; Ann Bermingham, *Landscape and Ideology: The English Rustic Tradition, 1740-1860*; Leslie Parris, *Landscape in Britain, c. 1750-1850*; Conal Shields and Leslie Parris, *Constable: The Art of Nature*; and Leslie Parris, Ian Fleming-Williams, and Conal Shields, *Constable: Paintings, Watercolours and Drawings*.

4. Elisabeth Inglis-Jones, *Peacocks in Paradise*, p. 190, gives 1803 as the date of Stothard's first visit to Hafod but does not substantiate it; Stothard was finishing his work at Burleigh House during the summer of 1803, so a visit to North Wales is unlikely. In a letter to Cumberland dated 15 September 1805, Johnes writes of an "old acquaintance of yours Stothard who is now here"; British Library Add MSS 36, 500 f. 220.

5. Inglis-Jones, *Peacocks*, p. 21, says that the house already owed a great deal to Stothard's advice and plans; Johnes consulted him often about the interior arrangement and furnishings.

6. Letter from Stothard to Rebecca cited in ibid., p. 218.

7. Cited in ibid., p. 236.

8. Bray, *Life of Stothard*, p. 56.

9. Inglis-Jones suggests this additional visit, *Peacocks*, p. 225.

10. Stothard's drawing for Chantrey's monument is located in a private collection in London. Francis Chantrey (1781–1841) traveled with Stothard to Paris in 1815. Like Stothard, he was employed by Thomas Hope and Samuel Rogers. Stothard introduced him to Johnes, who then commissioned the memorial to Mariamne; Margaret Whinney, *Sculpture in Britain, 1530 to 1830*, pp. 217–19.

11. A journalist for *The Chromolithograph*, 17 October 1868, p. 33, notes a letter received from Robert Stothard that "furnishes important corroborative evidence of the well-known fact that the design for Chantrey's famous 'sleeping children' commemorating the daughters of Mrs. Robinson in Lichfield Cathedral, was made, not by Chantrey but by his father. 'I was present' writes Mr. Robert Stothard, 'when my father, after Chantrey accompanied him on his usual walk, designed them at night.'" Whinney, *Sculpture*, p. 219, states that Mariamne's monument "marked an important stage in the break-down of the eighteenth-century tradition; for it had no allegory, but was instead a semi-realistic treatment of a death-scene, on a scale never so far attempted . . . it is a death-bed scene fraught with sentiment." Whinney cites the following contemporary reaction to this monument when it was exhibited at the Royal Academy in 1817: "Such was the press to see these children . . . that there was no getting near them: mothers with tears in their eyes, lingered, and went away, and returned; while Canova's now far-famed figures of Hebe and Terpsichore stood almost unnoticed by their side."

12. According to Andrew Wyld, London, the companion landscape drawing to *Farms in a Wooded Landscape* is a view in Dovedale; thus both were probably executed on Stothard's only known trip to Derbyshire in 1824.

13. Constable spoke of Stothard throughout his life with the highest veneration for him both as a man and as an artist. Two drawings can be identified that Constable probably executed on one of their joint excursions: *Coombe Wood June 5th 1812* and *Richmond Hill*. The softness and delicacy with which Constable's pencil touches the paper may reflect Stothard's similar handling of the pencil. Stothard's adherence to a more precise, topographic treatment may have influenced Constable in his tightened control over his medium at this time; see my article "Some Unpublished Landscapes by Thomas Stothard and Their Influence on John Constable."

Constable also may have followed Stothard's lead in his development of a broad, horizontal format in landscape compositions dating from about 1812. This thesis was developed by Charles Rhyne in response to my article; see Rhyne, "Constable Drawings and Watercolors . . . Part II. Reattributed Works." Although the exact nature of Stothard's influence on Constable remains speculative, there is no question that the two artists shared a sympathetic response to nature.

14. *Press Cuttings*, p. 1160.

15. Bray, *Life of Stothard*, p. 149, notes this latter commission but cannot identify the subject.

16. The pair of silver-gilt sideboard dishes are engraved on the reverse with the Arms of Hugh, Third Duke of Northumberland. They are thirty-five inches in diameter, stamped with the maker's mark of Paul Storr for Storr & Co. (Rundell, Bridge & Rundell), London, 1813; one

weighs 360 oz., the other 364 oz. 10 dwt. When this pair was auctioned at Sotheby's on 3 May 1984, the sales catalogue noted that they "were acquired as secondhand in 1822, when, as stated in Rundell's account dated 21st, 22nd, and 29th June, their cost of £252 7s. for one and £255 3 s. for the other, calculated at 14s. per ounce." The same document indicates charges of £6 17s and 7s. 6d. respectively to "Paid Expences to Wanstead 3 days, attending Sale and Carriage of Plate home," and "Paid Cartage and assistance"; see Sotheby's, *Sales Catalogue,* 3 May 1984, lot 105.

17. Christie, Manson and Christie, *Catalogue of the Remaining Portion.*

18. This letter is in the extra-illustrated edition of Bray's *Life of Stothard,* Boston Public Library.

19. The candelabra, vase, and shield were made to order by the firm of Green, Ward and Green, rivals of the Rundell firm.

20. Bray, *Life of Stothard,* pp. 150–51.

21. Robert T. Stothard, "Stothard and Blake," claims that Stothard painted this picture in 1804–1805, although this is very unlikely.

22. Bray, *Life of Stothard,* p. 140; Whitley notes that in 1897 Stothard's *Canterbury Pilgrims* was in a private exhibition and that it "was shown first in the Strand, at the house of Lee the perfumer, and afterwards in Berners Street" (*Art in England 1800-1820,* p. 216). In addition, the closing lines of an unidentified newspaper or magazine article included in the *Royal Academy Collection of Engravings by Thomas Stothard* by Frost states, "Canterbury Pilgrims was now on exhibition at the house of Cromek."

23. Letter from Cromek to Blake cited in the anonymous review of *Life of Stothard* by Bray, *Gentleman's Magazine,* 1852, pp. 149–50.

24. Hall, ed., *The National Gallery,* entry no. 6.

25. Walter Scott, *Life of Dryden,* cited in the anonymous review, *Gentleman's Magazine,* 1852, p. 150. The *Proposal for a Print after Stothard's Canterbury Pilgrims* declares that Stothard obtained "fidelity from the best authorities; from the British Museum, & other Public Depositories of rare manuscripts; from Monumental Remains; from the authority of Chaucer himself; & from ancient illuminated manuscripts, painted in his time, which serve to corroborate the Poet's testimony. . . . Gentlemen of the first taste in the Antiquarian Society, & particularly those who are celebrated for their knowledge of the ancient costume of this country, have been consulted: the Picture has derived considerable advantage from the liberal manner in which several of them came forward, & offered their libraries to Mr. Stothard's examination." An unidentified article of 21 March 1807 included in the Whitley *Scrapbooks* in the British Museum states that Hoppner "had yesterday the honour of presenting Stothard's 'Canterbury Pilgrims' to H. R. The Prince of Wales at Carlton House. The style in which the picture is painted reminds the connoisseur of the works of Holbein, Albert Durer and pictures of that period. His Royal Highness, with a discrimination that proved his acquaintance with works of art, immediately made the same observation. . . . His approbation was confirmed by his graciously permitting Mr. Cromek to dedicate the print to him."

26. Letter from Hoppner to Cumberland cited in Bray, *Life of Stothard,* p. 137, and in its entirety in William Carey, *Critical Description of the Procession of Chaucer's Pilgrims to Canterbury, Painted by Thomas Stothard, R.A.,* pp. 12–13.

27. Newspaper or magazine article included in the *Royal Academy Collection of Engravings by Thomas Stothard.*

28. This sonnet was copied into the extra-illustrated edition of Bray's *Life of Stothard,* Boston Public Library.

29. Farington notes in his *Diary* on 17 February 1818: "Landseer called. . . . He spoke of the Print from Stothard's 'Chaucer's Pilgrims' from which an Engraving begun by Schiavonetti & finished after His death by Heath having had 200 proofs taken off & abt. 500 other impressions, the Plate had been worked upon by Worthington, an Engraver, formerly pupil to Bromley, the Engraver, witht. Heath's knowledge who says He has spoiled the plate. Worthington had the care of it for Mrs. Cromek, the Proprietor. There were 700 subscribers to the Plate."

30. Letter of 13 September 1813 from Stothard to Mr. J. Benson of Doncaster, cited in Bray, *Life of Stothard,* p. 144; the original is included in the extra-illustrated edition in the Boston Public Library. The original painting was bought by Harte Davis of Bath for £300 (Bray, *Life of Stothard,* p. 400). It was once in the Miles collection, Leigh Court, and is now in the Tate Gallery. The copy for Rogers is perhaps the 15 1/2 x 14 1/2" oil version recently in the collection of Pierre Jeannerat, London. The version for Boddington sold at Christie's on 9 June 1866, lot 342, to Lady Ashburton and sold again at Christie's, 25 April 1975, lot 35, to an unknown buyer. An oil on panel version (11.5 x 41 cm) is in the Stanford University Art Gallery (84.206).

31. One version in pencil and watercolor heightened with white (4 x 13 1/2") was sold at Christie's 18 June 1980, lot 108. The catalogue entry noted another smaller watercolor version in a private collection.

32. Bray, *Life of Stothard,* p. 143; Bray says that Alfred Stothard told her that his father never pressed for the additional payment of the promised £40 but that "Mrs. Cromek sent him a number of impressions of the plate of the Pilgrims instead of it. Of course he was at liberty to sell them if he could; but Mr. Stothard had neither leisure nor inclination to turn printseller."

33. This is a summary of the basic source, which is J. T. Smith's version in *Nollekens and His Times* (1828); cited by Bentley, *Blake Records,* pp. 464–66; see also Martin Butlin, *The Paintings and Drawings of William Blake,* p. 475, and Claire Pace, "Blake and Chaucer: 'infinite variety of character.'" Aileen Ward (Department of English, New York

University) and Alexander S. Gourlay (Department of English, Iowa State University) are currently working on this thorny problem. I would like to thank Gourlay for the following additional citations dealing with the Blake-Chaucer issue: Karl Kiralis, "William Blake as an Intellectual and Spiritual Guide to Chaucer's *Canterbury Pilgrims*," *Blake Studies* 1:2 (Spring 1969):139–91; Warren Stevenson, "Interpreting Blake's *Canterbury Pilgrims*," *Colby Library Quarterly* 13 (1977):115–26; Orphia Jane Allan, "Blake's Archetypal Criticism: *The Canterbury Pilgrims*," *Genre* 2 (Summer 1978):173–89; Alice Miskimin, "The Illustrated Eighteenth-Century Chaucer," *Modern Philology* 77 (1979): 26–55; Betsy Bowden, "The Artistic and Interpretive Context of Blake's 'Canterbury Pilgrim,'" *Blake, An Illustrated Quarterly* 13:4 (Spring 1980):164–92; and Mary Ellen Reisner, "Effigies of Power: Pitt and Fox as Canterbury Pilgrims," *Eighteenth-Century Studies* 12:4 (Summer 1979): 481–504.

34. Cited in Bray, *Life of Stothard*, pp. 141–43; the original is included in the extra-illustrated edition in the Boston Public Library.

35. Flaxman remained a close friend of Stothard throughout his life; the beginning of a quarrel between Blake and Flaxman about 1805 suggests that Flaxman took the part of Stothard and Cromek in this dispute; G. E. Bentley, Jr., "Blake's Engravings and His Friendship with Flaxman," p. 187.

36. Only the *Prospectus* was published in 1836. Streatfield's collections for this history of Kent are now in fifty-two volumes in the British Library (Add MSS 33878–33939).

37. An identical drawing of this subject is in the Pierpont Morgan Library, #1964.19, *Knight Kneeling before St. George,* pen and black ink, yellow, gray, and gray-brown washes, circular, diameter 8 3/4"; another identical drawing is in British Museum sketchbook #201.b.7 with the inscription by Stothard's son Robert: "sketch made for Rev.d Tho.s Streatfield, his ancestor receiving the honor of knighthood at the Battle of Poirtiers."

38. Typical of Stothard's eclectic working procedure, preliminary studies for this project survive in a variety of techniques. For example, there exists in the Huntington Library and Art Gallery a silhouette-style drawing that is squared for transference of the *Battle of Poirtiers where Edward the Black Prince Is Taken Prisoner by the King of France.* Several related sketches are in the more finicky technique associated with Stothard's later style. The extra-illustrated Bray's *Life of Stothard* in the Princeton University Rare Books Library (ND 497 S 88 B71f EX) contains a study for figures from this series with the inscription: "Two figures composing the right-hand end of the subject of the Battle of Poirtiers where Edward the Black Prince takes prisoner the King of France; one of the outlines made from history for the Rev.d Thomas Streatfield as the center of the group the Death of Thomas Moore in Rogers' Poems was one of them besides the Bride

of Tricimaine by Scott." *British Museum Catalogue of Prints and Drawings,* entry 78, says of a duplication of one of these drawings: "Sir Thomas Moore's Farewell to His Daughter," "pen & ink outline (traced), 7 5/8 x 12"," "Engraved (the central group only) by W. Finden, p. 111, Rogers' *Poems,* 1834."

39. Letter in the extra-illustrated edition of Bray's *Life of Stothard,* Boston Public Library.

40. This drawing would seem to depict the Markham Picture Gallery due to its similarity to a sketch included in the letter quoted later in this paragraph and cited in n. 41.

41. "I am as pleased as you can be concirning [*sic*]. I have no determinate idea as to their relief from the wall. [M]ay not this be governed by the relief the frames of the pictures will have" (letter in the extra-illustrated edition of Bray's *Life of Stothard,* Boston Public Library). This letter is unidentified and undated, but internal evidence indicates it was written to Markham in 1813.

42. Letter in the extra-illustrated edition of Bray's *Life of Stothard,* Boston Public Library. One letter from Stothard to Markham in this extra-illustrated edition states: "I wished very much to have answered your last wherein you acknowledge the receipt of the pictures but as I have much to say to you in answer to some observations of my last sketches of the room. . . . You give me great pleasure by your approval of the picture Burgundy."

43. Letter in the extra-illustrated edition of Bray's *Life of Stothard,* Boston Public Library.

Notes to Chapter 5: Influence of the Market in Stothard's Last Years

1. These sources can be reconstructed via Stothard's "Catalogue" of the books in the Royal Academy, which he probably compiled while he was the Librarian and which still survives in the Royal Academy Library.

2. British Library Add MSS 36, 504 f. 91.

3. In 1811 Stothard exhibited *The scene of Boccaccio's Tales* at the Royal Academy. Although this subject is associated with his later Watteauesque mode, none of his contemporaries mentioned Watteau as a source for this painting. Perhaps it was treated in his earlier Rubensian manner and later modified for his illustrations to Boccaccio that were published in 1825. *San Souci* was painted for Robert Balmanno, according to a note by Balmanno in his collection of prints after Stothard, now in the British Museum; cited by Selby Whittingham, "What You Will; or some notes regarding the influence of Watteau on Turner and other British Artists," p. 8.

4. Stothard exhibited a *Fête Champêtre* painting at the 1818 Royal Academy exhibition and another at the 1826 exhibition; Bray, *Life of Stothard,* p. 241. This painting was

bought in 1818 by Lady Swinburne. Its location has been unknown since it was lent by Sir John Swinburne to the British Institution in 1841; see Whittingham, "What You Will," p. 9. Whittingham suggests that the watercolor in the Ashmolean Museum (see Fig. 49) accords with the descriptions of a watercolor that belonged to Rogers. He further posits (p. 8) that two pen-and-wash drawings in the British Museum are sketches for this painting.

5. One of the newspaper reviews of the exhibition commented that *Sans Souci* was "in the style of Watteau . . . finished with all that richness of colouring and gaiety of effect hitherto thought peculiar only to Watteau" (*Press Cuttings*, p. 1094). Although many paintings in English collections during this period were attributed to Watteau, it was probably Stothard's direct exposure to the French context for these paintings combined with his own artistic predicament that induced him to use Watteau as a model at this particular date. For a discussion of Watteau paintings in English collections, see Whittingham, "What You Will," p. 2.

Strong colorist effects were not, however, a new development in Stothard's art, but in keeping with his usual mode of work in oil painting. His adoption of a Rubensian mode in about 1796 had been noted by several contemporaries. Bray says that Stothard's first painting in a Rubensian mode was his *Victory*, exhibited at the Royal Academy in 1796 (*Life of Stothard*, p. 35).

In addition, one of the qualities that Stothard found much to his liking upon viewing Raphael's *Transfiguration* in the Louvre in 1815 was its brightness of coloring. He also was drawn to the Venetian color school. As he wrote in about 1813 to Markham: "I have thought of sending you the picture of Burgundy & Orleans & next the Diana [*Diana and Nymphs Bathing*, exhibited at the 1816 Royal Academy exhibition] which last I very much desire your opinion of & if disapproved of return it immediately it is an attempt if I have not succeeded in the Venetian manner" (letter in the extra-illustrated edition of Bray's *Life of Stothard*, Boston Public Library. I have dated this letter to about 1813 and have identified its recipient as Markham on the basis of evidence within the letter).

It was probably his attraction to coloristic displays that led Stothard to Watteau. In his borrowings from Rubens, Titian, and Watteau, Stothard imitated their color schemes for the same purpose: the decorative potential of color.

6. Whittingham argues that the Scottish artist Andrew Geddes (1783–1844) was the first artist of this period to use Watteau as a model. He painted conversation pieces in the style of Watteau from 1812 to 1814. See "What You Will," p. 6.

7. See n. 36 to Chap. 2.

8. Whittingham argues that it was Turner's admiration for the color school of painters, extending from Giorgione

onward, that accounts for his borrowings from Stothard; see "What You Will," pp. 2–25.

9. *Press Cuttings*, pp. 1133–34.

10. Ibid., p. 1500, May 1827 review of Hobday's Gallery of Modern Art Exhibition.

11. In a letter of 7 October 1821, now in the Thomson MSS in the National Library of Scotland, George Thomson wrote to Stothard: "I feel much obliged to you also in your kind condescension in the undertaking to do Allan's Designs in the manner of Retcsh's [*sic*] for me."

12. Thomson also helped Flaxman obtain an important commission for a statue of Robert Burns in about 1821; see Irwin, *John Flaxman*, p. 185.

13. The following is a summary of the prices Thomson paid Stothard for various projects mentioned in the Thomson Correspondence MSS in the National Library of Scotland:

10 August 1815: three guineas for designs after Allan and five guineas for original drawings

30 November 1816: two pounds to alter an engraving

7 June 1821: six guineas and ale for the exchange of a painting

22 July ca. 1822: five guineas for a watercolor and five guineas to alter a painting

19 January 1823: three guineas for an outline drawing and five guineas to exchange a painting

24 February 1823: four guineas to engrave an outline

August 1824: five guineas for an original drawing, three guineas for a drawing after Allan, and five guineas to alter a painting

14. Based on J. Cuthbert Hadden's biography, *George Thomson, The Friend of Burns: His Life and Correspondence*, it is possible to make the following estimate of Thomson's financial status: Thomson began work in 1780 at £40 per annum, in 1784 he earned £70, in 1794 he earned £100, in 1797 he earned £150, and in 1824 he earned £300. In his old age, Thomson was able to invest over £1,300 in Caledonian Railway and to purchase house property. Since his father was a schoolmaster and his wife had no known inheritance (she was the daughter of an army lieutenant) and he supported a large family of two sons and six daughters, his capital must have come from profits realized in his publishing enterprises, although he always claimed that he was losing money on these ventures.

15. Thomson did not perceive the absurdity of commissioning accompaniments to Scottish nationalistic tunes from men such as Beethoven who did not speak English, much less Scottish.

16. Hadden, *George Thomson*, p. 114.

17. T. Crouther Gordon, *David Allan of Alloa, 1794-1796: The Scottish Hogarth*, pp. 64–65.

18. Cited in ibid., p. 57.

19. Letter of August 1824 from Thomson to Stothard,

Thomson Correspondence MSS, National Library of Scotland.

20. This letter is recorded in Maggs Sales Catalogue of 1925, No. 2376, which is included in the Whitley *Scrapbooks*.

21. Letter in the Thomson Correspondence MSS, National Library of Scotland.

22. Letter in the Thomson Correspondence MSS, National Library of Scotland.

23. Letter in the Thomson Correspondence MSS, National Library of Scotland.

24. Letter in the extra-illustrated edition of Bray's *Life of Stothard*, Boston Public Library.

25. Letter in the Thomson Correspondence MSS, National Library of Scotland.

26. Letter in the Thomson Correspondence MSS, National Library of Scotland.

27. Letters in the Thomson Correspondence MSS, National Library of Scotland. Another of these letters that refers to the *Tullochgorum* design is dated 11 October 1824. In this letter, Thomson requests: "I would be much obliged to you if you will change the head of the male dancer in the foreground of the coloured Drawing—making him look at the female, as in the pen sketch." Indeed, the two surviving drawings seem to record this alternation.

28. Letter in the Thomson Correspondence MSS, National Library of Scotland.

29. Letters of 5 July 1813, 5 May 1827, 22 July ca. 1822, 7 June 1821, and 17 January 1823 in the Thomson Correspondence MSS, National Library of Scotland.

30. Letters of 8 August 1815 and 4 May 1821 in the Thomson Correspondence MSS, National Library of Scotland.

31. *Francis Douce (1757-1834) Albums*, d. 24 f. 315, Bodleian Library, Oxford.

32. Benjamin Robert Haydon, *Diary*, ed. Willard Pope, 17 July entry.

33. Cited in the *Dictionary of National Biography*, Stothard entry.

34. *Press Cuttings*, p. 1709.

35. Mrs. Flaxman acquired a large collection of Stothard's drawings and engravings; see Allan Cunningham, *The Lives of the Most Eminent British Painters;* cited by Irwin, *John Flaxman*, pp. 7–8.

Robert Balmanno gave his large cache of drawings and prints by Stothard to the British Museum; Samuel Boddington's collection of prints after Stothard came to the Huntington Library in 1951 by gift from Mrs. and Mrs. Carl F. Braun. There were six paintings by Stothard in the Vernon Gallery and ten in the Sheepshanks collection.

Bray, *Life of Stothard*, pp. 61–62, notes that the largest contemporary collection of Stothard's work was that of Samuel Rogers. According to Bray (p. 237), there was also a collection by James Heath, the engraver. Charles Heath's paintings and drawings by Stothard (which probably contained the collection formed by his father, James) sold at Sotheby's 23–28 July 1840 (John Gage, ed., *Collected Correspondnece of J. M. W. Turner,* p. 259). In a letter in the Boston Public Library of about 1813 to an unknown correspondent, perhaps Markham, Stothard reports, "Mr. Heath who is a partner in the work & is to engrave them [Stothard's designs for Scott's *Rokeby]* chiefly & who collects my designs wherever he can meet them, persuaded them he moreover is in love with the drawings & wishes to keep them to himself."

Gage, ed., *Collected Correspondence of Turner,* cites the following additional collections: Chantrey's selection of paintings by Stothard, sold at Christie's 30 April 1853 and 15 June 1861 (p. 244); Thomas Lawrence's drawings by Stothard, sold at Christie's 17 June 1830 (p. 264); Hugh Andrew Johnstone Munro of Novar's (?–1865) twenty-two paintings by Stothard (p. 272); Rogers's collection of paintings and drawings, sold at Christie's 28 April 1856 and following days (p. 279); Benjamin Godfrey Windus's (1790–1867) small collection of drawings by Stothard (p. 300). Watts's large collection of drawings by Stothard is cited by Whittingham, "What You Will," p. 35.

Frederick Locker, the author and the owner of the "Rowfant Library," formed a large collection of Stothard prints in the nineteenth century that is now in the Huntington Library. In a letter dated 20 March 1872 to another Stothard collector, W. J. Tiffin, Frost describes his collection of 3,500 prints (now in the Royal Academy Library) and lists other contemporary collections: "1. The Balmanno Collection in British Museum (mostly choice artists proofs), 2216 2. The Sir Westmacott Collection, now in R A Library. Large number but not choice impressions - 2590 3. The Sir S. Boddington. Do.[ditto] bought by Harvey Bookseller S. James's st (sold for £50) 4. Miss Kearsley, Alfred Place mostly unique—very choice Collection; proofs of 'Atlas Pocket Books,' 5. My Own. 12 Vol. Folio—The whole Collection of R. Chambers T L S 2131 forms the foundation only of mine, with selections from collections that have been dispersed the last 20 years, namely—T. Haviland Burke . . .sold 1852

    W. Pickering -1856

    *Dr. Eavering[?] (part of)1853

    *S. Rogers -1856

    *Utterson -1857

    JSR Westmacott -do [ditto]

    *R Cook RA -do

    Hawkins of Rignor Park Sussex - do

    Windus of Tottenham -

    *Miss Denman (Flaxmans) -

    *A. Stothard.. Jr [?]

    *I bought largely of all those marked *

There possibly may be other collections, in private hands but I doubt much if any prints would be found in them that are not in the above collections named." This letter is now in the collection of Jeremy Mass.

36. Cited in *The Chromolithograph*, 26 September 1868, p. 375.

SELECTED BIBLIOGRAPHY

I. Principal Archives Containing More Than One Hundred Drawings by Stothard

England

London

British Museum, ca. 600 drawings

Victoria and Albert Museum, ca. 300 drawings

Nottingham

Nottingham Castle Museum, ca. 550 drawings

United States

Boston, Mass.

Boston Public Library, ca. 115 drawings

San Marino, Calif.

Henry E. Huntington Library and Art Gallery, ca. 110 drawings

II. Manuscript Sources

England

Cambridge

Fitzwilliam Museum: Flaxman Correspondence 1786–1814, Flaxman MSS

London

British Museum: Cumberland Papers 1748–1825, Add MSS 36, 491–36, 522; Flaxman Papers 1780–1826, Add MSS 39, 780–39, 792; Rev. John Mitford, "Recollections 1847–56," vol. VIII, Add MSS 32, 566; Stothard Correspondence 1781, Add MSS 39, 168 f. 88

Royal Academy: Anderson Collection MSS; Royal Academy Council Meetings MSS

Victoria and Albert Museum: Stothard Correspondence 1801, Box I 86 JJ(ii)

Oxford

Bodleian Library: Francis Douce Albums

Private Collections

Giles Mitchell: MSS paper on Thomas Stothard based on the Nottingham Castle Museum Collection, ca. 1974

T. P. P. Clifford: MSS catalogue of the Thomas Stothard Collection in the Manchester City Art Gallery, ca. 1974

Windsor

Royal Archives: Joseph Farington Diary 1793–1821 (Typescript in the British Museum)

Scotland

Edinburgh

National Library: George Thomson Correspondence 1815–1833, Thomson MSS

United States

Boston

Boston Public Library: Stothard Papers bound into the extra-illustrated edition of Anna E. Bray's *Life of Stothard*, 4 vols., in the Wiggins Collection, Prints and Drawings Department

III. Printed Sources

Adburgham, Alison. *Women in Print, Writing Women and Women's Magazines from the Restoration to Accession of Victoria.* London: George Allen and Unwin, 1972.

Allan, D. G. C. *William Shipley, Founder of the Royal Society of Arts, a Biography with Documents.* London: Hutchinson, 1968.

Allen, Brian F. "Francis Hayman and the English Rococo." Ph.D. dissertation, the Courtauld Institute of Art, University of London, 1984.

Allen, B. Sprague. "William Godwin as a Sentimentalist." *Publications of the Modern Language Association,* no. 33 (1918):1–29.

Allentuck, Marcia Epstein. "Narration and Illustration: The Problem of Richardson's 'Pamela.'" *Philological Quarterly* 51, no. 4 (October 1972):874–87.

Altick, Richard D. *The English Common Reader: A Social History of the Mass Reading Public, 1800–1900.* Chicago: University of Chicago Press, 1957.

Anonymous. Review of *The Life of Thomas Stothard, R.A.* by Anna Eliza Bray. *Gentleman's Magazine,* 1852, pp. 146–50.

Ashton, Geoffrey. *Shakespeare and British Art.* New Haven: Yale Centre for British Art, 1981.

Baiardi, Ottavio Antonio, comp. *Catalogo Degli Antichi Monumenti . . . Di Ercolano.* 9 vols. Naples, 1754/5.

Balmanno, Robert. *Scrapbook of Printed Material on Thomas Stothard.* No. NN.6.18 located in the Department of Prints and Drawings, British Museum, London.

Barrell, John. *The Idea of Landscape and the Sense of Place (1730-1840): An Approach to the Poetry of John Clare.* Cambridge: Cambridge University Press, 1972.

———. *The Dark Side of the Landscape: The Rural Poor in English Painting, 1730-1840.* Cambridge: Cambridge University Press, 1980.

Barry, James. *Lectures on Painting by the Royal Academicians Barry, Opie and Fuseli.* Ed. Ralph N. Wornum. London: Bell, 1889.

———. *The Works of James Barry, Esq. Historical Painter.* 2 vols. London: T. Cadell & W. Davies, 1809.

Bartoli, Pietro Santi, comp. *Gli Antichi Sepoleri.* Rome, 1727.

Bennett, Shelley M. *British Narrative Drawings and Watercolors in the Huntington Collection, 1660-1880.* San Marino, Calif.: The Huntington Library, 1986.

———. "Changing Images of Women in Late-Eighteenth-Century England: 'The Lady's Magazine,' 1770-1810." *Arts Magazine* 55 (May 1981):138-42.

———. "Some Unpublished Landscapes by Thomas Stothard and Their Influence on John Constable." *Master Drawings* 17 (Autumn 1979):273-77.

———. "Thomas Stothard's Adaptation to the Semi-Industrial Arts," *Eighteenth Century Life* 7 (January 1982), pp. 19-31.

Bentley, G. E., Jr. "A. S. Mathew, Patron of Blake and Flaxman." *Notes and Queries* 203 (1958):168-78.

———. *Blake Books: annotated catalogues of William Blake's writings in illuminated printing, in conventional typography and in manuscripts. . . .* Oxford: Clarendon Press, 1977.

———. *Blake Records.* Oxford: Clarendon Press, 1969.

———. "Blake's Engravings and his Friendship with Flaxman." *Studies in Bibliography* 12 (1959):161-88.

———. "Notes on the Early Editions of Flaxman's Classical Designs." *Bulletin of the New York Public Library* 68 (May 1964):277-308; (June 1964):361-81.

Bentley, G. E., Jr., and Martin K. Nurmi. *A Blake Bibliography.* Minneapolis: University of Minnesota Press, 1964.

Bermingham, Ann. *Landscape and Ideology: The English Rustic Tradition, 1740-1860.* Berkeley, Los Angeles, and London: University of California Press, 1986.

Besterman, Theodore. *The Publishing Firm of Cadell and Davies: Select Correspondence and Accounts 1893-1836.* London: Humphrey Milford, 1938.

Bindman, David. *Blake as an artist.* Oxford: Phaidon, 1977.

———. "Blake's 'Gothicised Imagination' and the History of England." In *Essays in Honour of Sir Geoffrey Keynes,* edited by Morton D. Paley and Michael Phillips, pp. 29-49. Oxford: Clarendon Press, 1973.

———. *William Blake: Catalogue of the Collection in the Fitzwilliam Museum, Cambridge.* Cambridge: The Syndics of the Fitzwilliam Museum, 1970.

———. *William Blake: His Art and Times.* The Yale Center for British Art and The Art Gallery of Ontario, 1982.

Bishop, Evelyn Morchard. *Blake's Hayley.* London: Victor Gollancz, 1951.

Blunt, Anthony. *The Art of William Blake.* New York: Columbia University Press, 1959.

———. "Blake's Pictorial Imagination." *Journal of the Warburg and Courtauld Institutes,* 1943, pp. 190-212.

Boase, T. S. R. *English Art 1800-1870.* Oxford: Clarendon Press, 1959.

———. "Macklin and Bowyer." *Journal of the Warburg and Courtauld Institutes,* 1963, pp. 148-77.

Brailsford, H. N. *Shelley, Godwin and Their Circle.* New York: H. Holt & Co., 1913.

Bray, Anna Eliza. *The Life of Thomas Stothard, R.A. with Personal Reminiscences.* London: John Murray, 1851.

———. "Reminiscences of Stothard." *Blackwood's Edinburgh Magazine,* 1836, pp. 669-88, 753-68.

Bruntjen, Sven. "John Boydell (1719-1804): A Study of Art Patronage and Publishing in Georgian London." Ph.D. dissertation, Stanford University, 1973.

Burke, Edmund. *A Philosophical Enquiry into the Origin of Our Ideas of the Sublime and Beautiful.* 2d ed., 1769; rpt. New York: Garland Publishing, 1971.

———. *A Philosophical Enquiry into the Origin of Our Ideas of the Sublime and Beautiful.* Edited by J. T. Boulton. London: Routledge & Kegan Paul, 1958.

Burke, Joseph. *English Art 1714-1800.* Oxford: Clarendon Press, 1976.

Bury, Shirley. "The Lengthening Shadow of Rundell's." *The Connoisseur,* pt. 1 (February 1966):79-86 and pt. 2 (March 1966):152-58.

Butlin, Martin. *William Blake: A Complete Catalogue of the Works in the Tate Gallery.* London: The Tate Gallery, 1971.

———. *The Paintings and Drawings of William Blake.* New Haven and London: Yale University Press, 1981.

Butlin, Martin, and Evelyn Joll. *The Paintings of J. M. W. Turner.* New Haven and London: Yale University Press, 1977.

Calloway, Stephen. "Attitudes to the Mediaeval in English Book Illustration c. 1800–1857." Master's thesis, Courtauld Institute, London, 1975.

Carey, William. *Critical Description of the Procession of Chaucer's Pilgrims to Canterbury, Painted by Thomas Stothard, R.A.* London: T. Cadell & W. Davies for R. H. Cromek, 1808.

Christie, Manson and Christie. *A Catalogue of the Beautiful Original Sketches, and Some Finished Pictures, with a Large Collection of Drawings and Studies, in Colours and Indian Ink, of that Charming Artist, Thomas Stothard, Esq. R.A., Deceased . . . which will be sold by auction . . . June 17, June 18, and June 19, 1834.*

———. *A Catalogue of a Choice Collection of Pictures, and Drawings, by the late Thomas Stothard, R.A. . . . which will be sold by auction . . . Wednesday, June 25, 1845.*

———. *A Catalogue of the Remaining Portion of the Finished Pictures, and Sketches in Oils by that Delightful and Elegant Artist, Thomas Stothard, Esq. R.A., Deceased . . . also, a few Drawings, and his Collection of loose Prints . . . and other Books of Prints . . . which will be sold by auction . . . March 25 and March 26, 1835.*

Clayden, P. W. *The Early Life of Samuel Rogers.* London: Smith, Elder & Co., 1887.

———. *Rogers and His Contemporaries.* 2 vols. London: Smith, Elder & Co., 1889.

Collins, A. S. *Authorship in the Days of Johnson; Being a Study of the Relation between Author, Patron, Publisher and Public 1726-1780.* London: Robert Holden & Co., 1927.

Colvin, Sidney. "Children in Italian and English Design; Part III: Stothard." *The Portfolio,* 1871, pp. 154–60.

Constable, John. *The Letters of John Constable, R.A. to C. R. Leslie, R.A. 1826-1827.* Edited by Peter Leslie. New York: Richard R. Smith, 1931.

Constable, W. G. *John Flaxman.* London: University of London Press, 1927.

Cook, Davidson. "Burns and Stothard." *The Bookman* 52 (September 1917):167–70.

Cormack, Malcolm. *Constable.* Oxford: Phaidon, 1986.

Coxhead, A. C. *Thomas Stothard, R.A.: An Illustrated Monograph.* London: A. H. Bullen, 1906.

Croft-Murray, Edward. *Decorative Painting in England 1537-1837.* 2 vols. London: Country Life, 1970.

Crown, Patricia Dahlman. "Edward F Burney: An Historical Study in English Romantic Art." Ph. D. dissertation, University of California, Los Angeles, 1977.

Cumberland, George. *Thoughts on Outline, Sculpture and the System that Guided the Ancient Artists in Composing their Figures.* London: Robinson, 1796.

Cummings, Frederick, and Allen Staley. *Romantic Art in Britain, Painting and Drawings 1760-1860.* Philadelphia: Philadelphia Museum of Art, 1968.

Cunningham, Allan. *The Lives of the Most Eminent British Painters.* London: George Bell & Sons, 1880.

Dayes, Edward. *The Works of the late Edward Dayes, containing Professional Sketches of Modern Artists.* Edited by E. W. Brayley. London, 1805.

Delieb, Eric. *The Great Silver Manufactory: Matthew Boulton and the Birmingham Silversmiths.* London: Studio Vista, 1971.

Dibdin, Thomas. *The Bibliomania; or Book-madness.* London: Longman, 1814.

Dictionary of National Biography. Edited by Sir Leslie Stephen and Sir Sidney Lee. Oxford: Oxford University Press.

Dotson, Esther Gordon. "Shakespeare Illustrated, 1770–1820." Ph.D. dissertation, The Institute of Fine Arts, New York University, 1973.

Earland, Ada. *John Opie and His Circle.* London: Hutchinson & Co., 1911.

Eaves, T. C. Duncan. "Graphic Illustration of the Novels of Samuel Richardson, 1740–1810." *Huntington Library Quarterly* 14 (1951):349–83.

Erdman, David V. *Blake: Prophet Against Empire; A Poet's Interpretation of the History of His Own Times.* Princeton: Princeton University Press, 1954.

Essick, Robert N. *The Separate Plates of William Blake: A Catalogue.* Princeton: Princeton University Press, 1983.

———. *The Works of William Blake in the Huntington Collections. A Complete Catalogue.* San Marino, Calif.: The Huntington Library, Art Collections, Botanical Gardens, 1985.

Essick, Robert N., ed. *The Visionary Hand: Essays for the Study of William Blake's Art and Aesthetics.* Los Angeles: Hennessey & Ingalls, 1973.

Essick, Robert N., and Roger R. Easson, *William Blake: Book Illustrator: A Bibliography and Catalogue of the Commercial Engravings,* 2 vols. American Blake Foundation, 1972, 1979.

Finer, Ann, and George Savage, eds. *The Selected Letters of Josiah Wedgwood.* London: Corey, Adams & Mackay, 1965.

Fisher, Stanley W. *A Dictionary of Watercolour Painters 1750-1900.* London: W. Foulsham & Co., 1972.

Flanagan, J. F. *Spitalfields Silks of the Eighteenth and Nine-*

teenth Centuries. Leigh-on-Sea, England: F. Lewis Publishers, 1954.

Flaxman, John. *Lectures on Sculpture.* London: John Murray, 1829.

Fleming-Williams, Ian. *Constable, Landscape Watercolours and Drawings.* London: The Tate Gallery, 1976.

Foley, Matthew Joseph. *English Printing & Book Illustration 1780-1820.* Ann Arbor, Mich.: University Microfilms International, 1977.

Gage, John. *Colour in Turner, Poetry and Truth.* London: Studio Vista, 1969.

Gage, John, ed. *Collected Correspondence of J. M. W. Turner.* Oxford: Clarendon Press, 1980.

George, M. Dorothy. *London Life in the Eighteenth Century.* London: Kegan Paul, Trench, Trubner & Co., 1930.

Gilchrist, Alexander. *Life of William Blake.* 1863; rev. ed. London: J. M. Dent & Sons, and New York: E. P. Dutton & Co., 1945.

Goodison, Nicholas. *Ormolu: The Work of Matthew Boulton.* London: Phaidon, 1974.

Gordon, T. Crouther. *David Allan of Alloa 1794-1796: The Scottish Hogarth.* England: Published by Subscription, 1951.

Grylls, Rosalie Glynn. *William Godwin and His World.* London: Odhams Press, 1953.

Hadden, J. Cuthbert. *George Thomson, The Friend of Burns: His Life and Correspondence.* London: John C. Nimmo, 1898.

Hagstrum, Jean H. "Blake and British Art: The Gifts of Farce and Terror." In *Images of Romanticism: Verbal and Visual Affinities,* edited by by Karl Kroeber and William Walling, pp. 61-80. New Haven: Yale University Press, 1978.

———. *William Blake: Poet and Painter.* Chicago: University of Chicago Press, 1964.

Hall, S. C., ed. *The National Gallery; Comprising the Pictures Known as the Vernon Collection.* 3d series. London: Virtue & Co., n.d. [ca. 1855].

Hammelmann, Hans. *Book Illustrators in Eighteenth-Century England.* Edited and completed by T. S. R. Boase. New Haven & London: Yale University Press, 1975.

Hardie, Martin. *Watercolour Painting in Britain.* Edited by Dudley Snelgrove with Jonathan Mayne and Basel Taylor. London: Batsford, 1966-1968.

Haskell, Francis. *Rediscoveries in Art.* Ithaca, N.Y.: Cornell University Press, 1976.

Haydon, Benjamin Robert. *Diary.* Edited by Willard Pope. Cambridge, Mass.: Harvard University Press, 1960.

Hayes, John. "The Ornamental Surroundings for Houbraken's 'Illustrious Heads.'" *Apollo,* supp. (January 1969):1-3.

Hayley, William. *The Life of George Romney, Esq.* London: T. Payne, 1809.

Heath, Dudley. "Some Hitherto Unpublished Drawings by Thomas Stothard, R.A., of Child Life." *The Connoisseur* 31 (October 1911):99-103.

Heleniak, Kathryn Moore. *William Mulready.* New Haven and London: Yale University Press, 1980.

Herrmann, Frank. *The English as Collectors: A Documentary Chestomathy.* London: Chatto & Windus, 1972.

Herrmann, Luke. *British Landscape Painting of the Eighteenth Century.* London: Faber & Faber, 1973.

———. *Turner: Paintings, Watercolours, Prints & Drawings.* London: Phaidon, 1975.

Hind, Arthur M. *The Process and Schools of Engraving.* London: British Museum Publication, 1952.

Hodgson, J. E., and Fred A. Eaton. *The Royal Academy and Its Members.* London: John Murray, 1905.

Hogarth, William. *The Analysis of Beauty.* Edited by Joseph Burke. Oxford: Clarendon Press, 1955.

Holcomb, Adele M. "A Neglected Classical Phase of Turner's Art: His Vignettes to Rogers' *Italy.*" *Journal of the Warburg and Courtauld Institutes* 32 (1969):405-10.

Hopkins, Robert H. *The True Genius of Oliver Goldsmith.* Baltimore: The Johns Hopkins Press, 1969.

Hunt, Leigh. Section on Thomas Stothard from his *Journal* included in Stothard Album c. 102*no. 55, Department of Prints and Drawings, British Museum, London.

Hutchinson, Sidney C. *The History of the Royal Academy 1768-1968.* London: Chapman & Hall, 1968.

———. "The Royal Academy Schools, 1768-1830." *Walpole Society* 38 (1962):123-91.

Inglis-Jones, Elisabeth. *Peacocks in Paradise.* 1950; rpt. Shoreham-by-Sea, Sussex: Service Publications, 1971.

Irwin, David. *English Neoclassical Art; Studies in Inspiration and Taste.* London: Faber & Faber, 1966.

———. "Flaxman: Italian Journals and Correspondence." *Burlington Magazine* 51 (1959):212-17.

———. *John Flaxman, 1755-1826; Sculptor Illustrator Designer.* London: Studio Vista/Christie's, 1979.

Irwin, David, and Francina Irwin. *Scottish Painters, At Home and Abroad 1700-1900.* London: Faber and Faber, 1975.

Jephson, Henry. *The Platform: Its Rise and Progress.* 2 vols. London: Frank Cass & Co., 1968.

Jones, E. Alfred. *The Gold and Silver of Windsor Castle.* Letchworth, England: The Arden Press, 1911.

——. "Gold and Silver Plate in the Royal Collections." *The Connoisseur* 99 (May 1937):247–56.

——. "Thomas Stothard, R.A., as a Designer of Silver Plate." *The Connoisseur* 119 (March 1947):58.

Jones, George. *Sir Francis Chantrey, Recollections of His Life, Practice and Opinions.* London: Edward Moxon, 1849.

Keynes, Sir Geoffrey. *Blake Studies; Essays on his Life and Work.* 1949; 2d ed., Oxford: Clarendon Press, 1971.

——. "George Cumberland 1754–1848." *The Book Collector,* Spring 1970, pp. 31–65.

Keynes, Sir Geoffrey, ed. *The Letters of William Blake.* London: Rupert Hart-Davis, 1968.

King, Pauline Grace. "Thomas Stothard and the Development Toward Victorian Romanticism." Ph.D. dissertation, University of Chicago, 1950.

Klingender, Francis D. *Art and the Industrial Revolution.* London: Noel Carrington, 1947.

Knight, Charles. *Shadows of the Old Booksellers.* London: Peter Davies, 1927.

Lindsay, Jack. *J. M. W. Turner: His Life and Work.* London: Cory, Adams & Mackay, 1966.

Lippincott, Louise. *Selling Art in Georgian London; The Rise of Arthur Pond.* New Haven and London: Yale University Press, 1983.

Mankowitz, Wolf. *Wedgwood.* London: B. T. Batsford, 1953.

Mayer, Dorothy Moulton. *Angelica Kauffmann, R.A. (1741-1807).* Gerrards Cross, Buckinghamshire: Colin Smythe, 1972.

Mayo, Robert D. *The English Novel in the Magazines 1740-1815.* Evanston: Northwestern University Press; London: Oxford University Press, 1962.

Monkhouse, Cosmo. "The Earlier English Water-Colour Painters; Part VII Figure Painters: Stothard, Blake, Cattermole, & etc." *The Portfolio,* 1888, pp. 127–33.

Muir, Percy. *Victorian Illustrated Books.* London: B. T. Batsford, 1971.

Mumby, Frank Arthur. *Publishing and Bookselling.* 5th ed. London: Jonathan Cape, 1974.

Olney, Clarke. *Benjamin Robert Haydon, Historical Painter.* Athens: The University of Georgia Press, 1952.

Oman, Charles. "A Problem of Artistic Responsibility: The Firm of Rundell, Bridge and Rundell." *Apollo,* March 1966, pp. 174–84.

Pace, Claire. "Blake and Chaucer: 'infinite variety of character.'" *Art History* 3 (December 1980):388–409.

Parris, Leslie. *Landscape in Britain, c. 1750-1850.* London: The Tate Gallery, 1973.

Parris, Leslie, Ian Fleming-Williams, and Conal Shields. *Constable, Paintings, Watercolours and Drawings.* London: The Tate Gallery, 1976.

Perry, Norma. "John Vansommer of Spitalfields: Huguenot, silk-designer, and correspondent of Voltaire." *Studies in Voltaire and the Eighteenth Century* 60 (1968):289–310.

Pointon, Marcia R. *Milton and English Art.* Manchester: Manchester University Press, 1970.

Press Cuttings from English Newspapers on Matters of Artistic Interest 1686-1835. 6 vols. Album P.P.17.G in the Victoria and Albert Museum, London.

Pressly, Nancy L. *The Fuseli Circle in Rome: Early Romantic Art of the 1770s.* New Haven: Yale Center for British Art, 1979.

Proposal for a Print after Stothard's Canterbury Pilgrims. London, February 1807.

Pye, John. *Patronage of British Art.* London: Longman, Green & Longmans, 1845.

Reeve, Level. "Fine Arts." *The Literary Gazette,* 1851, pp. 923–24.

Reynolds, Graham. *The Later Paintings and Drawings of John Constable.* New Haven and London: Yale University Press, 1984.

Reynolds, Sir Joshua. *Discourses on Art.* Edited by Robert R. Wark. San Marino, Calif.: Huntington Library, 1959.

Rhyne, Charles S. "Constable drawings and watercolors in the collections of Mr. and Mrs. Paul Mellon and the Yale Center for British Art: Part II. Reattributed Works." *Master Drawings* 19 (Winter 1981):392–95.

Ridgway, R. S. *Voltaire and Sensibility.* Montreal and London: McGill-Queen's University Press, 1973.

Roberts, R. Ellis. *Samuel Rogers and his Circle.* New York: E. P. Dutton & Co., 1910.

Robinson, Henry Crabb. *Henry Crabb Robinson on Books and their Writers.* Edited by Edith T. Morley. London: J. M. Dent and Sons, 1938.

Rosenblum, Robert. *The International Style of 1800: A Study in Linear Abstraction.* New York: Garland Publishing, 1977.

Rudé, George. *Hanoverian London 1714-1808*. Berkeley & Los Angeles: University of California Press, 1971.

———. *Paris and London in the Eighteenth Century, Studies in Popular Protest*. New York: The Viking Press, 1970.

Sammuels, Allen M. "Rudolph Ackermann and the English Dance of Death." *The Book Collector* 23 (Autumn 1974):371–81.

Sandby, William. *The History of the Royal Academy of Arts*. London: Longman, Green, Longman, Roberts & Green, 1862.

Sells, A. Lytton. *Oliver Goldsmith: His Life and Works*. New York: Harper & Row Publishers, 1974.

Shields, Conal, and Leslie Parris. *Constable: The Art of Nature*. London: The Tate Gallery, 1971.

———. *John Constable, 1776-1837*. London: The Tate Gallery, 1969.

Smith, Elton Edward, and Esther Greenwell Smith. *William Godwin*. New York: Twayne Publishers, 1965.

Stothard, Robert T. "Stothard and Blake." *The Athenaeum*, No. 1886 (19 December 1863):838.

Strong, Roy. *Recreating the Past: British History and the Victorian Painter*. London: Thames and Hudson; New York: The Pierpont Morgan Library, 1978.

Symmons, Sarah. "The Spirit of Despair: Patronage, Primitivism and the Art of John Flaxman." *Burlington Magazine*, October 1975, pp. 644–50.

———. *Flaxman and Europe. The Outline Illustrations and Their Influence*. New York & London: Garland Publishing, 1984.

Thompson, E. P. *The Making of the English Working Class*. London: Pelican Books, 1968.

Thornton, Peter. *Baroque and Rococo Silks*. London: Faber & Faber, 1965.

University of Chicago, David and Alfred Smart Gallery. *Alderman Boydell's Shakespeare Gallery; an exhibition of a selection of the engravings made after the paintings commissioned by Alderman Boydell*. 4 Oct.-26 Nov. 1978. Introduction by Richard W. Hutton; catalogue by Laura Nelke.

Utter, Robert Palfrey, and Gwendolyn Bridges Needham. *Pamela's Daughters*. New York: The Macmillan Co., 1936.

Vaughan, William. *German Romanticism and English Art*. New Haven and London: Yale University Press, 1979.

Vogler, Richard Allen. "Cruikshank and Dickens: A Review of the Role of Artist and Author." Ph.D. dissertation, University of California, Los Angeles, 1970.

Wark, Robert R. "James Barry." Ph.D. dissertation, Harvard University, 1952.

———. *Drawings by John Flaxman in the Huntington Collection*. San Marino, Calif.: Henry E. Huntington Library and Art Gallery, 1970.

———. *Drawings from the Turner Shakespeare*. With a Bibliographic Note by Shelley M. Bennett. San Marino, Calif.: Henry E. Huntington Library and Art Gallery, 1973.

Watkins, David. *Thomas Hope (1769-1831) and the Neo-Classical Idea*. London: John Murray, 1968.

Watt, Ian. *The Rise of the Novel: Studies in Defoe, Richardson and Fielding*. London: Chatto & Windus, 1967.

Webb, R. K. *The British Working Class Reader, 1790-1848: Literary and Social Tension*. London: George Allen & Unwin, 1955.

Weinglass, David H., ed. *The Collected Letters of Henry Fuseli*. Millwood, N.Y.; London; Nendeln, Liechtenstein: Kraus International Publications, 1982.

Whinney, Margaret. "Flaxman and the Eighteenth Century." *Journal of the Warburg and Courtauld Institutes* 19 (1956):269–83.

———. *Sculpture in Britain, 1530 to 1830*. Baltimore: Penguin Books, 1964.

Whitley, William T. *Art in England 1800-1820*. New York: The Macmillan Co.; Cambridge: Cambridge University Press, 1928.

———. *Art in England 1821-1837*. New York: The Macmillan Co. Cambridge: Cambridge University Press, 1930.

———. *Scrapbooks of Printed Material on British Artists*. Located in the Department of Prints and Drawings, British Museum, London.

Whittingham, Selby. "What You Will; or some notes regarding the influence of Watteau on Turner and other British Artists." *Turner Studies* 5, pt. 1 (Summer 1985):2–25 and pt. 2 (Winter 1985):28–49.

Wiles, R. M. "Middle-Class Literacy in Eighteenth Century England: Fresh Evidence." In *Studies in the Eighteenth Century*, edited by R. F Brissenden, pp. 49–67. Canberra: Australian National University Press, 1968.

Williams, D. R. *The Life and Correspondence of Sir Thomas Lawrence*. 2 vols. London: Henry Colburn & Richard Bentley, 1831.

Williams, Iolo. "An Identification of Some Early Drawings by John Flaxman." *Burlington Magazine* 52, pt. 1 (1960):246–50.

———. *Early English Watercolours and Some Cognate Draw-*

ings by Artists Born Not Later Than 1785. 1952; rpt. Bath, England: Kingsmead Reprints, 1970.

Williams, John [pseud. Anthony Pasquin]. *Memoirs of the Royal Academicians.* London, 1796.

Wilson, Mona. *The Life of William Blake.* Edited by Sir Geoffrey Keynes. Oxford: Oxford University Press, 1971.

Wilton, Andrew. *Turner in the British Museum: Drawings and Watercolours.* London: British Museum Publications, 1975.

INDEX

W

Walker, J., 68, 81
Walker, William, 33
Walpole, Horace, 84
Walton, Izaak, 86–88
Ward, James, 23
Watteau, Antoine, 53–55
Watts, Alaric A., 63, 85, 87, 88
Watts, Isaac, 60, 88
Wedgwood, Josiah, 5–7, 12, 17, 41, 42
Wellington, Duke of, 42, 44
West, Benjamin, 23, 34
Westall, Richard, 25, 34, 42, 43
White, James, 69
Whittaker, George, 85, 88

Wilkie, David, 52
Williams, John [Anthony Pasquin], 23
Windus, Benjamin Godfrey, 60
Wollstonecraft, Mary, 14
Wordsworth, William, 26
Wright, J., 74
Wright, John Masey, 34
Wright of Derby, Joseph, 13
Wright, W., 83

Y

Young, Edward, 75, 80, 86

Z

Zimmerman, Johann Georg, 85

PHOTO ACKNOWLEDGMENTS

The Ashmolean Museum, Oxford, Fig. 49

The Boston Public Library, Boston, Figs. 7, 8, 11, 35

The British Museum, London, Figs. 1, 13, 14, 17, 21, 24, 38, 42, 50; from Stothard Album 200*c.1, Figs. 16, 18, 19, 22, 23, 25; from Stothard Album 199+b.14, Figs. 37, 39; from Stothard Album 199*b.14*, Fig. 47

The Castle Museum, Nottingham, Figs. 2, 29

Her Majesty Queen Elizabeth II, Fig. 41

The Fitzwilliam Museum, Cambridge, Figs. 10, 33, 34

The Library of the Getty Center for the History of Art and the Humanities, Santa Monica, California, Fig. 3

The Henry E. Huntington Library and Art Gallery, San Marino, California, Figs. 4 (152250), 5 (152250), 6 (181067), 20, 27, 28, 31, 32, 36, 40, 46, 51, 52, 53 (152250)

The National Portrait Gallery, London, Frontispiece

Mr. Dennis Oppé, England, Fig. 12

The Tate Gallery, London, Fig. 45

The Victoria and Albert Museum, London, Figs. 9, 15, 30, 44, 48

The Wellington Museum, Apsley House, London, Fig. 43

The Osborn Collection, Beinecke Rare Book and Manuscript Library, Yale University, New Haven, Fig. 26.